AMERICAN
INTELLIGENCE

AMERICAN INTELLIGENCE

Small-Town News and
Political Culture in
Federalist New Hampshire

BEN P. LAFFERTY

UNIVERSITY OF MASSACHUSETTS PRESS
Amherst and Boston

Copyright © 2020 by University of Massachusetts Press
All rights reserved
Printed in the United States of America

ISBN 978-1-62534-461-8 (paper); 460-1 (hardcover)

Designed by Sally Nichols
Set in Deathe Maach and Adobe Jenson Pro
Printed and bound by Maple Press, Inc.

Cover design by Frank Gutbrod
Cover art by Mophart Creation *Workshop printers intaglio*, vintage engraved illustration.
Magasin Pittoresque, 1852, Shutterstock.com.

Library of Congress Cataloging-in-Publication Data

Names: Lafferty, Ben, author.
Title: American intelligence : small-town news and political culture in
    Federalist New Hampshire / Ben Lafferty.
Description: Amherst : University of Massachusetts Press, [2019] | Includes
    bibliographical references and index. |
Identifiers: LCCN 2019019875 | ISBN 9781625344601 (hardcover) | ISBN
    9781625344618 (paperback) | ISBN 9781613767054 (ebook) | ISBN
    9781613767047 (ebook)
Subjects: LCSH: Newspaper publishing—New Hampshire—History—18th century.
    | Publishers and publishing—United States—History—18th century. |
    Journalism—New Hampshire—History—18th century. | Press and
    politics—New Hampshire—History—18th century. | Journalism—Political
    aspects—United States—History—18th century.
Classification: LCC PN4739.N35 L34 2019 | DDC 071.42—dc23
LC record available at https://lccn.loc.gov/2019019875

British Library Cataloguing-in-Publication Data
A catalog record for this book is available from the British Library

Portions of the research in chapters 2 and 6 appeared in "Joseph Dennie and *The Farmer's Weekly Museum*: Readership and Pseudonymous Celebrity in Early National Journalism," *American Nineteenth Century History*, 15, no. 1 (2014): 67-87. Used by permission.

TO MUM, DAD, AND JOE

CONTENTS

PREFACE

This book was conceived of in all the hubris of youth. My ambition was to map out every single piece of news shared between newspapers that came from, or ended up in, the state of New Hampshire. I became preoccupied with the idea of individuals living simultaneous to one another but operating in different worlds of information. The most famous example of this phenomenon in American history is likely the Battle of New Orleans in 1815, a bloody struggle that took place two weeks after the signing of the Treaty of Ghent, in which peace between Britain and the United States had been agreed. Hundreds of men died in a war that both sides had stopped fighting, simply because there was no means of rapid communication between a city in the lowlands of Europe and the banks of the Mississippi.

I became fascinated with the uncountable number of daily occurrences, small and large, that were shaped by people's access, or lack of access, to timely information. The merchant and the artisan would be reacting to data regarding market forces that might be weeks or even months old. Voters would cast their ballots, based not on the world as it was in real time, but on the last scrap of rumor or newsprint that had come into town. Somebody voting in an election in an isolated frontier town would have an entirely different window into reality than someone in a bustling commercial harbor. America might be at peace or at war, booming or in a slump; indeed, somebody might be dead or alive, depending on the recency of the information at hand.

This monomaniacal obsession with charting the flow of information led me to spend thousands of hours tracking and comparing news articles as they appeared in the American press of the 1790s. As I did so, encouraged by friends and colleagues who fortunately treated my compulsion with benign interest, I began to see that the patterns I saw emerging were taking place in the broader context of an evolving and turbulent young country. The early American newspaper is not just a point of entry to understanding the beginning of the United States; it was an influential player on the historical stage and did as much shaping of American society and politics as it was shaped by them in turn.

The book that you now hold in your hands still has, I think, evidence of my original ambition running through it. However, in the end, it has become about other things too. Printers and editors were not mindless nodes and transmitters of information; they had personalities and motives and agendas of their own. So too did readers, whose preferences and desires shaped the system around them. What began as a macrohistorical book about vast, impersonal networks ended up being far more about people than I had anticipated. It took me the best part of a decade to realize that an impersonal network isn't a network at all.

The notion for this book was germinated almost a decade ago, and in the course of that time so many people and institutions have shown me kindness that I will inevitably forget someone who assisted or supported me along the way. To them, sorry, and thank you.

Early on in this project I received a good deal of sage counsel from Iwan Morgan, who, while not an early Americanist, always encouraged me to write a book that people might want to read (should the fruits of that advice not be evident here, the fault is entirely mine). I also received critical guidance from both Adam Smith and Simon Newman, who both managed the difficult balancing act of reassurance and critical comment.

The staff, librarians, and archivists of the American Antiquarian Society helped me navigate the manuscript correspondence of editors, without which a chapter of this book would have been impossible. My presence at AAS was made possible by the Fulbright Commission, who have supported me twice in my career. I have also been astutely directed by the staff of the Manuscript Reading Room at the Library of Congress, and the Adams Reading Room hosted much of the writing. My thanks go to all three institutions. A significant portion of the research that underpins this book was also made possible by the generosity of the Canterbury Christ Church University research committee, who afforded me the opportunity to visit archives and spend time writing.

Richard Pult did far more than he had to in helping find this book a home, at a point at which I came as close as I have done to giving up. Brian Halley, of the University of Massachusetts Press, has handled my project with dispatch, discernment, and diplomacy. Rachael DeShano, production editor, has had the grace and forbearance not to point out when I have asked her questions regarding something that she had already explained to me. I should like to thank my anonymous reviewers, who provided a salutary mix of positive reinforcement and much-needed counterpoint. As to what follows, the virtues were magnified and the faults mitigated by their guidance.

My sometime colleague and now friend David Hitchcock has been a supply of both scholarly insight and encouragement. He is a historian and comrade of the first rank. So, Dave, thank you for doing so much of the heavy lifting, intellectual and otherwise.

My parents, to whom this book is dedicated, have been more supportive than I can begin to explain. My mum has been asking me questions for my entire life and asked some of the very first questions that led to this book. Always my first audience, she has read more work of mine than I recall writing; she has my eternal gratitude. My dad has been an unceasing and unconditional well of support and affirmation. I have always labored under the surety that I am never walking alone. My brother, Joe, I would like to thank for his wit and levity, at times when I have been in short supply of both commodities.

Finally, while I am giving thanks, I owe the book itself a debt. My research brought me to Washington, D.C., and to Lauren Skala, who, with all respect due to Joseph Dennie, Ebenezer Andrews, and the rest, was the most important discovery I have ever made on a research trip.

—Ben Lafferty
FEBRUARY 2019

AMERICAN INTELLIGENCE

INTRODUCTION

Never was there given to man a political engine of greater power.
—Reverend Samuel Miller

The newspapers of late-eighteenth-century America are curious historical artifacts. While it might be cliché to point out that today's organ of public record is tomorrow's bird-cage liner, the unprepossessing physical character of a Federalist-era journal makes the inverted alchemy from journalism to wastepaper all the more tangible. Printed on a single folded sheet of paper, folded to make four "pages," they were made to be consumed and set down in a casual manner. The amount of subsequent readers that each individual copy had, as they frequently passed between numerous sets of hands, attests simultaneously to both their value and their lack of status. People wanted to read newspapers, but most felt little need to keep them. Their value was wholly transitory and ephemeral.

How did these zephyr creations come into being? Fortunately, the men (and they were *almost* all exclusively men)[1] who made them had a natural proclivity for setting things down in writing; historians, therefore, know a good deal about them. Some print shops were one-man operations; editing, manufacturing, marketing, accounting, and retail would be handled by a single worker-proprietor. Jeffrey Pasley has called printers the "intellectual elite of the early American working class," despite the occupation having "its cerebral and prestigious aspects, it was still a dirty, smelly, physically demanding job."[2] His labor might possibly have been supplemented by an apprentice[3] or occasional hired hand, but all of the skilled jobs would generally be conducted by the owner. Printers could work alone, but those who had an interest in expanding their operations and circulation had to hire out or take on indentured apprentices. James Tagg has estimated the time taken to produce eighteen hundred copies of a newspaper as between fifteen and thirty man-hours.[4] And if a particularly ambitious printer had an even grander vision of expansion, a second press would be necessary. This was the model that characterized most provincial printers in the eighteenth century. Larger concerns would naturally lead to a division of labor. The most common type of partnership tended to complement technical proficiency and machinery with intellectual capital. In such cases, the physical production and distribution would be undertaken by one man and the editing, writing, and advertising by the other. In some cases, the work was supplemented by unpaid laborers in the form of family members, apprentices, and slaves. Such arrangements made sense; some talented journalists were wholly incapable of turning out a newspaper each week, and many printers had a need for regular and well-written prose. However, many of these relationships were short-lived, perhaps indicating their inherent instability. Some leather-aproned, ink-stained artisans doubtless found the pretensions of these foppish, college-educated aesthetes insufferable, and many of the editors quickly found compiling a weekly news sheet for the rural yeomanry to be beneath them. The most straightforward problem was that a printing business would have to be very successful to support two full-time workers. A few printing firms, normally the beneficiaries of large government contracts, were able to expand and take on multiple employees, but these were for the most part located in large cities like Philadelphia, New York, or Boston.

In the past couple of decades, scholars of American journalism, and more broadly of American political culture, have made great strides in locating the position of the newspaper within the society of the early national period. Rather than viewing newspapers in the abstract, historians have increasingly come to interpret print as being part of a "popular political sphere," which along with festivals, parades, public speaking, clubs, and societies shaped American political interactions under the first party system.[5] This work acknowledges that newspapers existed in a world alongside other forms of media and symbolism and that in fact they enjoyed symbiotic relationships with these phenomena. Thomas Leonard writes persuasively about the cultural significance not just of the printing of news but also of its reading, when he explains that "social norms were reinforced as people read the news." Leonard's argument, that newspapers had greater meanings and social roles than can be conveyed by straightforward textual analysis, is a compelling one. "Community ties," he writes, "were demonstrated in the simple act of getting news because, at a minimum, some cooperation, some surrender of privacy, some tipping of the hand was called for. Public spaces displayed the diversity of arguments, revealing who read what; in homes, readers were watched and knew their place. Often, the setting for news was part of its message, for the setting required that a role be played." By conceptualizing the reading of newspapers as an act of community creation, Leonard substantially broadens both their significance and their interpretive scope as historical objects. Newspapers go from being packages of information about external events to vectors of cultural and social mores, and they information they carried, says Richard Brown, "could have a whole different significance depending on where you lived and who you were."[6]

News was gathered by editors in a variety of ways, but it was usually come by opportunistically. "With a printer in charge of a newspaper," Charles Clark has noted, "the collection of news was still largely a passive affair. Whether copying from the London colonial prints, printing letters containing news from the 'country' in his own province, or writing up what they heard from the local grapevine, the printer took, by and large, what came to him." A few editors had the means and the inclination to employ reporters and stenographers, but most made do with secondhand accounts. These came in from different sources. Local news might well be handed in by patrons of the printing shop or friends of the printer. In some cases, it is obvious that a story has been related orally to an editor, who has then adapted it for the paper. Editors also relied heavily on correspondence. Newspaper correspondents were not the trained journalists of later eras, but rather were private citizens whose only interest in the newspaper was that they read it. They held to no code of professional ethics, nor did they undergo any scrutiny or fact checking. Howard Tumber has argued that "during the first 'information age,' from 1476 until the second half of the nineteenth century, journalism could be classed as 'unprofessional.'" Journalists, he contends, "were not a distinct group, nor were they fulfilling their 'responsibilities' toward 'the public.' They were actively engaged in political life and were simultaneously publishers, writers and political theorists."[7] Many stories headed with the phrase "we have it by a reliable gentleman in . . ." were the product of these exchanges. Correspondents proffered not only eyewitness accounts of events but also hearsay, political diatribes, religious sermons, poems, jokes, and a plethora of other ephemera. The steadiest source of news from the wider world was other newspapers. Networks of exchange between editors meant that newspapermen tended to have access to a broader spectrum of newspapers, from a much larger geographic region, than regular readers. The introduction of the United States Postal Act, with its heavy discount for newspaper deliveries,[8] regularized and incentivized these exchanges. Plagiarism and attribution meant little in eighteenth-century journalism; stories and articles were cut-and-pasted by practically all editors. Will Slauter has described the process by which a newspaper editor, when challenged with space to fill, wielding a large pair of shears, "leafed through his newspapers to find the right amount and cut it out on the spot." Journalism as we currently understand it was, according to Jean Chalaby, "an invention of the nineteenth century." Editors of sympathetic political views could pool their resources toward a common goal. The coordinated dispersal of materials responsible for the political downfall of Hamilton in the Reynolds affair is a prime example of cooperation among editors of like mind. Alexander Hamilton became embroiled in an extramarital affair with the reputedly lovely, and devious, Maria Reynolds. In the end he found himself blackmailed by her husband and drawn into a scandal involving his former associate William Duer and insider treasury intelligence. While Hamilton managed to suppress the full details of the imbroglio for five years, James Callender eventually "broke" the story that ruined Hamilton's already tarnished reputation.[9]

The manufacturing process of newspaper production did not undergo any radical transformations from the colonial period until the early nineteenth century. The process of manufacture started with the setting of type. Each page was laid out in individual letters and punctuation marks, pieced together from engraved blocks, and separated by spaces. This was the skill-intensive stage of newspaper production. Not only was type small, sticky, and difficult to keep track of, but mislaid type could render a whole print run unusable.[10] Small printers had to go page by page, stopping to reset the type each time; only a printer with a large inventory would have the requisite selection of letters and punctuation to be able to lay out a whole newspaper in one sitting. As difficult as this job was under the best of circumstances, conditions were often adverse. Poor lighting was the biggest problem, but cold could make the handling of metal type especially vexing. If typesetting required dexterity and concentration, then pressing was a task that demanded patience, endurance, and not a little strength. Pressing print was a multistage process: each individual page had to be secured in place, drawn into the press on a conveyor, and imprinted. This final act was done by the turning of a large handle, the "devil's tail,"[11] and the whole process had to be undone for the page to be removed. When we consider the size and weight of a typical printing press, and the thousands of times these processes were repeated, the physical toll of this work is not to be underestimated. Printing was an occupation that demanded brawn as well as brain.

While presses had been refined somewhat in the eighteenth century, no "eureka" innovation revolutionized the industry. Printers, therefore, had to contend with familiar challenges. Start-up costs could be high for American printers. In 1801 Samuel Chase had to raise $8,000 in capital to found his *Anti-Democrat* in Baltimore.[12] The business necessitated the acquisition of good type. While possessing different fonts could add visual diversity to a paper, of greater practical interest to most printers was access to a variety of font sizes. Larger and bolder type was used for headlines, but small fonts could allow editors to squeeze a dense piece of legislation, or a military field report, onto a single page. Less well-established printers could not hope to keep a wide variety of fonts at hand. Most type was imported from Europe in the 1790s. Prior to the 1790s, attempts to establish foundries for type in America had been thwarted by more competitive British manufacturers. The American type industry would not truly take off until the success of Binny and Ronaldson's Philadelphia foundry in the 1800s.[13] The cost of purchasing (or manufacturing) type was one of a printer's main overheads, but not the only one. Ink did not come cheap, and one needs only to sample late-eighteenth-century papers to see how ink intensive they are. There was a marked preference for thick, dark text, and heavy saturation. While the extra cost incurred may have been trifling per sheet, spread over thousands of copies it mounted considerably. The messy nature of printing meant that rags were in constant demand. In New Hampshire alone, during the 1790s 140 advertisements were taken out by printers requesting rags from their customers, some offering remission of subscription dues or even cash.

Once the paper was made, the greater challenge remained: selling it profitably. "Consciously or unconsciously," Dan Berkowitz has written, editors factored in "expectations from local advertisers that help pay both salaries and bills, as well as the expectations of community members who form the subscriber base that shapes and justifies advertising rates."[14] Finding and marketing to customers was often the obstacle that drove otherwise fine publications out of business. Most papers operated mainly on a subscription model. While individual issues could be purchased at the print shop, the lack of a merchandising network meant that direct retail made up only a small part of the newspaper business.[15] Subscription rates among weekly papers averaged about three dollars a year,[16] and chasing down recalcitrant subscribers was a perennial headache for the purveyors of newspapers. In order to get papers out to customers, post riders were frequently employed by printers with far-flung readerships. These men were responsible not only for delivering papers but also for collecting payment.

A newspaper could rarely sustain a print shop alone. Even if the publication was successful, the nature of the subscription model meant that printers often suffered long periods without any significant income. Privately published books and pamphlets provided business in the short term. Occasionally, matters of widespread public interest would spur sales for a printer; when Benjamin Franklin Bache got hold of an early copy of the Jay Treaty, he was reported to have produced some thirty thousand copies.[17] Other ephemera, such as advertising leaflets or sheet music, could also fill out a printer's portfolio. Many print shops kept items with no link to the business whatsoever, as frequent advertisements for sundries and patent medicines attest. Government contracts provided the steadiest and most dependable sources of income, for those lucky enough to be granted them. These inevitably required patronage and suggested that a printer becoming successful might have more to do with courting the local establishment than bravely exposing scandal and corruption. Jeffrey Pasley has demonstrated the not inconsiderable overlap between office holding and printing in the 1790s. This reliance on patronal largesse would "eventually transform many American editors and their papers into actual working parts of the political system."[18]

This book is not primarily focused on the production of newspapers in the sense outlined above. Instead, it is preoccupied with how information, in the form of newspapers, traveled around the Federalist-era United States. The most valuable work on the logistics of eighteenth- and nineteenth-century information transmission in America remains Allan R. Pred's *Urban Growth and the Circulation of Information: The United States System of Cities, 1790–1814*. Pred, not a historian but a geographer, provided in-depth statistical analysis that goes beyond newspaper distribution, examining postal services and transportation networks, among much else. His maps constitute an ordnance survey of information; through analysis of regional and city newspapers, Pred charted the lag in the transmission of knowledge, undulating in what he dubbed "spatial bias." His studies demonstrated that news did not travel with equal velocity in straight lines; it was reliant on trade and nascent postal services for transmission. As news traveled the young republic's dirt roads and rivers, infrastructure as well as geography played a part in determining who knew what, and when. Population density too played a major role, having a greater correlation to the availability of information than relative proximity to major urban centers. Americans in the Union's remotest reaches could be separated by many months in political time. While Pred's focus was on the developing interdependence of major cities, his work implicitly demonstrates the interdependence of town and country not only in economics, his principal preoccupation, but also in culture. "For lesser news," he observed, "small-town papers customarily depended directly on the press of the city within whose hinterland they were situated and indirectly on the sources of that press. Conversely, small-town weeklies supplied large-city papers with hinterland news."[19]

Pred's focus on cities is understandable. First, his primary scholarly interest was not newspapers in isolation but rather in leveraging data about newspapers into an understanding of urban culture and networks; in-depth analysis of rural or small-town journalism would not have fitted into his schemata. Second, there was the problem of sources. While a very large amount of tedious work is still unavoidable in replicating the type of work that Pred was engaged in, historians at one time would be consulting microfiche, or indeed hard-copy newspapers themselves, instead of a searchable database, making a geographically dispersed study impossible. He was forced to artificially narrow his sample groups to make his task humanly feasible. His "mean public-information time lags for Philadelphia in 1790," for example, made use of "48 seasonally stratified issues" from two newspapers from that city.[20] Pred and his contemporaries were not able to quickly parse different newspaper content and therefore were not able to benefit from observing the interplay between content and transmission. Pred was also unable to control for the human element in this study. Certain sorts of news items were not reproduced in the same frequency as others, and some items (political poetry and essays, for example) were not always deemed worthy of immediate inclusion in papers that received them. In this book types of political content have been broken down into categories, which permits us to observe differences in their rates of transmission. Furthermore, we are now able to conduct studies of this kind not by following the trajectories of whole newspapers, but by following the routes taken by thousands of articles, all sorted by type. This approach, which acknowledges the cut-and-paste style of American journalism typical of the age, seems much more faithful when re-creating the communications network in the abstract. Pred acknowledged the challenges of doing such research in a predigital age:

> The arbitrary selection for the maps of one or two papers at a given time and place need not have biased the data. Admittedly, it is likely that editors differed considerably in their selection of stories, and this may have been mirrored in paper-to-paper variations in the frequency with which specific nonlocal places were mentioned. However, such editorial preferences and prejudices should not have affected the time consumed from the occurrence of the nonlocal event to its local publication. Moreover, there is some danger that time lag means for particular non-local places might be distorted when based on a small number of values randomly clustered in one season. This danger is magnified if the news source is another paper that appeared only weekly. However, the possible impact of such distortions on the contour of isolines was usually offset by more broadly-based means obtained for other nearby places.[21]

Due to the constraints upon him, his graphical representations of information time are somewhat crude compared to what is achievable today. The empirical data compiled for this book suggests that the "isolines" that he used to present the boundaries of information space-time are not actually terribly useful in portraying the complexity of news and knowledge availability. Information did not travel in straight lines, or at the same rate in multiple directions, but instead moved fractally. News that might take two weeks to reach a city three hundred miles away might take a month to reach a village one hundred miles away. Pred's work remains a remarkable empirical accomplishment before we even make exceptions on the grounds of available technology. While he is utilized by economic historians of the period (his name crops up with some regularity in the *Journal of Economic History*), perhaps his largely quantitative approach explains why his work has been underutilized by historians not only of politics and culture but of journalism itself. A myopic focus on source, without reference to Pred's "information accessibility" indexes, tells us much about one journalist's beliefs and opinions but very little about those of his readers and community. This book is an attempt to answer the sort of questions Pred was posing in the 1970s, by using the wealth of electronically accessible resources now at our disposal. Even when it disputes his findings and conclusions, it is intellectually indebted to his work.

The digitization of newspaper archives has revolutionized the type of work that can be done in this field, and scholars are increasingly cognizant of the fact that OCR searchable archives allow for the application of research methods impossible with hard-copy newspapers or even microfiche.[22] Content analysis, formerly conducted on a document-by-document basis, becomes possible across vast, and easily defined, amounts of text, spread across numerous sources. The recent work of Rachel Hope Cleves is an exemplar of what can be done with this technology. Her content analysis across a variety of databases charts the impact of the French Revolution in the United States.[23] Finding links between separate documents has also been greatly enabled, which is a vital capability if we are to consider the development of news culture not as the acts of isolated individual actors but as the product of a cultural community. These new possibilities in methodology offer means of testing old hypotheses and answering previously unanswerable questions. What was the relationship between the newspapers of small country towns and those of the burgeoning urban centers? Where did news come from, and how was news about the wider world gathered and distributed in far-flung rural communities? How did developments in transportation, commerce, and federally subsidized mail delivery affect the distance and direction that news traveled and the time it took to do so? Were the newspapers of small-town printers passive recipients of an emerging national culture, mere echo stations helping to spread a centralized and mandated political-culture message, or creative participants in the process of national development, or, indeed, active antagonists against such a process?

Scholars have previously used the data available to them to reason laterally. In order to calculate relative "informational" importance in the realm of European news, Pred used shipping quantities as the main corollary with information flow, based on the not unreasonable assumption that freight and information are interrelated factors.[24] Therefore, he came to the conclusion that New York is the most important entry point for information in the United States. Rather than trying to solve these problems laterally, we can now conduct direct statistical samples of newspaper content, rather than trying to extrapolate from other, more readily available, data. With this new intelligence, some questions might require revised responses. The tone of political journalism changed from 1790 to 1800; did the changes that were going on in the business and infrastructure of that sphere help to bring about the partisanship that has previously been attributed to party political factors?

New Hampshire offers an excellent opportunity to explore key issues in late-eighteenth-century political journalism. First, the state provides a range of newspapers across different locations while providing a small-enough field of study to be manageable. Lynn Warren Turner described these fertile conditions when he wrote: "The educational renaissance of the 1790s was not confined to the schools, but spread its benefits as well for those institutions and agencies that were the means of adult education. On the eve of the Revolution, New Hampshire boasted only one newspaper, the New Hampshire Gazette, which was circulated among a mere handful of wealthy patrons. By 1790, the state supported six newspapers, and the press pushed inland as far as Keene and Walpole." A literate population had been a defining characteristic of New England culture throughout the eighteenth century and had created the conditions for a sophisticated print culture. According to Paul Starr, male literacy in New England was about 85 percent in 1760 and female literacy about 60 percent (a figure that Starr thinks was probably an underestimate). This, combined with religious and commercial factors, led to Boston becoming the center of the printing and book trade in the North American colonies and gave the region as a whole the most vibrant and active print culture for most of the eighteenth century. This was in stark contrast to the colonial Chesapeake, which was, in Starr's words, an "almost entirely . . . pre-Gutenberg, scribal culture." The development of print culture in late colonial and early national America varied a good deal by region. Trish Loughlan rightly points to the "provincial and plural nature" of printing and notes that in various parts of the country, print was the exclusive domain of the privileged. According to Richard Kielbowicz's data, in 1800 New England had 23.2 percent of the U.S. population and 29.9 percent of the newspapers, while by contrast the South had 43.1 percent of the population and just 27.8 percent of the newspapers.[25] This discrepancy was not just in the raw numbers of newspapers available in each region, but also in their dispersal. At that moment, no newspapers were being published in the state of South Carolina outside of Charleston, leaving most of the state dozens of miles away from the nearest newspaper printer. In places like New Hampshire, on the other hand, printers and their newspapers were dispersed throughout the state.

New Hampshire existed in the hinterland of city and country. While Boston, to its southeast, exerted considerable political influence, it was not dominant, nor did its reach extend to the state's northern and western borders. New Hampshire acted as a political borderland, with Republican Vermont its immediate western neighbor. While New Hampshire certainly constituted a part of the New England political milieu, the presence of such firebrand editors as Matthew Lyon on its doorstep provided an interesting contrast and challenge to the Federalist orthodoxy. There are easily enough newspapers to make statements based on statistical research meaningful (a study like this one of Georgia, for example, would suffer from small sample sizes and lack of publication diversity), but small enough that all available examples can be accounted for. The depth of newspaper production, as well as the lively culture of correspondence, was also no doubt encouraged by the high rate of literacy in the state. The richness of these resources has been enhanced by the excellent historical society of the state that has done a superb job of collating and preserving the historical newspaper collection; no state has a flawless archive of newspapers, but New Hampshire's is wonderfully close. A study of New Hampshire also provides an interesting counterpoint to the prevailing historiographical themes found in the study of journalism. Most historians prefer to focus on the Democratic-Republican side of the partisan journalism phenomenon. New Hampshire, at least in print, ranked as one of the most orthodoxly

Federalist states in the Union and allows us to probe the sometimes overlooked role of the conservative reaction to the Republican challenge of the late 1790s.

Why, though, in a broader sense, does any of this matter? Beyond their own experience, what difference does it make to a historian whether a farmer in Hillsborough had subscriptions to no newspapers or to twenty? Is it of interest to any but the most eccentrically encyclopedic how many times a week the post rider of the *Recorder* or the *Spy* or the *Courier* went out on his rounds? The first answer is that rich bases of data about the movement of information allow us to test old answers to old questions and perhaps to ask a few new ones. Did John Fenno, Philip Freneau, Franklin Bache, and all the rest matter to the extent that most historians have supposed? The act of writing, particularly political writing, holds no metaphysical power to transform society. Indeed, early U.S. history is not the only field in which scholars have attached far more importance to an author than any of his or her peers might have. Readers matter as much as writers, as historians like David Paul Nord have ably demonstrated. His concept of the "reader-citizen," for whom knowledge of current events was an essential component of national identity, is the ultimate outcome of early American journalism. As it is difficult to develop a widespread, integrated look at readership through anecdotal written materials, we must turn to data instead, to reveal patterns of distribution and consumption, to uncover the American reader.

In popular narratives, there is a tendency to regard developments through the spectrum of wholly mechanical innovations: printing, telegraphy, telephony, broadcasting, cable and satellites, the World Wide Web. While new technologies have played transformative roles, it is important that we avoid falling into an unthinking technological determinism. James Curran argues that exclusively technological explanations tend to "see new communications technology as inherently subversive. In some contexts, print was harnessed to sustain the social order, while in others print played a part in challenging it. What mattered above all else, was the wider context which strongly influenced print's content and reception."[26] It is helpful to broaden the meaning of the term *technology* beyond improvements in the inner workings of a mechanical or electronic device.

Instead, the technology of systems, the methods of organization and the deployment of existing human tools, can as often provide a far more telling insight into ongoing changes in society. The Internet makes for an excellent example. There is no singular piece of equipment that can adequately define what the Internet is or what it does. Take a modem, a fiber-optic cable, a laptop computer, or a server out of the context of a globe-spanning computer network, and they become inert, albeit intricately manufactured, lumps of plastic, silicon, and lithium. A significant portion of the corporeal technology from which the Internet is constructed predates it considerably. Nor is it possible to account for its now apparent ubiquity with reference to any particular piece of ingenuity in terms of either hardware or software. Most of the things for which the Internet is now so widely lauded and decried, uses for which it has now become an apparently indispensable part of countless human lives, were perfectly feasible twenty years ago and indeed performed by small groups of outliers. It is not the hardware or the code that makes the Internet so historically important; it is the culture that embraces and integrates it, the businesses that either are destroyed or made possible by it, and the people who choose to communicate and live with it. Technology in the narrow sense has no power, no historical significance, without an animating human will, without the spark of an idea. The achievement of an innovation matters, of course, but so does its implementation and use. Without an organization and social systems that enable and encourage utilization of technology, such systems lack meaning. The Internet consists of the people who use it just as much as the circuitry and transistors it runs on.

There is always a risk, in seeking explanations for apparently "modernizing" moments, in looking past the complex and nuanced ways that people had lived before. "Because we live in a media-rich age," William Gilmore has argued, "historians of print and written literacy often have underestimated the breadth of human communications ability in past societies and so, when they considered it at all, have also underestimated broad participation in cultural life." If the phenomenon of the Internet was the result of a combination of electric hardware and historical timing, then the rise of the newspaper in the early United States seems to be based almost exclusively on the latter. The history of printing can be measured in millennia in China, and movable type has existed in the West for centuries. The basic means of distribution, horse riding, extends back to prehistory, allowing for a few developments in stirrup and saddle manufacture along the way. The ability to manufacture and distribute newspapers was available to people long before a handful of Americans started doing so. As Charles Steffen has put it, "In the end, what underlay the expansion of newspaper circulation in the early national era was not a single technological breakthrough like the steam-powered cylinder press, or a new marketing strategy like selling papers by the issue rather than by yearly subscription, or a government policy of subsidized newspaper delivery like that provided in the Post Office Act of 1792. Newspapers were both agents and emblems of the larger culture in which they were embedded."[27] If we consider the number of archived newspaper articles by decade through the eighteenth century, then the picture is one of gradual growth up until the Revolution, followed by a sudden abundance. In the period 1790 to 1799, more newspaper articles were published (5,594,119) than in the ninety preceding years from 1700 to 1789 (2,593,830).[28]

These statistics must be qualified with a few admissions. Any quantitative study of communication is beset by the vicissitudes of what Josh Durham Peters has called "historical transmission." The corpus of evidence that any historian must work with is always incomplete, whether in the form of the countless unaccounted-for days in biographical research or the under-the-counter transactions that plague historians of trade. For those attempting to understand the flow of communication, the pitfalls take on a multitude of forms. Some of these come in the form of conscious human "gatekeeping." What publications did a collector make special efforts to acquire? Which ones made their way into the hands of an archivist, and which remain tucked away in an attic or cellar? Some of what determines what we have and what we don't is sheer accident. A fire claims one crate of newspapers but spares another. Some types of paper and ink degrade more quickly in some conditions than others.[29]

Therefore, a caveat is necessary. Anybody who claims that they can, with absolute certainty, make definitive quantitative claims about the flow of news (or, for that matter, any other commodity) is engaging in delusion. All the data presented in this volume is reflective of the material studied by the author. Between the researching for and publication of this book, new material will have been cataloged and digitized. In addition, the data was produced by a single highly fallible researcher, whose own understanding of its transmission and content evolved over the course of the research. In my research for this project I read, in total, more than eleven thousand discrete pieces of newspaper content, ranging from editorials, advertisements, and sermons to shipping reports and jokes. I can state with certainty that I have misinterpreted, failed to contextualize, and even misread some of what I was looking at. I have shown three different people a blotched or faded piece of print and have received three different guesses as to what it might say. My hope is twofold. First, I hope that in most cases I have compensated for these errors with volume, so that the statistical anomalies caused by mistakes are watered down by the number of other "data points." One misunderstood article in a sample of ten undermines the validity of any conclusion drawn from the statistics it produces. One misunderstood article in a hundred is regrettable but falls within what pollsters call the "margin for error." My second hope is that you, forbearing reader, can recall this note of equivocacy wherever numbers are concerned.

The data shows that the growth of the press occurred alongside growth in both population and economy, and therefore to some extent reflects the development of early American society as a whole. More newspapers of the late eighteenth century have survived intact than from earlier periods of production. Nevertheless, the prodigious growth in news is undeniable. In the decade of the 1790s, more news was published than for the entirety of the preceding *century*. The year of 1800 saw the publication of more newspaper articles (781,767) than the not uneventful decade of the 1770s (489,784). As Simon Newman has observed, "There had been a veritable explosion in the number of newspapers printed and available in the late eighteenth-century America, from the forty odd that had served some three million colonists on the eve of the revolution to well over one hundred by the early 1790s and more than two hundred by the turn of the century."[30] This phenomenon was not limited to the number of different newspapers available but extended to the overall reach of their circulation. For every hundred households, there were between eighteen and nineteen newspaper subscriptions in the 1780s; by the 1820s, there were more than fifty.[31] This was a remarkable upheaval, as incredible as any information boom of the digital age, and one achieved with none but the most minor advancements in mechanical and transportation technology. Given the lack of a single transformative machine or process, we must look elsewhere for an explanation to this phenomenon.

Richard R. John, in describing the "communications revolution," identified three important developments: the periodic press, the postal service, and the stagecoach industry. Such phenomena acted in concert to provide the infrastructure for a "distinctive informational environment" that expedited the emergence of a broader national economy, popular partisanship, and participation in interstate voluntary organizations.[32] Infrastructure and institutions, more than inventions, account for these dramatic changes; systems, even if they came about via accident and expediency in roughly equal parts, are technology too. The one that became the means of information distribution in the early national period was as much composed of culture as it was technology. A culture of information sharing, of passing news on, both orally and in print, to one's acquaintances was an integral part of the infrastructural development that contributed to the meteoric rise in information dissemination. A technology of systems emerged not of any sentient design, but with the reflexive self-correction and adaptation of the organism. Human activity, in politics, business, religion, poetry, and entertainment, created America's first extensive knowledge network.

CHAPTER ONE

"DOMESTICK SUMMARY"

A Short History of
New Hampshire
in the Federalist Era

As the close of the eighteenth century approached, New Hampshire was a state with more geography than history. Amid its deep forests and forbidding mountains, its mosquito-addled summers and frostbitten winters, it is a wonder that colonial society took root at all. The Native tribes that had occupied the area, the Abenaki and the Penacook, had been largely driven out in the seventeenth century. While the first years of the United States coincided with something of a demographic boom in the new state, with the population growing by 40,000 inhabitants from 1786 to 1791,[1] it remained a second thought for most other Americans. In 1790 the state had a population density of just over fifteen people per square mile, with a population of 141,885 (including 158 slaves).[2] Massachusetts, by comparison, exceeded thirty-five people per square mile. No town in the Granite State exceeded 5,000 in population; the largest, Portsmouth, boasted 4,720 inhabitants, making it the thirteenth-largest town in the United States.[3] And Portsmouth was, by any measure except perhaps the political, New Hampshire's most important urban center; no other town could claim a population greater than 3,000, with Gilmantown (2,610), Amherst (2,369), and Rochester (2,852) the next largest. That the five largest towns in the state represented about a tenth of its population gives us some indication of the rural, even frontier, character of the state, especially as those figures included many individuals living in surrounding hinterlands and farming communities. The population was relatively concentrated in the southern and the eastern counties, with about 103,000,[4] almost three-quarters of the state's population, living in the three most southerly counties: Cheshire, Hillsborough, and Rockingham. This southern band, relatively well peopled and settled, was home to dozens of hamlets and villages, with land mainly turned over to agricultural pursuits. The remainder of the state was sparsely populated. Grafton, a large county occupying most of the Northwest, had a total population of just over 13,000, and only two towns, Hanover and Lebanon, exceeded 1,000 residents.[5] In the North, communities were small and scattered, surrounded by a mixture of farms and undeveloped land, and were in a transitory phase between recognizably frontier and agrarian life. "Between 1780 and 1830, each of the Upper Valley counties were settling into a more stable pattern of rural life," William Gilmore has written. "Grazing, subsistence farming, and small-scale commercial farming dominated the economy. Some artisan and semi-skilled labor was available, as were professional services."[6] These developments did not take place overnight, but the couple of generations covered by Gilmore's time frame were certainly aware of their effects.

By 1800 the total state population had risen to 183,858 (now with only 8 slaves),[7] a rise of 29.6 percent, slower than the national growth rate of 35 percent. Growth was not evenly distributed. Portsmouth grew to 5,339, a rise of 13.1 percent, while Concord went from 1,738 inhabitants to 2,052, a shift of 18.1 percent. With the overall state population outgrowing its major towns, New Hampshire underwent the phenomenon of becoming *less* urban over time, with the Census recording a fall of 3.3 percent to 2.9 percent of the population living in town.[8] While the towns lagged, the fringes flourished. The aforementioned Grafton County, running along the new Vermont border, boomed in population, rising 56.3 percent to 23,093. Strafford, to the north of Rockingham, a county bordering what would become the state of Maine, rose from 23,609 to 32,614, an increase of 38.1 percent. What Lynn Turner dubs the "Old Colony," the eastern, more urban portion of the state containing its most venerable settlements, had, in 1790, 27.2 percent of the New Hampshire population, while the frontier possessed a mere 8 percent. By 1800 the Old Colony's share had fallen to 21.7 percent, and the frontier's had risen to 11.3 percent. Population growth in New Hampshire mostly took the form of geographical expansion over urban consolidation. The majority of the state's residents could be found in communities of fewer than 1,000 people, and these small enclaves were being spawned at a remarkable rate. The 1800 Census recorded population details for fifteen new towns and registered eight as no longer inhabited.[9] While the population in the South and the East continued to grow, the center of demographic gravity shifted northward and westward as the decade progressed. Such trends were influenced by a multitude of factors, though developments in transportation had a significant impact. "Not only were her towns on the seaboard and in the interior strengthened by the natural growth of their population," wrote George Barstow in the mid-nineteenth century, "but multitudes of adventurers from the northern section of Massachusetts, invited by the cheapness of her land and the extent and fertility of unoccupied domains, had found their way along the valley of the Connecticut, nearly to its sources, and, after occupying its intervals, gradually extended their settlements among the hills and valleys of the back country." While Barstow was perhaps guilty of indulging in a little romantic nostalgia about the land of his boyhood, he gives a clear impression of its rustic nature and of the transformation that was taking place within it. "Points, at an earlier period apparently inaccessible, were reached by the advancing tide of emigration; and neither the lack of roads, the absence of schools and religious privi-leges, or the other innumerable privations incident to a settlement in the wilderness were sufficient obstacles to stay its progress. Even the recesses of the White Mountains, whose snow-clad mountains . . . were reached at this early period."[10] New Hampshire was, in the Federalist period, in a state of social flux. The locus of its economic, political, and cultural power was being contested between commercial towns and the pastoral country. While versions of this schism were being played out across America, the peculiarities of New Hampshire's history, geography, and culture gave the division some of its special character.

Portsmouth was, by the 1790s, the foremost center of commerce in the state. By acting as New Hampshire's primary merchant port, and thereby providing the conduit for the export of its raw materials, the import of sundries and luxuries and intelligence from the Old World, it accumulated much of the state's financial and cultural power. When the Polish author Julian Ursyn Niemcewicz was traveling through the United States in the late 1790s, he left this account of the town:

Portsmuth [sic] is one of the old cities in America. It had 5,000 inhabitants. It covers a rather extensive area. All the houses are of wood; as in all American cities there are houses in which the splendour substantially surpass others. Their owners, privileged by wealth, live on a higher plane. Though by the Constitution and at law there is neither nobility nor distinction of birth, though equality is well secured, wealth rejects it and creates differences between men.

Portsmuth extends along the Piscataqua river and has the most favourable situation for trade. The river is a mile in width. Its depth everywhere is so great that the biggest warships can enter and leave, which advantage is as great in peace as it is dangerous in time of war. The waters run swift as an arrow's flight. This speed and the deep-flowing channel change and cool the air, making this town one of the healthiest in America. . . .

More than two hundred ships may be seen in this port. The biggest trade is to the West Indies and Europe, and is in fish, barrel staves, salt butter, meat, etc. If the voyage is successful, this produce brings a profit of 250 per cent. They are changed in the West Indies for coffee, sugar, cotton, or more often during wartime for English bills of exchange which may later be redeemed for *dry goods* or various English wares. The merchants, in spite of today's losses, are rich and closefisted. . . . The land hereabouts is not very fertile.[11]

As Niemcewicz indicates, Portsmouth's prosperity was based on trade rather than agriculture or forestry, placing it in contrast to most of the rest of the state. New Hampshire's short strip of coastline between the northern and southern parts of Massachusetts gave Portsmouth a pre-eminence in the state's maritime interests that a town of its size might not have otherwise enjoyed. Timothy Dwight, the president of Yale, on his travels found its harbor swarming with vessels. "The commerce of Portsmouth," he recorded, "employed in the year 1800 twenty-eight ships, forty-seven brigs, ten schooners, two sloops, and one bark, besides twenty coasting vessels, and a still greater number occupied in fishing."[12] Such a fleet certainly did not make Portsmouth a maritime center of the first rank, but it was an important regional port that served a growing network of inland communities.

While Portsmouth could not compete with Boston in commercial terms, it did provide a point of ingress for goods, people, and information. Robert Lovett, a merchant, portrayed the town as an important gateway to the state, arguing that he and his fellow traders served as an important link between the New Hampshire hinterland and the wider world and as a hub for not only shipping but also land-based transportation. "It is situated," he explained, "on the Oyster River, where it enters Great Bay, which in turn leads to the Piscataqua River, and out to sea at Portsmouth." For men like Lovett, location was paramount not just from the vantage point of business, but with regards to the practicalities of transportation. "Large ships could not navigate in Great Bay, and a small craft, known as a gundelow, was developed to carry goods between Portsmouth and Durham, Newmarket, Exeter and other towns on rivers entering the Great Bay. A bridge was constructed across the Piscataqua in 1794, to the west and north of the present one, and a turnpike in 1796."[13] Simple though such improvements might have been, they afforded new opportunities for merchants.

Indeed, according to most accounts, for those engaged in the business of moving goods from one place to another, times were exceedingly good. Trade benefited from a number of favorable conditions. Conflict overseas drove a demand for products in which the state was naturally rich, particularly in lumber and fish. This demand for New Hampshire exports in turn spurred the production of new maritime vessels; eight were constructed in the Piscataqua during 1790, with twenty being constructed in 1791 and the number only increasing from there. "At the same time," historian Jere Daniell has written, "the money supply increased so quickly that by the summer of 1791, knowing men" agreed that it was "full plenty enough for the benefit of the trade," and a year later farmers' produce was reported to fetch "the highest prices and quickest money ever known." Merchants and others with capital offered loans on reasonable terms."[14] These benign circumstances, along with high agricultural prices, the preponderance of easy credit, and speculative opportunities, led to a land boom. Portsmouth, along with a few other towns, received the bulk of this dividend; it was certainly the principal beneficiary in the boom in shipping. There is some indication of Portsmouth's bustling character thanks to the few official records that remain. In 1798 the town had 686 homes worth $100 or more, of which 16 were built three stories or higher. The merchant elite dominated the town, with the wealthiest tenth controlling 50 percent of the town's assets. For the most part, poverty seems to have been a relatively minor problem, with the majority of people living in two-story wooden houses of reasonably sound construction.[15] While the habitations seem to have been comfortable enough, the rather haphazard nature of the town's growth caused Timothy Dwight to turn up his patrician nose: "There are in Portsmouth thirty-one streets, thirty-eight lanes, then alleys, and three public squares. The squares are not remarkable either for their size or their beauty," he sniffed. "A few of the streets are wide and pleasant; most of them are narrow and disagreeable. The town was laid out without any regard to regularity. Had the contrary system been pursued, very few would have been equally handsome."[16] Besides offending Dwight's aesthetic sensibilities, the town as described was clearly a place of some note; indeed, his sneering rather suggests that it was a place more preoccupied with the making of money than in delighting passing scholars. Businesses were piling up atop one another by the decade's end. An article in the *New Hampshire Gazette* described "a dwelling house and very large store, with six shops in front, owned by John Melcher (late printer) and occupied by himself as a dwelling house, and Henry Burley,

Wm. Garlan, Robert M'Cleary, N. S. And W. Peirce as a Bookstore and Printing-Office."[17] Such bustling activity, with six shops crowding into one building, suggests a vibrant and lively commercial culture.

The town could also, in its own modest way, boast its own clique of intellectuals and would-be philosophes. John Melcher, publisher of the state's most venerable newspaper, the *New Hampshire Gazette*, had been instrumental in the setting up of the town's public library, and he, along with a small group of others, was involved in what might be described as a broad project of public betterment. Michael Baenen, a historian of the Portsmouth Athenæum (an institution with transparently classical aspirations), writes that "the demise of the Portsmouth Library collection did not deprive the residents of Portsmouth of access to the expanding world of print. The town was well positioned to supply newspapers, books, and periodicals to its own residents and those of its rural hinterland."[18] The town's first printing office had been established by Daniel Fowle in 1756, after he moved his operation from Boston to avoid a libel prosecution by the government of Massachusetts; he would go on to publish the first book in the colony.[19] From 1793 onward Portsmouth supported at least two newspapers at any given time. There were a variety of booksellers, some of whom also operated small-circulation libraries. Supplementing these provisions were the newspaper reading rooms, which not only served a public eager for commercial and maritime dispatches, but also acted as important meeting places for like-minded individuals, provided vital commercial and shipping news, and served as commercial gathering places. "None of these institutions, however," Baenen notes, "met the same needs as those addressed by a 'social' or 'public' library."[20] It was into this void that civic-minded individuals, men like the creators of the Athenæum, inserted themselves. Such private intellectual institutions did serve an important function, although they could hardly be said to be democratizing in either their reach or their remit.

About 90 percent of the New Hampshire populace were literate, as compared to around 60 to 70 percent in the mid-Atlantic region, the product of an economic, religious, and political culture that took learning to be as much of a public good as a private one and a state government that took an active part in promoting it.[21] A number of different causes for this prevalence of learning have been attributed, including high rates of school enrollment, a laity with a need to personally engage with scripture, and the rapid commercialization of rural society.[22] In 1791 the legislature, responding to concerns about the state of rural schools, mandated the expansion of the education system, further expanding the accessibility of learning. George Barstow, who was at once an advocate and a chronicler of these measures, provided the fullest contemporary account, writing that "from the close of the revolution, an increased regard for schools and institutions of learning began to be cherished among our citizens. During the present year, an academy was incorporated at New Ipswich, being the second institution of the kind in the state. The burthens occasioned by the war having been in some measure removed from the people, their attention was more generally directed to the importance of common schools, and more liberal provision was made for their support." If the revolution had represented something of a backward step for public education in New Hampshire, when in Barstow's words the schools "had been almost universally prostrated by the turmoils and dangers of the war," then the peace brought an opportunity for renewal and development. According to Barstow, such policies were, in spirit at least, intended to have a leveling effect, extending "its advantages to the rich and the poor—the citizens of the most populous and flourishing towns, and the scattered dwellers among its mountains." Even if the general standard of the education was somewhat rudimentary and rote, it did unquestionably create one of the most literate societies not only in early national America but in the entire Western world. "Under the influences of a reviving interest in the cause of education," Barstow proudly recorded, "academies and public schools, generously endowed and liberally supported, sprung up at short intervals, and within a brief period of time, in the principal towns and villages of the state." In 1791 academies were established in Atkinson and Amherst. As Barstow explains, these institutions then produced teachers who went on to provide elementary and secondary education across the state. "A taste for learning was suddenly diffused through every part of the community," he wrote, and expounded more generally on New Hampshire's literary culture, excellent schools, and educational patronage, claiming that nearly "every family in the state" had access to books and education, should they choose to avail themselves of the opportunity. Historians have generally concurred with Barstow's assessment, deeming it, in the words of Lynn Turner, the "educational renaissance of the 1790s." An important step in this process began with a statewide act fixing the level at which taxes funding schools and academies would be set (which aped similar statues established in Massachusetts earlier in the century). This new guarantee of funding for general education meant that even the most benighted counties were obliged to maintain a basic provision. The legislation also mandated the teaching of grammar, reading, mathematics, and geography, as well as Latin in the grammar schools found in larger towns.[23]

In addition to Latin syntax, schools were also expected to provide a strong dose of moral instruction and guidance. While not necessarily religious institutions in the strictest sense, schools were obliged to adhere to a Christian ethic both in their curriculum and in their broader social role. Education served the pragmatic purpose of creating good citizens, and few in New Hampshire in the 1790s would have objected to the proposition that, despite an avowedly secular social compact, good also meant godly. And even if schools were not in the business of directly catechizing the young, they provided the skills necessary for full engagement with holy scripture. Such a commitment was not to be taken lightly, and its cardinal significance was not lost on publicly minded men. According to Belknap, one John Phillips of Exeter, "excited by the melancholy prospect," established and funded the Phillips Academy in 1781, having also played a pivotal role in the creation of a similar institution in Andover. The result of this mixture of public and private efforts was, in the words of Turner, "that the state became distinguished in the early nineteenth century for its leadership in this field of education."[24] This would prove to be fertile ground for a vibrant culture of print.

New Hampshire was also burnished by a few intellectual figures of national reputation. Foremost among these was the historian and inveterate correspondent Jeremy Belknap. He achieved widespread fame for his authorship of *The History of New Hampshire*, which was widely lauded as innovative in both its scholarship (which emphasized archival research and empiricism, an approach that was more noteworthy then than today) and its style. It attracted the notice of no less a figure than Alexis de Tocqueville, who noted, forty-five years after its publication, *"The History of New Hampshire, by Jeremy Belknap,* is a work held in merited estimation. . . . The reader of Belknap will find in his work more general ideas, and more strength of thought, than are to be met with in the American historians even to the present day." Belknap was also a prolific source of all types of written media and an active public intellect. He "spent most days crouched at his writer's desk for long hours, scribbling memoranda, narratives, letters, transcriptions, verse and sermons . . . ," Russell Lawson has noted. "Belknap was the founder of the Massachusetts Historical Society, and the finest naturalist of northern New England. His accounts of the White Mountains of New Hampshire are some of the best natural histories of the late eighteenth century."[25] His works were widely published throughout the United States, and he dined with Adams and Washington. That a town the size of Portsmouth could boast such luminaries was an indication that it was not only a place of commerce but one of culture as well.

Concord, the town that would become the state's capital and the second most important publishing center, was more typical of the inland towns that dotted New England. With a population of around 2,000, it sat as the hub of a farming area that had, in 1725, been divided into 103 equally sized lots that had been granted to new arrivals. While those plots had been apportioned, consolidated, inherited, and sold over the subsequent eighty years, the essential patchwork of wooden farmsteads and tilled soil persisted, at the center of which lay the town itself. According to J. M. Opal, it sustained seven dry-goods stores, six taverns, about a dozen artisan shops, as well as assorted smaller stores. There was a stout schoolhouse, a pair of bookshops, and, from 1798, a circulating library. The residents of Concord also seem to have belonged to a fairly equitable society, with extremes of neither poverty nor wealth to be found. Partly due to a yeoman prosperity, and partly due to a vigilant, not to say formidable, town constable, the town pauper roll remained empty for decades. While Opal does mention that some merchants of the town did do very well for themselves, with a William Duncan owning both large commercial enterprises and tracts of land, he notes that Concord generally lacked the cosmopolitan, college-educated gentlemen who filled the highest echelons of early American society. The great bulk of townsmen tilled the soil. "Reputed for bravery and diligence, yeomen commanded respect."[26] Concord was very much part of an agricultural economy and culture. Bound to seasonal and market vagaries, the economies of such towns could be fraught with instability.

Outside the commercial and political capitals of Portsmouth and Concord, the 1790s were an important time for the development of many New Hampshire towns. Walpole, lying on the western border of the state beside the Connecticut River, was a typical example of a community created by the westward flow of migrants. It resembled an increasingly familiar midsize New England community, with stores, offices, and schools. As the decade progressed, this rather remote place became home to doctors, lawyers, tanners, hatters, blacksmiths, and, yes, printers, the typical signs of a burgeoning rural center beginning to take on the more complex, commercial forms of the town. This in turn led to the building of roads and stagecoaches and then the influx of more people. In such small ways did the forces of the American market revolution transform places like Walpole. That such a town could have been home to the nationally famous *Farmer's Weekly Museum*, a publication to be much discussed in this book, also makes it a case study in what David Jaffe has called the "Village Enlightenment," the process by which a community of ideas grows symbiotically with that of business. Jeremiah Mason, a Walpole lawyer, and beneficiary of all this bustling activity, recalled in his memoirs:

> This was a brisk, active village, with several traders, and many industrious mechanics, and two or three taverns. . . . Walpole was, at that time, a place of more business than any other in that vicinity, and was much resorted to by the people of the neighbouring towns. There was also a considerable trade from a distance, passing on what was called the great river road. . . . The inhabitants of that part of the Connecticut River valley were then just passing from the rude and boisterous manners of first settlers to a more civilized, orderly, and settled state. There was more motion, life, and bustle in the older parts of the country.[27]

As the "rude and boisterous manners" passed into memory, a place like Walpole surely became a more convivial spot for would-be public intellectuals like Joseph Dennie, editor of the *Farmer's Weekly Museum*. And if the waning of the frontier spirit that had characterized places like Walpole in colonial times might set off a romantic pang in a modern reader, it seems not to have troubled the hardheaded Mason.

Indeed, why would one mourn the creation of a "civilized, orderly and settled state" when, even in the confines of New England, new vistas awaited? As New Hampshire's population grew, people tended to spread out into unoccupied land rather than concentrate in the established centers. Villages and hamlets, like Peterborough, with a population of 997 in 1790,[28] were scattered across the state. When the area was incorporated in 1760, almost everyone in Peterborough grew their own food, produced their own clothes, and concocted herbal remedies for their ailments. Its industrial capital consisted of a water-powered saw and a gristmill, and retail business was conducted out of a single store. With the exception of one dirt road wide enough to allow for the passage of a yoke of oxen, these hubs were linked by winding footpaths hewn out of the forest. "Trails for a man on foot," Elting Morison wrote, "or a horse and rider took wandering courses east and west to connect the town with other small settlements in the region. Not many travellers made their arduous way along these paths, nor had they much cause to do so." In many respects, Peterborough was less a town and more a loose assortment of more or less isolated subsistence farms. The house of William McNee, a wood and brick structure with a chimney sufficient to service three fireplaces and a Dutch oven, would be a typical example of the domestic architecture (among the affluent, at any rate) of rural New Hampshire. With the town having quadrupled in population over the course of thirty years, the 1790s saw the construction of the first true road through it.[29] It was in villages like these that New Hampshire did much of its growing in the latter part of the eighteenth century.

New Hampshire's political complexion can be challenging to reconcile with general narratives of the Federalist period. During the 1780s, the southwest portion of the state had voted against the ratification of the Constitution; however, after the establishment of the federal government, most of those Anti-Federalists were successfully absorbed into early national-era politics.[30] And while New Hampshire could not accurately be called a one-party state, at times it can be hard to tell the difference. Federalist dominance, at the state level at least, often seemed so ensured that many counties failed to produce a single opposition candidate. Tellingly, Philip Foner's book *The Democratic Republican Societies, 1790–1800* contains chapters on Pennsylvania, New Jersey, Connecticut, New York, Massachusetts, Vermont, Delaware, Maryland, Virginia, Kentucky, and North and South Carolinas; among all of these, New Hampshire is a conspicuous omission, an indicative statement concerning the extent of opposition politics within the state itself. The state seemed to conform to some conventional preconceptions about the atmosphere of the very first years of the republic. Jere Daniell provides a typical perspective, writing of the period from 1790 to the end of 1794 that "the citizens of New Hampshire had enjoyed a political tranquillity unknown since the days of Bennington Wentworth," the midcentury colonial governor.[31] The state had a reputation, both among its own citizens and from afar, for good governance and sensible if unspectacular leadership. The policies of the newly formed federal government, and more specifically the first Washington administration, were widely credited with the general feeling of order and prosperity that seemed to prevail. Federalism, in the form it took in the 1790s, is a difficult political philosophy to concisely summarize, given that both its objectives and its means of achieving them were somewhat amorphous. Like most political movements, it contained factions that spent a good deal of time and energy arguing about what its priorities ought to be. However, there are certain facets of its agenda that were common to the majority of its adherents: an "energetic" government that would play an active part in various aspects of public life, including in the encouragement of economic development, a strong military that would discourage the machinations of predatory foreign powers, and a sophisticated financial system like the one that had developed in Britain over the previous two centuries. All of this would be organized under the enlightened leadership of men of "virtue." The government that these men would constitute would be representative in this sense that its deliberations would represent the interests of all of its citizens; the legislators themselves, however, would not be representative of that massed citizenry. Positions of power would be held by men of education, worldly experience, and refinement, men versed in the classics and liberal philosophy. It was democracy in the sense that shepherds, tanners, and millers might have an equal say in public matters, what James Madison described as "men who possess most wisdom to discern, and most virtue to pursue the common good."[32]

For the most part, the former opponents of the new status quo either pledged their allegiance or, at the very least, kept their misgivings to themselves. Washington's pacific and noninterventionist inclinations were broadly in line with those of most New Hampshire residents in the early part of the decade. "Thus," Daniell writes, "by 1794 the anxiety of a decade earlier had all but disappeared. The people of New Hampshire were happy with the formal structure of government, the system of politics which determined who should rule, and the style and policies of men presently in power. Public officials—whether elected or appointed—found their authority respected. The state as a whole was united by the mutual commitment of virtually every citizen to the ideals and ethics of republicanism." After the tumultuous years of the revolution, most citizens basked in a period of stability and calm. Perhaps more important, the ramshackle Articles of Confederation had been replaced by a system that, seemingly, could be made to work. "Our government appears at the last to be happily settled," wrote Jeremy Belknap to former governor John Wentworth in the spring of 1791, "and every friend to virtue and good order must wish it permanency. I hope that twenty-five years of controversy and revolution will be sufficient for the space of time which I have to exist on this globe. Where I to live to the age of Methuselah," he concluded, "I should not wish to see another such period."[33]

Indeed, New Hampshire newspapers could not help but congratulate their readers as to their good fortune, living as they did at the center of sense and order in the universe. "It must redound to the honor of New Hampshire," the *Recorder* noted, "when it is known, that from the time of passing of the Revenue Law to the present moment, not one breach of that act has taken place in this district." Indeed, so pervasive was the state's sense of equanimity that some journalists paused to wonder if it marked a new epoch in human experience. "Last Thursday the Superior Court of this state finished their session at Plymouth, which ends the circuit for this spring," began an article in the *New Hampshire Spy*, a Portsmouth newspaper. "It is very remarkable that through the whole circuit, not a single bill of indictment was found by any grand jury.—This fact involves two alternatives—either that people have grown more virtuous, and that there is no need of laws penal, and grand juries—or that the grand juries or Attorney General are grown more negligent than formerly—we rather impute it to the first, as the cause."[34] This sense of well-being had tangible sources. Cooperation among the state's political elders, a successful legislative system, and falling taxes all contributed, and the 1791 convention to amend the state constitution was a success. Before the writing of the state constitution, Josiah Bartlett was elected its "president" with 95 percent of the popular vote, and when challenged for the newly created governorship by John Langdon in 1793, he still received 75 percent. Bartlett had been a prominent public figure since the 1770s, at various times a member of the Continental Congress and the New Hampshire Supreme Court, and by the beginning of the 1790s was unquestionably New Hampshire's foremost elder statesman. Bartlett was a paragon of the eighteenth-century public gentleman. In addition to his military service, he was the first president of the New Hampshire Medical Society and acted as an associate judge for the state.[35] He had served as a largely apolitical figurehead, lending his unimpeachable reputation to the fledgling state government, a sort of local George Washington, before retiring due to ill health in 1794 and dying the following year. Even before he withdrew from the public stage, however, Bartlett's patrician political philosophy, like that of many of his generation, was rapidly fading in pertinence. While his persona was able to hold state politics together, his anti-ideological approach could not work over the long term; in this too he resembled Washington.

The era in which it was considered unseemly for a gentleman to campaign for office, lest he seem too nakedly ambitious, was drawing to a close. While Bartlett might, in his patrician manner, remain above the fray, others threw themselves into electioneering with gusto. John Sullivan helped found the *New Hampshire Spy* newspaper in large part to further his political career,[36] and William Plumer[37] developed a reputation as a savvy backroom operator.[38] This new generation of New Hampshire politicians better understood the future of American democracy as the sort of theatrical competition that it was becoming rather than the sort of classical (really mythical) civic self-sacrifice that men like Bartlett hoped it to be.

This stirring of political energy gained momentum in the second half of the 1790s. While the state remained solidly Federalist in federal elections, a confluence of factors conspired to complicate the picture at the state level. After the death of Bartlett, John Taylor Gilman became de facto leader of the New Hampshire Federalists and was a key member of the state establishment, the so-called Exeter Junto.[39] A Hamiltonian in his political economy, he had made a fortune speculating in Continental securities, a fact that did not sit well with the former foot soldiers of the revolution, who felt that their hard-won victory was being profited upon by financiers, and farmers, who feared falling agricultural prices. His protax policies were formulated with the intention of building up the government coffers in case of emergency, as well as strengthening the fledgling apparatus of administration.[40] A chief source of his popularity was his fervent rhetoric against the French Revolution, the increasingly anarchic nature of which alarmed the stolid New England electorate, who feared similar scenes of bloodshed and terror spreading into the United States.[41] The French Revolution divided Americans along cultural as well as political lines. Some Americans reveled in reports of revolutionary valor and affected the cockades and sashes of the Jacobin Club. For others, it represented an almost apocalyptic collapse of civilized life; many were especially affronted by the apparent assault on organized religion (even if the faith under attack was Catholicism).[42]

John Langdon, the foremost Republican in the state, became a vocal critic of the apparently increasingly Hamiltonian foreign policy the Federalist Party was following. A dominant figure in Portsmouth politics,[43] Langdon had been a delegate to the Second Continental Congress, a senator, and America's first president pro tempore and later governor of the state, whose personal popularity meant that Portsmouth was solidly Republican by the latter half of the decade. Newspaper reports suggested that large numbers of Portsmouth residents turned out for Republican parades and public events.[44] During the Revolutionary War, Langdon (along with Bartlett) had been an opponent of paper money, arguing for taxation and anti-inflationary book balancing when taking part in the Continental Congress, although these views shifted over time.[45] Langdon was no populist in his political philosophy, being a wealthy capitalist privately dismissive of the contribution that common people might make to the democratic process. However, he was a highly effective demagogue and expertly managed a political machine that cultivated the support of the town's many dockworkers, artisans, and sailors. As Louis-Guillaume Otto, the French chargé d'affaires during the period of the Constitutional Convention, commented, "One of the most interesting and likeable men in the United States . . . Mr. Langdon had made a great fortune in commerce, he is the Robert Morris of his State, making a great expenditure and making many citizens devoted to him due to his liberalities."[46] Langdon used his considerable influence to attack the government for what he saw as a slavish acquiescence to antirevolutionary British machinations.

Such open criticism of the administration by a prominent political figure was unheard of in New Hampshire even five years earlier. When this transition in the style and substance of New Hampshire politics took place is the subject of some disagreement among historians. Lynn Warren Turner places the schism a couple of years earlier than Daniell when he writes, "Nothing except vague and conflicting personal antagonisms divided the leaders of New Hampshire in 1792. Within a few months, however, these men were to find themselves arrayed in hostile ranks under banners inscribed Federalist and Republican, fighting at the side of other men with whom, in many cases, they had exchanged heavy blows during the paper money struggle at the ratifying convention." This disintegration of the relatively tranquil politics of manners between men of basically similar backgrounds and persuasions into real disagreements over policy reflected changes taking place across America. However, as the decade progressed, the most incendiary debates raged not over the Bank of the United States and the outlines of fiscal policy but regarding events overseas. As Turner has it, "Not political theory, not economic interest, not class hatreds, but a war raging three thousand miles away divided the people of New Hampshire into hostile political parties. The French revolution and the continental battles growing out of it had been noticed occasionally in the foreign disputes printed four or five months after the event in New Hampshire newspapers, but for three years these had aroused little interest." As the wars between revolutionary France and Great Britain took on a global dimension, suddenly the conflict, and its ramifications, seemed rather more immediate. On the one hand, there was a new sister republic fighting for *Liberté, Égalité, Fraternité*, which had apparently renounced Christianity and was spiraling into dictatorship under a brilliant and ambitious young general. On the other hand were the old imperial masters, against whom many living Americans had taken up arms, and with which most still felt the ties of language, culture, and common ancestry. Most New Hampshire residents, like most New Englanders, chose the latter. That being said, men like Langdon, who had been a supporter of Hamilton's banking measures, were by 1794 becoming much more forthright in their condemnation of British interference and in their praise of France. Langdon explained that he "wished to see the revolutionary spirit of seventy five again revived" and identified with the "Intrepidity, Justice, and Magnanimity" of the French.[47]

The bisection of foreign and domestic interests helped account, in large part, for the tensions between New Hampshire's solidly Federalist status in national politics and its more complicated local affairs. For the majority of New Hampshire residents, antipathy toward France (or, more specifically, toward the French Revolution) did enough to ensure a political unification that transcended boundaries of class, region, and interest. In state politics, however, where economic concerns were more pertinent, the state was divided between East and West, as well as town and country. Exeter, Durham, Dover, Barrington, and Nottingham, the "Old Colony," all adhered to Federalist doctrine, as did the conservative and relatively populous region of the Merrimack Valley, notably Concord, Amherst, Chester, Londonderry, and Gilmantown. For the most part, these towns made up the commercial, political, judicial, and cultural hubs of the state, and as such they wielded considerable power in the legislature. The agricultural areas of the Connecticut Valley were also conservative but were less aligned to the manufacturing and financial interests of Hamiltonian Federalism. While they supported Gilman in most cases and shared in the general Francophobia, their divergent economic interests, and to some extent cultural values, sometimes put them at odds with the eastern Federalist establishment, who could not necessarily rely on their unqualified backing. Portsmouth was, under John Langdon, the state's principal Democrat-Republican stronghold.

While southern New Hampshire was being divided up in accordance with an emerging pattern across the United States, then the inchoate politics of the northern frontier stood apart. A transient population and an emergent economy contributed to the general air of instability, but the region was also preoccupied with rather different issues than both the settled agricultural West and the more urbanized East. The political networks that dominated the more southerly climes, headed by consummate networkers like Gilman and Langdon, were ineffective at managing these disparate and disorganized districts. The region also contained a mixture of different economic interests, a combination of rugged woodsmen and the wealthy speculators who controlled large tracts of land. The imposing physical impediment provided by the White Mountains meant that for long stretches, particularly in the winter months (a season that could in practical terms last up to six months),[48] the region experienced long periods of isolation. Neither Federalists nor Republicans could rely on support from the northern parts of the state, which would act as a decisive factor in subsequent elections.[49]

New Hampshire's political establishment was one of the least progressive with regard to religious freedom in the United States. Along its northern frontier, which was home to the most diverse array of Christian sects and dominations, political debate was frequently dominated by resentment toward a seemingly repressive elite. While the state constitution had been ratified in 1784, it was not until the 1790s that the legislature got around to implementing certain parts of it.[50] One such section was Article 6, which read: "The several parishes, bodies, corporate, or

religious societies shall at all times have the right of electing their own
teachers, and of contracting with them for their support or maintenance, or both. But no person shall ever be compelled to pay towards the
support of the schools of any sect or denomination. And every person,
denomination or sect shall be equally under the protection of the law;
and no subordination of any one sect, denomination or persuasion to
another shall ever be established."[51] In practice, this meant that if towns,
as incorporated entities protected under the article, elected and hired a
church minister, a resident of the town would need to prove, in court,
that they belonged to a distinct religious sect to escape payment of any
taxes associated with the hiring.[52] Considering that many migrants,
especially to the frontier, had been displaced by religious intolerance,
and indeed many of its townships had been founded as the result of
church quarrels, this article was contentious across the northern part
of the state. The original constitution provided no real protection from
persecution. Normally, this took on the character of exclusion from
town affairs, as the town meetinghouse, usually controlled by Congregationalists, was able to bar Baptists, Quakers, and others. While religious
freedom would gradually permeate New England over the course of the
next few decades, sectarian minorities in New Hampshire would have
to wait until the nineteenth century for consistent and lasting progress
in terms of their civil liberties. In pamphlets and sermons, the smaller
Christian communities were the objects of vitriol, and the newspapers
occasionally joined the fray. Baptists were the frequent targets of scorn,
caricatured as a wild rabble, sometimes in terms that likened them to
Native Americans. "A BAPTIST preacher, in the District of Maine, who
was eternally vociferating against learning, one day took his text in the
law of Moses, where it says that the tent or tabernacle shall be covered
with *badger's skins*," went one article in the *Rising Sun* with characteristic scorn. "But unluckily he read *beggar's skins*, and begun his sermon
as follows:—My beloved, what great advantages we have in our day
compared with those under the law, we, whether poor or rich, have our
lives secured to us; but those, whose lot was cast under the law, should
they be poor and obliged to beg, why then flap goes their skin to cover
the tabernacle with." According to the *Spy*, the taking of Presbyterian

communion was a "hazard" to one's eternal soul, "but to receive it from the bishops, or episcopal clergy, has no hazard at all as to its validity."[53] The system of taxation too was biased toward Congregationalists and other denominations with settled constituencies. In order to fully benefit from the law, churches needed fixed addresses and dedicated pastors. Baptists and Methodists, who in New Hampshire tended to rely more on itinerant preachers and ministries, had little use for such mandated imposts.

Few of the clichés used to describe Federalist-era politics survive a detailed inspection of the situation at the grassroots. The two sides in the first party system were often divided as much by their personal interests as their ideologies. The Federalists, the old assumption goes, were the money men, those who profited from, and encouraged, the arrival of paper specie and complex financial instruments and who desired the ascent of both big business and a supportive big government. The Democrat-Republicans were America's natural physiocrats, whose livelihoods depended not on paper but on the soil, whether by tilling it or owning it, urban carpetbaggers set against yeoman farmers and slaveholders. Such a dichotomy, however, fails to encapsulate the nuances of New Hampshire's unique strain of political culture. "If this was strictly true," Turner observes of the Federalist and Republican stereotypes, "no state in the Union would have been more Republican than New Hampshire in 1799." Why would, were it that simple, the Republicans be at their strongest in the most densely populated commercial town in the state, led by a speculator, while the farmers solidly turned out in support of Federalist candidates? It is in circumstances such as these that the Beardsian approach, attempting to account for political differences through differences in social background, can offer only partial explanations. Issues of geopolitics and religion intersected with the supposed class interest of the parties, and of course both sides were subject to the capricious whim of that relentless dynamo of the political turbulence: event. In 1798 the Republicans spectacularly miscalculated when attempting to attack John Adams on the subject of America's French ministers. The people of New Hampshire took the resultant XYZ Affair, in which papers revealing France's attempted extortion of the United States were made public, almost personally; the insult united them behind President Adams and the Federalist Party's local representatives. The Republicans, who now seemed dangerously subversive and in league with foreign malefactors, were crushed in the next set of elections. In 1799 Gilman was elected with some 86 percent of the vote, and Republicans were hounded from the state legislature. That same legislature went on to become Adams's most loyal supporter in the Union, with the resolution supporting his policies taken up by the unanimous result of 127 to 0.[54]

The Republicans, however, were not alone in making errors of judgment. Perhaps careless from the seemingly unassailable position, the high-water mark of Federalist dominance in 1799 would rapidly recede. One mistake was fighting too hard and too long to keep the state capital in Exeter, the stronghold of Federalist organization. This reinforced the fears that many voters held of an aristocratic "Exeter Junto" hoping to cling to power by unconstitutional means. Perhaps the gravest error was the party's attempts, in 1800, to control the state Union Bank for political ends, the levying of taxes for use in speculation, and eventually to attempt to conceal corrupt practices. This all provided plenty of grist for the opposition mill, and one contributor to the *Dartmouth Gazette* sounded a typical note of alarm. "On enquiring of our Member a few days ago, what the General Court had done in their late long and tedious session at Exeter," reported the correspondent, "I found he could not distinctly recollect anything of a public nature, except the assessment of a new State Tax of *Twenty-seven Thousand Dollars*, and an appropriation of a sum supposed to be Twelve or Fifteen Thousand Dollars, for the purchase of twenty-four shares in the *New-Hampshire Bank*." Such a maneuver was grist to the mill of those who saw the Federalists as little more than a gang of financial opportunists and insider traders. "I confess I was not a little surprised to hear of such unexpected transactions. With regard to the Tax, I did not apprehend that the Legislature would, at a juncture like the present, be induced to require new taxes on people, but on the most urgent occasion. . . . It may therefore be considered a tax laid on the people, not merely to meet the exigencies of Government, but for the less honourable purpose of *speculating in Bank Stock*."[55]

From 1800 onward, the development of a truly competitive two-party system took place, one in which Republicans could challenge Federalists across the state.[56] The eventual rise of the Republican Party was not, however, a consequence solely of shifting political demographics. Many people, including politicians, made the gradual transition over toward Jeffersonian Republicanism. Nicholas Gilman, the junior member of the New Hampshire delegation to the Constitutional Convention and a Federalist congressman, is a case in point. Few contemporary accounts of Gilman exist. William Pierce was measured in his appraisal when he noted, "Mr. Gilman is modest, genteel, and sensible. There is nothing brilliant or striking in his character, but there is something respectable and worthy in the Man." A French attaché was less reserved: "a young man of pretensions; little liked by his colleagues; one calls him by derision to the Congress. He has however the advantage of having represented his State in the great Philadelphia Convention and having signed the new Constitution. This circumstance proves that there is not a great choice of things to do in this State, at least the most sensible and skilful men are not rich enough accept a public position."[57] Nevertheless, Gilman provides the model that characterized many New Hampshire Federalists. Despite being a strongly pro-Hamilton Federalist during his time in the state house of representatives, he, like his fellow convention delegate Langdon, eventually drifted toward the Republicans during his time in the state legislature, which he occupied until 1805, and he was elected as a Jeffersonian U.S. senator from 1805 until his death in 1814, at age fifty-eight.[58]

In some respects, this account fits with some common narratives concerning politics and political culture in the early national period: the decline of elite, patriarchal politics and the foreshadowed ascendancy of mass democracy, the many eventually, inevitably, triumphant over the few. To be certain, popular participation in politics had an enormous impact on political culture. Whether the election of 1800 was a "revolution" or not, it is clear things were changing even in conservative New Hampshire. However, nationally speaking, New Hampshire did remain a bastion of Federalism, and while it would be swept up in the landslide of 1804, it was one of only five states to return to the Federalist fold in

1808. As Sean Wilentz points out with regard to 1800, "Although the Republicans put up a spirited, long-shot fight in New England (and nearly captured the Massachusetts statehouse), they did not win a single [electoral] vote in the region." What is also certain, and will be discussed at much greater length later in this book, is that politics in New Hampshire in the 1790s became steadily more coarsened, more mean-spirited, and for all the light and heat produced offered little in the way of tangible improvement. The tranquillity of petty county-town fiefdoms was exchanged for the tumultuous enmity and recriminations of Federalists and Republicans. This shift, when it came, unsettled people accustomed to the old order, and they frequently gave vent to their anxieties in their local newspaper. "Governors, Senators, Judges, Counsellors, Printers, Speakers, Clerks and even Door Keepers," lamented one such correspondent, "must 'budge because they are in place.' Men whose services in the cause of their country—whose wisdom, virtue and ability place them beyond the tongue of everything but democratic slander, have been ousted; to make way for time-servers whose only claim to office is their inveterate enmity to order and good government; and unceasing opposition to the Republican Constitution of the United States." This natural flux of office holding, and the waxing and waning of factions, might seem unremarkable to a modern audience, but it isn't difficult to imagine why they might have provoked unease in the first generation of independent Americans. There was also often a strain of xenophobia that little effort was made to conceal. "Mr. Barnley has been forced to resign; and Messrs Mayo and M'Craw have been violently hurled from their office," the writer concluded, "because they were not Robespierrean Democrats, Tom Paine Christians, and M'Kean wild Irishmen." The Federalists did not have a monopoly on anxiety. One correspondent to the *Republican Ledger* of Portsmouth bemoaned living in a state run by "a few overbearing men who have amassed immense fortunes, by fraud, deception and hypocrisy." The people of the United States, he wrote, "earn their money with too much labor, to have it squandered away by the intrigues of a few artful individuals."[59] New Hampshire was finding, all too quickly, that living free came with its own set of costs.

CHAPTER TWO

"DEVILS AND DIATRIBES"

The Business of the Early American Newspaper

THE PRINTER now earnestly calls on every person indebted to him, either for the GAZETTE, or otherwise, to make immediate payment, which at this time, will be essentially serviceable to him; many of his customers have been induced, though often called upon, to suffer their Newspaper accounts to be long standing, much to his disadvantaged, he is persuaded owing to the smallness of their accounts, they thought them of little consequence to the Printer, and would let them run on 'till they accumulated to a larger sum, and then pay off, but assures those, his subscriptions are very numerous, and when his accounts are made up, even quarterly, amount to a very considerable sum for him:—every person acquainted with the nature of his business, knows he cannot prosecute it to advantage without large sums of ready money. He now rests persuaded, that no person indebted to him, will take it amiss, when presented with his bill, but discharge the same as readily as he was served on command.

—*New Hampshire Gazette*, November 16, 1793

The men who created the United States' first newspapers had a few obvious things in common. They were educated, whether through formal schooling or autodidactic self-discipline. They conducted business on inconsistent profit margins and were participants in an unstable and precarious market. During the 1790s alone, of the twenty-five individuals who tried their hand at publishing a newspaper in the state of New Hampshire, only one, John Melcher, managed to keep control of a newspaper for the entire decade. Most did not make it beyond two years.[1] Fortunes could be made in publishing, but financial ruin was far more probable. Beyond these common traits and challenges, however, marked gradations existed within the trade. Creating a newspaper demanded a mixture of artisanal craftsmanship and qualitative judgment. As Ralph Brown observes, "Well into the nineteenth century the country printer was almost always a jack-of-all-trades." We are familiar with the ink-spattered, hard-handed men engaged in what Jeffrey Pasley has called the "dirty, smelly, physically demanding" business of printing. The quintessential self-made American man, Benjamin Franklin is by far the most famous and emblematic of eighteenth-century printers, but the Horatio Alger narrative was not the only one to feature in the American press. Savvy political operators and journalistic innovators such as Philip Freneau, whom Gordon Wood credits with "altering the terms of the national debate" and effectively framing American first partisan dichotomy, were also key players in early American print.[2] Indeed, the names most familiar to modern readers—Freneau, John Fenno, Benjamin Franklin Bache—are so recognizable because of how exceptional they were. These were men who dealt mostly in the rarefied air of ideas and rhetoric, men who were able to hand over their broadsides and essays to the skilled laborers who manufactured the newspapers. Most journalists, beyond their own social networks, went largely unappreciated or unacknowledged. Indeed, the professional and public identities of those who produced and wrote for newspapers were frequently, and intentionally, hidden from public view.

These bifurcated identities could prove fruitful. Benjamin Russell managed to maintain a successful business empire while remaining one of the most widely read conservative journalists in the republic.[3]

There were also entrepreneurial opportunities for printer-editors in the increasingly crowded marketplace of American publishing. Hudson and Goodwin, proprietors of the *Connecticut Courant*, a paper with roots in the Revolution, in addition to their printer's shop owned shares in a pair of paper mills and had moved into book publishing, with their most popular editions selling thousands of copies. Over time, however, even newspapers that had been run successfully by printer-editors began to draft in dedicated wordsmiths, as when George Goodwin hired Theodore Dwight to provide copy and editorial assistance.[4] The paper was then at both its most profitable and its most influential, moving to new premises and increasing circulation.[5]

From 1790 to 1800, the number of news publications in the United States rose from 92 to 234. Meanwhile, the number of weekly publications more than doubled, while daily newspapers tripled.[6] These newspapers were not only more numerous but also becoming more expansive and standardized. Not everybody prospered in this apparently heady boom period, however. While some proprietors like Russell, Hudson, and Goodwin built substantial networks of print and distribution, most struggled to make ends meet. The incredibly high attrition rate experienced by newspapers tells only part of the story: most of those that survived beyond the typical two years were often saddled with debts, and most failed to make enough money to sustain themselves; most printers relied on other sources of income to supplement their livelihoods. Given the outlook of a small-town weekly newspaper, deciding to start one seems to have been an act of either bravery or delusion. Most who tried seem to have had a little of both.

In the fall of 1792, Ebenezer Andrews, a printer of Boston, was taking inventory. In the latest of a series of increasingly despondent and irate missives to his friend and business partner Isaiah Thomas, he admitted, "I sometimes wish to be rid of the magazine, especially if we could get compensation for it. I have been making a calculation by which it appears to me that we do not get nearly so well paid for the magazine as for other work that we do."[7] His calculations were comprehensive and made for grim reading. On paper, his newspaper should have been making a reasonably robust turnover of £490 per annum, but Andrews had to account for losing more than 16 percent of his income for the year to "bad debts": subscribers and advertisers that had failed to pay or skipped town. His expenses were also mounting alarmingly. After laying out £70 for paper, £54 for copper printing plates, and a whopping £288 on journeymen labor (whom Andrews freely admitted to *under*paying), along with other sundry expenses, Andrews put the total profit for the year at £111. Even this figure, Andrews said, did not tell the whole story. While the physical manufacture of the copies was expensive and time-consuming, he and his presumably harried apprentices spent untold hours sending out papers and chasing recalcitrant subscribers.

The amount £111 a year was not a pittance in the early 1790s, but Andrews had ample reason to be dissatisfied. Given the weighty capital investments that printing entailed (equipment and printing stock being imported at great expense from Britain) and the costs of housing and feeding apprentices (of which Andrews kept twelve), such a return would have been considered disappointing in most other industries. When printers lacked the requisite number of apprentices to meet their work-load, or when the apprentices were not sufficiently trained to complete the task at hand, they had to turn to journeymen printing assistants. Such situations, almost uniformly, left all parties involved feeling cheated, exploited, and aggrieved. "The devil seems to have gotten into the Jour-neymen," railed Andrews. "They now want more than one shilling per token—and the next thing will be more than one shilling."[8] In keeping with trends among most types of skilled American artisan, they could usually command a substantially higher wage than their English coun-terpart, due to the relative paucity of trained labor, and the more sophis-ticated the work, the greater the disparity.[9] Altogether, the owner of a medium-size business in a major American city could be rightfully dis-gruntled by such a meager return on investment. There were also capital outlays to consider. A new set of type, ordered from Fry & Sons of Lon-don, cost Isaiah Thomas £106 (including shipping) on August 16, 1786.[10] Such an outlay might represent a printer's typical turnover for a three-month spell. Start-up costs were quite simply beyond the reach of those without good credit, generous backers, or independent wealth. In 1784 Thomas had type and settings worth £9,600 shipped from London.[11]

Publishing a newspaper could be the least efficient use a printer could make of his press. The huge labor investment in resetting type every week, along with tiny margins and mounting distribution costs, gave some printers pause. Andrews, upon reviewing his accounts for 1790, discovered that he had made far greater profits from the publication of a spelling book, a job that from the initial typesetting to sending the product to market took less than a month, than his newspaper had made in the whole year. A spelling book, or "grammar," a staple of medium-size presses, could be printed in huge quantities (Andrews printed thirty thousand in a single run), and plates could be reused many times. They required no complicated system of distribution, no constant updating, and customers (usually schools and academies) might purchase twenty or thirty at a time. Andrews confessed to a friend that he could see no practical business reason he should even bother putting out his paper at all, when it took up most of his own and his apprentices' time and made up a fraction of his income as compared to grammars, Bibles, and job work.[12] Yet he persisted, churning out a weekly paper that he was neither interested in nor noticeably profiting from. He was by no means unusual in this. Printers were also exposed to huge, and largely unavoidable, risk when taking on jobs. Sometimes materials unexpectedly became costlier, transportation difficult, or buyers pulled out; Matthew Carey of Philadelphia lost £100 on a single print run after miscalculating his costs in one such incident.[13]

Printers like Andrews and Thomas had, at least, the luxury of independence. For less fortunate or established printers, reliant on patrons or creditors, the margin between solvency and ruin could be slim. Such men had just enough autonomy to run the internal business affairs of their print shops as they saw fit, but they were tied into larger networks controlled by larger publishers. The distance between the amounts of money such a franchisee might receive and their costs was often irreconcilable. Leonard Worcester, in a despairing letter to his master, laid out the extent of his plight. "The newspaper to remain upon its present plan," Worcester explained, "three hands must be employed."[14] Worcester received £730 a year from Isaiah Thomas, who had provided the initial investment for the business. While this was a considerable sum, from it Worcester was expected to meet every single cost that might arise. In the winter of 1796, he calculated that between the cost of housing and feeding his apprentices (£230 per annum), maintaining and repairing his equipment (£100 per annum), as well as myriad other smaller expenses, he was left paying himself a salary of £85 a year. Crucially, though, he could not even depend on receiving that paltry sum, as any unforeseen expense, be it a rise in the cost of ink or the failure of a crucial piece of machinery, would ultimately come out of his own income. Part of Worcester's contract also involved surrendering more than a third of his annual turnover to his investors, regardless of whether he had made a profit or was able to pay himself. Despairing of his situation, Leonard Worcester did what seemingly was the only option available to him: he demanded more money (a 25 percent increase) and threatened to walk out when his demand wasn't met.[15] Worcester would, three years later, quit the printing business altogether, striking out to Vermont to become a minister. One only hopes that preaching the Word paid better than printing it.

Context played a large part in determining the chances of a printing business. In the winter of 1795, Elisha Waldo, a young man in the trade, was faced with a painful dilemma. Based in Brookfield, Massachusetts, Waldo could barely keep his enterprise afloat with the 310 subscribers he had accrued.[16] Brookfield, he was gradually coming to realize, was too small a market to sustain a newspaper in the long term. While he was desperately seeking customers at home,[17] he made a study of the various conditions necessary for a profitable and sustainable newspaper. Springfield, the nearest major town, had a large and literate population but, he noted, already boasted two active presses. Attempting to compete against established brand recognition and market share was, he concluded, a recipe for failure.[18]

Dissatisfied with his immediate options, Waldo scouted (either in person or by inquiring through friends) a number of potential new locations. Albany, New York, when he stumbled upon it, seemed almost too good to be true.[19] Waldo was astounded that such a community, with a population of nearly four thousand, and soon to be made the state capital, lacked not only a regularly printed newspaper but also an active printer. He had found his opening. That was until he stopped to consider a heretofore unencountered problem: the enormous expense of uprooting a printer's shop. Whatever advantages might lie in the printing trade, mobility was not among them. The tools of the trade were, for the most part, wrought of unwieldy and cumbrous cast iron and lead. Once transportation costs to New York were factored, it slowly dawned on him that he might as well start from scratch. Ultimately, he elected to stay in Brookfield, scratching along with his modest but reliable base of subscribers,[20] dreaming up ever more inventive ways of getting his product to a presumably eager public.

An interesting, and usually unspoken, truth about printers is that they seldom viewed their failures as anything other than a problem of distribution. Failures, the nearly universal assumption went, came down to the logistics of marketing, sales, and payments. Waldo, like most of his fellow printers, left no evidence that he devoted any thought at all to the possibility of attracting more readers by making his newspaper *better*. Editors generally gave more thought to satisfying advertisers than subscribers. The willingness of the consumer to buy any of a range of apparently interchangeable options was effectively taken for granted.

The average New Hampshire printer produced fewer than two thousand single-side sheets in a twelve-hour day, allowing for the production of a thousand "quarto" newspapers, which were doubled-sided large sheets.[21] However, most papers did not require anything like that capacity. While subscriber rates varied from town to town, for many country printers a circulation of four hundred was considered respectable.[22] Isaiah Thomas was being more candid than most when he noted, "It has always been allowed that 600 customers, with a considerable number of advertisements, weekly, will but barely support the publication of a newspaper." Milton Hamilton has underscored the importance of post riders in calculating readership and circulation numbers: "The average printer circulated five or six hundred copies weekly, a few in the village, but the greater share by post riders."[23] These post riders (men employed to deliver papers to subscribers) had to be paid, of course, either directly by the printer or by taking a share of the sale.

Printers sometimes collaborated with their ostensible rivals in other towns, proposing quid pro quo deals where both parties peddled subscriptions for the other's paper.[24] These relationships could even become formalized and were sometimes remunerative. One arrangement struck between two New England editors proposed a 5 percent commission for each subscriber one could find for the other's paper in their town.[25] Post riders acted, in a sense, as franchisees of the printer. Their job was not just to deliver the product but also to seek out and secure new customers. "A man some time since," recalled Elisha Waldo, "made application to me to ride as far as Connecticut and carry our papers—he did not produce as many subscribers as expected." In order to make their way into the market, they would frequently run loss-leader deals. Isaiah Beese, a post rider and newsagent, wrote to one publisher: "Your magazine is very well liked, a number of persons talk of taking it, but only two have subscribed as yet. . . . Send on a few numbers monthly, six will do, I will do my best to dispose of them." This was common practice for many printers: give the product away for free, in the hope of attracting subscribers and cultivating word of mouth. Such tactics sometimes proved successful. Five months after he started distributing free copies of the paper, Beese placed a large order to meet the demand of his growing number of paying subscribers. If attracting new subscribers was difficult, and extracting cash from them was frequently Sisyphean, then the customers themselves also frequently met with frustration. Papers frequently miscarried or were rendered unreadable by the omnipresent sleet and snow of the long New England winters. Prompt customer service was also hard to come by. Isaac Story, of Marblehead, was forced to write four, increasingly vexed, letters before his subscription was canceled.[26]

An observant subscriber to a late-eighteenth-century newspaper would learn, in time, to expect certain things: political dispatches from Philadelphia, London, and Paris; the latest commodity prices from the Antilles; last Sunday's sermon; advertisements for hatters, wheelwrights, sign makers, and lawyers; bad jokes and awful poetry. Among these mainstays, they would grow accustomed to pleas from the printer for overdue subscription payments. This type of practice was not unusual in all business types found in rural and small-town communities. Bookkeeping was a vital part of the economy, particularly for an industry like newspapers, which relied on regular deliveries that were often provided by mail. "I confess to many of my *customers*, that I want payments more punctually; and to those who are *not*, that I want more custom," implored George Hough of Concord. "Some have made regular payments; and to such I render my grateful acknowledgements; But to those who are delinquent, and inattentive to paying, I most seriously address myself, and urge them not to put the '*evil day*' day further off."[27] It seems reasonable to suppose that not all of those subscribers whom Melcher and Hough, perhaps not coincidentally two of New Hampshire's longest-lasting printers, were addressing were negligent or destitute but rather in the habit of settling their account on their occasional trips into town. "Payments must be made quarterly, to enable the Editor to satisfy the demands of the paper makers, the boarding house, and various other necessary creditors," read an insert in the *New Hampshire Sentinel*. It goes on to illustrate the degree to which such printers were rooted in a rural or semirural community, informing subscribers that "WOOD, BUTTER, CHEESE, GRAIN and almost every article used in a family, will be as acceptable as the cash, if brought in season. The Editor promises to use every Customer well that will use him well."[28] The printer's livelihood was inextricably intertwined with the material economies of agrarian, pastoral, and artisanal life. The country printer could not afford to be choosy about what he took as payment. "Payment was made in kind rather than in coin," one recalled, "and every sort of procedure has legal tender at the printing office."[29] It was an invisible but essential part of his job to solicit, collect, account for, and eventually monetize the assorted miscellany.

If there was a sustainable living to be made in the newspaper trade, few seem to have found it. Taking the state of New Hampshire in the 1790s as a case in point, with the exceptions of John Melcher of the *New Hampshire Gazette* and Charles Pierce of the *Oracle of the Day*, most newspapers cycled through proprietors, printers, and editors with great rapidity; the average commercial life span of the New Hampshire printer was a little more than two years. Papers either were sold to the next optimist with money to burn or folded. Of the twelve newspapers newly established in New Hampshire in the 1790s, only half were still active at the end of the decade.

TABLE I. NEW HAMPSHIRE NEWSPAPER PUBLISHERS, 1790–1800

CONCORD	
Concord Herald	1790–1794: George Hough
Mirrour	1792–1794: Elijah Russell; 1794–1797: Elijah Russell and Moses Davis: 1797–1799: Moses Davis
DOVER	
Phoenix *cum* Sun	1792: Eliphalet Ladd; 1793: Eliphalet Ladd and George Homans; 1794–1800: Samuel Bragg Jr.
EXETER	
Gazetteer *cum* Herald of Liberty	1790–1794: Henry Ranlet; 1794: William Stearns and Samuel Winslow; 1795–1796: Samuel Winslow
HANOVER	
Eagle *cum* Darmouth Gazette	1793: Josiah Dunham; 1795–1798: John Mosely Dunham and Benjamin True; 1799–1800: Moses Davis
KEENE	
Columbian Informer	1793–1795: Henry Black; 1795: William Ward Blake
Rising Sun	1795: Cornelius Sturtevant, Abijah Wilder, and Elias Sturtevant
New Hampshire Sentinel	1799–1800: John Prentis
PORTSMOUTH	
New Hampshire Gazette	1790–1800: John Melcher
New Hampshire Spy	1790–1791: George and John Osborne; 1792–1793: John Osborne

Data compiled from the Library of Congress.

Most papers went through owners and editors frequently. Sometimes, these changes were unfortunately inevitable, as with the death of Henry Blake in 1795, at which point the editorship of *Columbian Informer* briefly passed to William Ward Blake. As can be seen in Table 1, the newspaper was often a family business, not just with the Blakes and Sturtevant of Keene but also with the Osbornes of Portsmouth and the

Dunhams of Hanover. Also worth noting is the career of Moses Davis, which began on the *Mirrour* of Concord, but then in 1799 decamped to the *Dartmouth Gazette* of Hanover. Printing was a business open to immigrants, but one that demanded skills and contacts. Durey has observed of British political émigrés looking to set up in the United States that "some who had previous experience in the higher branches of the print and publishing trades nevertheless had to start from the bottom." It did, though, as Durey points out, provide a path into American politics and society for such men. Cases such as James Thomson Callender and Joseph Gales of the *American Daily Advertiser* were examples of migrants who rose quickly.[30]

In bookkeeping terms, one of the most sizable set of assets a printer might possess was copyrights. Between them partners Isaiah Thomas and Ebenezer Andrews held copyrights worth an estimated £5,700, far in excess of any machinery or stock they had on hand.[31] Everton has observed, "Print was a business, and publishers were its merchants. As Bourdieu puts it, they are 'cultural bankers,' improved by definition in the manufacture and maintenance of various forms of capital."[32] The "capital" of the book was, to some extent, dependable. Bibles and dictionaries could be stockpiled and sold in a month, a year, or even a decade. Newspapers were more perishable and started to depreciate in value from the moment of their creation. While such amassed intellectual property looked good in an account ledger, it could present an unwary printer with a dangerously false sense of security. Printers like Thomas and Andrews calculated the total value of their copyrights by the amount they had *paid* for them; they had no sense, and no real way of ascertaining, what they would fetch on the open market, should they be sold. The fee one paid an author for the right to publish their work usually bore scant relationship to the eventual value they represented to the publisher. Each copyright represented a delicately calculated speculation for the publisher, and most long-term practitioners hedged their bets in volume and diversity. A successful hit, or a perennial seller, would cover the losses incurred by the many more copyrights that didn't succeed. The accounting system used, therefore, was akin to a gambler tabulating his income by tracking his wagers rather than his winnings.

Another set of complications arose when printers counted their intellectual property toward their assets. Text copyrights are among the least fungible commodities one can own; the potential market for them was, in the late eighteenth century, the handful of other printers who bothered to pay lip service to the infant laws on the subject. Thomas and Andrews owned the copyright to a huge number of texts: schoolbooks, encyclopedias, hymnals, grammars, poetry anthologies, translations of foreign texts. The first problem was that any publisher worth the name, in America or Britain, owned works that were, if not identical, then practically interchangeable so far as the reading public was concerned. A printer could appraise their capital however they wished, but if there wasn't a single person willing to part with cash for it, the listed value became largely academic. Numerous printers, teetering on the brink of insolvency, learned the hard way that their apparently ample cushion of salable equity was not worth the paper it was printed on.

The second problem would be entirely familiar to anyone looking to monetize "content" in this or any other age: piracy. American copyright law, like much else in the young Union, was informed by British precedent, in this case the Statute of Anne of 1710. The U.S. Copyright Act, passed in 1790, was far narrower in scope than our contemporary notions of intellectual property and the protections that the law affords today. The original duration of a copyright was a mere fourteen years, which the author had the right to extend once, creating a maximum duration of twenty-eight years. A young writer could reasonable expect, therefore, their rights to their work to expire within their own lifetime. What might be considered an infringement of copyright was also much more tightly defined. Copies, Lewis Hyde explains, "meant literal, verbatim reproductions; no one needed permission to make what are now called derivative works—translations, sequels, abridgements, and so forth." America's founders were wary of what were called "perpetual monopolies," and this view extended to intellectual property. Private rights were important, but so was the public interest.[33]

Even within these modest parameters, the Copyright Act was barely enforced or enforceable, even within the United States, and printed material from abroad was not regulated at all.[34] A printer might be able, albeit at great cost of time and money, to sue a local plagiarist, but they were altogether powerless in the face of international bootlegs. For northern New England printers, dozens of miles from the Canadian border, as well as the constant influx of British print into the seaboard ports, this presented an especially ominous threat. Furthermore, the Copyright Act extended only to maps, charts, and books; other types of printed material received no legal protection whatsoever.[35] Therefore, when a printer did fall on hard times, or was even foreclosed upon, they discovered that the things that held value were the corporeal accoutrements of the trade: printing blocks, rollers, presses, ink. They also discovered that once these had been hawked to the nearest opportunist, the intellectual property that had previously represented value only to the solitary constituency of themselves was now of use to precisely no one.

One way of ascertaining the precariousness of most printers' positions is to look into the amounts of money they squabbled over. A heated exchange of correspondence between Thomas and John Boyle, two of the biggest printing names in Worcester and Boston, respectively, threatened to escalate into legal action.[36] The dispute centered on which of the two men was to foot the bill for shipping costs incurred, which totaled less than three pounds. The bitterness with which two relatively successful and prosperous printers argued over such trifling sums reveals much about eighteenth-century notions of honor, but more about desperate straits such businessmen regularly found themselves in. Yet the printing business trundled on, and the profusion of weekly newspapers in the newly formed United States continued unabated. The question persists: Why? Once a publisher had good editions of a Bible, dictionary, and spelling book, or better yet a license to print official and state documents, the relatively trivial profits to be made in the newspaper trade, stacked up against the unavoidable risk, the constant need for new material, and the sheer amount of work involved in resetting type every week, it seems almost irrational that businessmen would go to such trouble for so little return. What motivated these entrepreneurs to persist in the face of a seemingly stark economic reality?

Despite the apparently bleak prognosis, there were some practical enticements for getting into the news-sheet business. While the paper itself might represent a net loss to the printing office, there could be other commercial compensations. Publishing a newspaper has to be seen in the broader context of a printer's entire operation. "The book-store at Walpole was one of [Isaiah Thomas's] most profitable investments," Green has observed, "because readers of the Farmer's Weekly Museum were influenced to buy books recommended by Dennie." Another, more cynical, reason for publishing a newspaper was the personal and political patronage it would frequently attract. Owning a press, but more important demonstrating one's ability to get printed matter into the hands of the public, frequently led to far more stable and lucrative government work in the future. Isaiah Thomas was appointed postmaster of Worcester, Massachusetts, by Timothy Pickering, the postmaster general of the United States, an easy transition since Thomas's print distribution meant that he was informally doing the job already.[37] Even the publishers of major papers eagerly sought these subsidies. John Fenno, printer of the *Gazette of the United States*, in 1789 received only ninety dollars from his six hundred subscribers. Fenno came to believe that any printer, even one with a popular paper, would need at least a "slice from the Printing loaf" that came from what he called the "executive printing business." Otherwise, he thought, "without auxiliary aid of this sort, I do not possibly see how I can get along."[38] Jeffrey Pasley has demonstrated the high volume of newspaper editors and publishers who were able, with the aid of their own periodicals, to springboard themselves into politics. Given the noticeably large numbers of lawyers who became journalists, journalists who became lawyers, and of either to run for office, newspapers became in the early years of the republic a well-marked route into a career in electioneering.[39]

Pragmatism aside, there was another, rather more complicated, set of reasons. Newspapers occupied a curious cultural hinterland in Federalist-era America, neither high art nor irredeemably lowbrow. They were, by turns, frivolous and sanctimonious, unscrupulous and self-righteous, politically indifferent and rabidly partisan. They would campaign against their competitors, report fictions and hearsay as gospel truths, and print virulent slander against the innocent. They purported to be bastions of truth and morality, yet existed week to week as vehicles of advertisements sold to the highest bidder. They were disposable, for the most part lacking recognized authors or a coherent editorial persona. Yet, undeniably, they were a crucial vector of culture in the early national period and touched the lives of Americans who otherwise would have been isolated from the debates and dichotomies that shaped the nation in those turbulent years. Despite how unequivocally bad much of the journalism and writing in the newspapers of the time was, editors were generally held in high esteem by their readers. To be sure, many (particularly from elite society) bemoaned the press's baleful influence, complaining that it promoted factionalism, populism, and national disunity. The tone of correspondents, however, and the fragments that are available to us from readers, suggests a different attitude. "Books and newspapers—which are now diffused even among country towns, so as to be in the hands of all, young and old—were then scarce, and were read respectfully, and as they were grave matters, demanding thought and attention," wrote Samuel Goodrich, recalling his youth in New England in the 1790s. Goodrich was at pains to point out that rather than being "toys or pastimes," or idle distractions "taken up every day, and by everyone . . . in the short intervals of labor, and then hastily dismissed, like waste paper," newspapers were considered objects of great value. To illustrate this, Goodrich explains the material lengths to which readers went to partake of the paper. "The aged sat down when they read, and drew forth their spectacles, and put them deliberately and reverently upon the nose. These instruments were not as now, little tortoise shell hooks, attached to a ribbon, and put on and off with a jerk; but were made of silver or steel, substantially made, and calculated to hold a firm and steely grasp, showing the gravity of the uses to which they were devoted." In all, Goodrich couldn't help but reflect on the passing of the world that he grew up in. "Even the young approached a book with reverence, and a newspaper with awe," he sighed. "How the world has changed."[40]

Comments like these were not uncommon, and when letters to the editors of newspapers are examined, the impression of reverence is further reinforced. "The newspaper was perused from its head to the last advertisement in the last column," Milton Hamilton observed. "Reading matter was scarce in most homes, and in many the newspaper and the

Bible had to fill the want." While it was important that printers were ordinary members of the community, with businesses to run and a dependence on social contacts, it also seems that they were respected, frequently distinguished towns- and village folk. As Pasley states, "Printing provided many a young working man with a substitute for the advanced education that only a tiny minority of early Americans could obtain." While they were artisans rather than members of the elite, they enjoyed a higher social status than most of their fellow artisans. As the possession of a printing press was something of a status symbol for a community, as well as providing the means to print useful official documents, their owners were far more likely to rub shoulders with local "government officials, political leaders, lawyers and clergymen," the most active participants in newspaper content, than other manual laborers were.[41] Running a newspaper was more than an entrepreneurial opportunity. In fact, anybody with a real interest in riches would have been well advised to steer well clear of the business altogether. What it did offer was the opportunity for men who, despite lacking the traditional qualifications of lineage or property, sought influence. The relatively lowly economic station of most printer-editors belies the power they held in forming and shaping communities.[42]

Owning, or editing, a newspaper put a person at the center of the community. Not only did they act as conduits for communication, but they stood alongside the minister, mayor, and tavern keeper as a locus of social and cultural life. Shopkeepers and tradesmen advertised through them. Farmers and speculators relied on them for up-to-date international prices. Politicians and preachers depended on them to organize gatherings and promulgate their messages. Like that other weekly institution of early American village life, the church, the newspaper actually permeated into the daily lives of those even who did not directly engage in it, as Thomas Leonard has demonstrated.[43] The paper served as fodder for barroom disputation, prayer-meeting reflection, and personal rumination. As people traded papers among one another, they were participating not only in discrete exchanges of information but also in a civic performance.

While they might not be as personally visible, few local notables could compete with the printer for name recognition, and this extended far beyond the immediate environs of the immediate locale. A James Giles, of Bridgeton, West Jersey, attached a note to his subscription to the *Worcester Spy*: "I have a strong desire to know whether Mr Isaiah Thomas, one of the proprietors of your paper, is the same person, who served in Lamb's Regiment of the Artillery during the war or not—if he is, I will thank you to be so obliging to note it on the next paper you send me."[44] Such personal communications were not uncommon; publishers were possibly the easiest people to reach in the entire United States, perhaps even including those who held high office. Their names, and place of business, were printed in books, newspapers, pamphlets, and countless other ephemera disbursed across the entire nation. It is no wonder that so many took assumed names.

Correspondence directed toward printer-editors, even when it expressed dissent on political lines, was usually written with courtesy and not a little obsequiousness (this is easily understood, of course; editors were under no obligation to print attacks against their character). While many letters of protest were written to newspapers, because of pseud-onymous authorship, the aggression tended not to redound directly to the editor. Many locally generated articles begin with a similar formula. "Mr. Printer, please give the following a place in your Sun,"[45] some read, or "Mr. Printer, PERMIT me through the medium of your useful paper, to acquaint the public with a mode of cultivating apple trees from cut-tings."[46] Articles with headlines like "Biography of WILLIAM STRAHAN, a late celebrated Printer,"[47] a well-known English printer, further attest to the standing that printers could achieve. While Pasley is assuredly correct that printing was a "dirty, smelly, physically demanding job," the manual aspects of the occupation probably strengthened this sense of social location. As Ralph Adams Brown put it, "The first journalists ... were men of many parts." They were, variously, printers (in the very practical typesetting, lever-pulling sense), editors, advertising managers, book publishers and retailers, stationers, government employees, real estate agents, tutors, political leaders, or post riders. While the likes of Robert Morris abhorred the sweating multitudes, the public voice of the new provincial newspaper, even when dogmatically Federalist like those of New Hampshire, most often presumed to speak on behalf of the yeomen and artisans, and too elevated a status would have served only to alienate the editor from his community of reader-consumers. "The Editor acknowledges with gratitude the generous encouragement of the public, in patronizing his infant establishment," ran a piece in the *Political and Sentimental Repository.* "As this is the season for payments, when the land is flowing with milk and honey, and the industrious husbandmen are reaping the rewards of their virtuous labors, let not the Printer be forgotten."[48] Such appeals situated the editor-printer within their village community.

Though the editors of New Hampshire's newspapers were articulate, earnest men, as evidenced by their style of thought and of prose, they were perceived as, and perceived themselves to be, a part of a broader social spectrum. Contemporary New Hampshire historian George Barstow provides a snapshot of the career of George Hough, publisher of the *Herald*:

> Towards the close of the year, printing was first introduced, on rather a limited scale, at Concord. George Hough, who was during his life engaged more than fifty years in the typographic print, came to Concord from Windsor, Vermont where he had been engaged, in company with Alden Spooner, in the publication of the Vermont Journal. His printing press, the first established in this state north of Exeter, was set up in a small building in front of the ground now occupied by the state-house; and the first issued from it was "Doddsley's Christian Economy," which was published in October. On the 5th of January, of the following year, he commenced the publication of a weekly paper, called the Concord Herald which, with several changes in title, was continued till 1805. Such was the first beginning of printers in Concord, where it has since increased to such an extent, as to entitle that place to a high rank among the principal publishing towns in the country.[49]

Part of the role of the printer-cum-publisher-editor was to be a participant in multiple spheres of social and cultural life. The best examples took care to cultivate contacts and sources not only from within their own professional and class spheres, but among those in the worlds of business, church, and government as well. William Bentley, the Salem polymath and journalist, held a regular levee of merchants and marine captains, who kept him abreast of events that went unremarked upon among the lyceums and salons of his own kind. Men like Bentley, in addition to making otherwise unusual contacts in their own community, could also call on professional, intellectual, and cultural networks farther afield. Living in the prosperous but still relatively peripheral Salem, Bentley noted that he "had no literary men of my society," and his publishing activities gave him access to the livelier discourse of Boston, both in correspondence and sometimes in person.[50]

The 1790s represent an important turning point in the understanding of what it meant to be a newspaperman. As networks of distribution and subscription expanded, the production process began to demand more of a printer's time. Meanwhile, these same developments meant that more news was available than ever before. The notion that an individual could be responsible for overseeing the manufacturing and commercial aspects of the business, while digesting a steadily increasing stream of news, sifting through correspondence, and writing editorials, came under challenge. In a world of increasingly plentiful information, it was necessary that someone serve as a filter to the growing deluge of news. The role of "gatekeeper," which according to Pamela Shoemaker is the "process by which the billions of messages that are available in the world get cut down and transformed into the hundreds of messages that reach a given person on a given day," has always been integral to what it means to be an editor; by the eighteenth century, however, the function was becoming indispensable.[51] While the traditional dual role of editor and printer remained common, some papers began to experiment with a more modernized division of labor, and the *Farmer's Weekly Museum* of Walpole demonstrated the most pronounced delineation of these positions in Federalist-era New Hampshire.

The *Museum*, despite its short life span from 1793 to 1799 (in which time it went into and out of business on more than one occasion), produced an unusually large quantity of original and sometimes controversial content, written for the most part by editor Joseph Dennie. The progeny of two prestigious and privileged families, he hardly fitted the mold of the Franklinesque "self-made man." The Dennies were, according to Harold Milton Ellis, part of the "Merchant aristocracy," and the Greens were "probably the most remarkable family in the annals of American printing" and "people of property and good standing, who enjoyed an excellent reputation for uprightness and for honesty and business."[52] Before settling in Philadelphia, Dennie was a model of late-eighteenth-century mobility. Having graduated in the humanities from Harvard, from 1789 to 1799 he lived in Boston, Lexington, Cambridge, Groton, Charlestown (New Hampshire), Boston again, and Walpole, changing address eight times, after embarking on a series of failed enterprises. Before establishing himself in Walpole, Dennie had practiced as a lawyer, having passed the bar at Keene in 1794 (indeed, he came to New Hampshire with the intention, or more probably under the pretense, of practicing law), and served as a part-time magazine and newspaper editor.

Dennie was a regular unpaid contributor to the *Farmer's Weekly Museum*, starting in October 1795, before Isaiah Thomas relinquished his partnership in the paper, and David Carlisle appointed Dennie editor. After co-owning the *Weekly Museum*, Isaiah Thomas went on to greater fame as author of *The History of Printing in America, with a Biography of Printers, and an Account of Newspapers* (1810), and founder and president of the American Antiquarian Society. Before achieving success, Thomas's life story, which he recorded in fragmentary form, tells us much about the economic situation and social standing an aspiring printer might enjoy. Thomas had signed on as an indentured apprentice in 1756 to the Boston printer Zechariah Fowle, at the age of seven. His travails in business and life included squatting in abandoned buildings, selling his printing stock to pay debts, and divorce. Evidently, though, opportunities existed, too. In 1796 Thomas's main print shop in Worcester held inventory of almost $40,000, and elsewhere he held controlling interests in five bookstores, three newspapers, and one of the best-regarded magazines in the country, in the form of the *Worcester Magazine*. When he accounted for his assets in 1802, he found himself to be worth $151,340, making him one of the wealthiest men in the country. By the end of his career, he had business interests in Walpole, Brookfield, and Boston; was a respected Grand Lodge Mason; and was operating his own paper mill.[53] Carlisle, on the other hand, was largely responsible for the business side of the *Weekly Museum*, having been entrusted with investment capital by Thomas. As Andrew P. Peabody described him in the nineteenth century, "Carlisle seems to have been, if not a ready writer, a wise purveyor. . . . [I]t is the token of the successful manager of a journal or magazine, not that he can write well, but that he knows where to look for good writers."[54] A New Hampshire native, Carlisle was entrusted by Thomas with a press with which to found the *Farmer's Weekly Museum*.[55]

Dennie initially drew a salary of $110 (a fairly modest sum for a man of his background and education) and continued the intermittent practice of law to subsidize his journalism. As time went on, he abandoned his legal practice to focus solely on his writing and editing, which seemed to better suit his temperament. "Dennie wrote with great rapidity, and generally postponed his task until he was called upon for *copy*," Joseph Buckingham, a young employee of the Walpole printers, recorded in his memoirs. "It was frequently necessary to go to his office, and it was not uncommon to find him in bed at a late hour in the morning." Buckingham also remarked on Dennie's fitful approach to writing, noting that "his copy was often given out in small portions, a paragraph or two at a time; sometimes it was written in the printing office, while the compositor was waiting to put it in type." One anecdote from Buckingham perfectly illustrates the famous editor's cavalier approach to the running of his paper:

> One of the best of his lay sermons was written at the village tavern, directly opposite the office, in a chamber where he and his friends were amusing themselves with cards. It was delivered to me by piecemeal, at four or five different times. If he happened to be engaged in a game when applied for copy, he would ask someone to *play his hand for him while he could give the devil his due.* When I called for the closing paragraph of the sermon, he said, "*Call again in five minutes.*" "No," said Tyler, "I'll write the improvement for you." He accordingly wrote the concluding paragraph, and Dennie never saw it till it was put in print.[56]

By 1798 his salary had increased nearly fivefold to just over $500, placing him squarely in the ranks of the comfortably off, particularly in a relatively small town like Walpole.[57] This rather propitious rise in such a short period of time is illustrative of the social mobility of editors.

The men who composed newspapers were remunerated for their labor to very different degrees from region to region, as well as from press to press.

This forms a part of a broader process that Pasley describes as the "gentrification" of the partisan press in America. The division of labor between those who "provided strictly mechanical services to Federalist political leaders," on the one hand, and the "young lawyer-literati," on the other, was far more evident among the newspapers sympathetic to (or backed by) the Federalist cause than the Republican. Part of the explanation can be found in Federalist attitudes toward class and labor. At the practical level, Dennie and his ilk were little inclined to engage in anything as strenuously proletarian as operating an iron printing press. Beyond this, there was an ideological dimension. The principle of a virtuous, enlightened elite that colored Federalist politics extended as well to journalism. "The most a Federalist printer could usually hope for," Pasley explains, "was to be the business manager of the operation, overseeing finances and production." The political agency was, in these cases, largely left to men like Dennie.[58] Dennie began to spend less time on his paper, before it collapsed in 1799, and he struck out for Philadelphia seeking the fame and fortune he confidently assumed his talents deserved.

For men like Dennie, therefore, involvement in a small-town newspaper had little to do with community engagement (he left for Philadelphia at the first opportunity), nor could a Harvard-educated lawyer with his family connections be too hard-pressed for cash. Instead, five or ten years spent editing a weekly newspaper might serve as a stepping-stone to a career in politics, publishing, or literature. Dennie would go on to assist with the editorship of the nationally circulated *Gazette of the United States*, no doubt due to the notoriety he generated at the *Museum*, before becoming the editor and chief writer of the literary magazine the *Port Folio*, which doubtless suited him better than reporting livestock prices and responding to letters from irate farmers. One of the reasons people did not stay in the trade for very long was not necessarily that they failed, but rather that they succeeded.

There is no single explanation as to why someone went into the early

American newspaper business. In fact, there were probably as many explanations as there were newspapermen. Some were well-to-do Harvard graduates with family money and nebulous ambitions. Others were working-class autodidacts with a little formal schooling and quixotic faith in one day turning a profit. Many were born into the trade, serving as apprentices and later inheritors of their fathers' businesses. Others wrote for the love of party, of abolition, of temperance, or of God. The only commonality between them all is that they were, in this moment of embryonic nationhood, participating in the creation, and the contesting, of a culture.

CHAPTER THREE

"DEAR MR. EDITOR . . ."

Reading the Early American Newspaper

To publish a good News-Paper is not so easy an Undertaking as many
People imagine it to be. The Author of a Gazette (in the Opinion of
the Learned) ought to be qualified with an extensive Acquaintance
with Languages, a great Easiness and Command of Writing and
Relating things cleanly and intelligibly, and in a few Words; he should
be able to speak of War both by Land and Sea; be well acquainted
with Geography, with the History of the Time, with the several Interests of Nations. Men thus accomplish'd are very rare in this remote
Part of the World; and it would be well if the Writer of these Papers
could make up among his Friends what is wanting in himself.

—Benjamin Franklin

Small-town American newspapers of the late eighteenth century
were remarkably uniform objects. They were, almost without exception,
four pages in length, and usually published no more than twice a week.
Unless given over to some event of particular notice (and presidential
elections, for example, seldom received such lavish treatment), little news
appeared on the front page, it being given over to advertisements, shipping
reports, and agricultural prices. Pages 2 and 3 typically contained the bulk

of the "news" content, with some papers opting to separate the centerfold into international and domestic affairs. The last page typically contained overflow content or late additions, along with poetry, a transcript of a local sermon, and more advertisements. Outside of some small embellishments on the front-page header, and a very occasional illuminated letter to begin a major article, they had little in the way of graphic content and were entirely monochromatic. News was drawn from a variety of sources: lifted directly from other newspapers, taken from the editor's private correspondence with distant acquaintances, or related by itinerants—merchants, preachers, and seamen. These considerations notwithstanding, the style, and particularly the preoccupations, of the journalism is shockingly redolent. If the printing is sometimes shoddy, the language is generally clear and comprehensible; it is the labor of the craftsman rather than the artist, usually emphasizing utility over expression. The parlor tricks of the journalist are all in evidence: hyperbole, the juxtaposition of moral outrage, and titillation. The content is a mixture of politics, religion, poetry, scandal (sex not normally being in the frame, but seldom far from it), commercial advertisement, and, on occasion, sport. Human obsessions and peccadilloes seldom change. What is remarkable is the extent to which the tenor of the reportage remains familiar. Along with the sober recounting of wars and royal successions are the anecdotal pieces, often recounted thirdhand, which are the instantly recognizable progenitors of our tabloid press, with their constant interplay of moral allegory and frivolous novelty.

One popular type of journalism could be filed under "animals do the darnedest things." The *Spy* ran the story of the "Pumping Cow," noting that "a very singular instance of sagacity, says a London paper, was lately observed in a young cow. . . . The animal being in want of water, went to the pump-well, and taking the handle between her horns, worked the pump and helped herself to drink!!!" The pieces concludes, "Ye *learned Pigs*—ye *calculating Horses*—and *ye dancing Dogs*, hide your diminished heads before this *pumping Cow*." The author, as they implied with their reference to other farmyard denizens, was working within the tropes of an almost formalized story type. Perhaps it is unsurprising that newspapers with names like the *Farmer's Feast*[1] and the *Rural Repository*[2] would contain so much correspondence about cattle, horses, and pigs;

people simply looked about and recorded what they saw. The Pumping Cow jostled for position on page 3 of the *New Hampshire Spy* with the killing of forty-seven Seneca chiefs, a peach-tree blight (along with useful instructions for disposing of ailing trees), an acid retort to an anonymous letter of the previous issue on the failures of democracy, and an "original anecdote" about three lawyers and an "old Dutch woman," the lawyers falling on the wrong side of the punch line.[3] While such an assortment could hardly be said to conform to a cohesive editorial vision, it certainly did not want for variety or diversion.

Articles of this whimsical style generally shared common themes: animals, of course, but also lavish descriptions of Old World decadence (whether tones of wonder or disapproval), tales of rustic gumption and bravery, and the vain and highborn coming a cropper, usually in self-inflicted circumstances. One piece, headlined "Anecdote of a Remarkable Instance of Canine Sagacity," from the *New Hampshire Spy*, contained all the usual ingredients. It related the tale of a French officer, "more remarkable for his birth and spirit than his riches," in the service of the Venetian republic, who had been snobbishly cast out of high society by scornful nobles. When being escorted from the lavish apartments of such a grandee, the officer's eye lit upon a display of ornate glassware laid out on a damask cloth. "He took hold of a corner of the linen, and turning to a faithful English mastiff who always accompanied him, said to the animal, in a kind of absence of mind, 'There poor old friend! You see how these scoundrels enjoy themselves, and yet how we are treated!' The poor dog looked up in the master's face, and wagged his tail, as if he understood him." The denouement of the story had a pleasing certainty to it. "The master walked on, but the mastiff slackened his pace, and laying hold of the damask cloth with his teeth, at one hearty pull brought all the sideboard to the ground, and deprived the insolent Noble of his favorite exhibition of splendor."[4] While a reader in Dover or Conway probably had never been to Venice, and may even have been hard-pressed to locate it on a map, stories like these related a familiar set of lightly comic moral lessons. It also mattered little if such a tall tale was true; this was not intended to be "news" in the sense of a factual report on an event. A dog acted impishly; an arrogant fop got his comeuppance. Such things were fodder for newspapers in the eighteenth century as they are for Twitter and YouTube in the twenty-first.

To the regular reader of eighteenth-century human interest pieces, such articles take on a familiar format. Indeed, some phenomena, such as a child running a mile in five or so minutes, seemed to hold near-infinite fascination for provincial editors and readers alike. Dozens of articles, nearly identical in content, differentiated only by locale and nomenclature, appeared in the New Hampshire press in the 1790s. "A young gentleman of the name of Mestayer," one breathlessly reported, "of London, only turned twelve years of age actually ran, within these few days past, on the bath road, one mile in five minutes and two seconds."[5] Prodigious children, like animals, were a favorite marvel of readers, and such stories traveled so well because they were decidedly not geospecific. The vagaries of Turkish politics, or a report on the new Louvre museum, might elude an audience in rural New England, but a boy running very quickly was relatable to all.

Papers also served as a source of diversion and entertainment. While the crossword puzzle was still more than a century away, editors (or their correspondents) posed their readers puzzles and curious lateral-thinking questions. Examples like the following littered the back pages of newspapers across America:

> *A correspondent handed in the following Riddle, and requests a solution.*
> I'm on tops of high hills, and in vallies so low,
> That I oftentimes suffer with frosts and with snow—
> I am beat with a stick, altho never to blame—
> I'm the wealth of the farmer—the husbandman's gain—
> I am lik'd by the lady—admir'd by the boy,
> And when I dance before him he leapeth with joy.[6]

Again, such content served a number of different purposes. First, it might turn the reading of a newspaper from a solitary or performative act into a collaborative one. Families might ponder these problems together, or they might occupy a half hour of idle tavern chatter. They also provided newspapers with more lasting value; one might cut out an interesting riddle and send it to a friend. Finally, they invited interaction with the editor, encouraging readers to write in their solutions. Riddles and poetry were often woven together, with one such rhyming puzzles beginning:

> Tis you, fair ladies, I address
> Sent to adorn your life
> And she who first my name shall guess
> Shall first be made a wife.[7]

A disproportionate number of these games, headed with titles like "A Riddle for the Ladies," were aimed at women.

While editors frequently provided such genial diversions for their readers, they sometimes published general-interest pieces that, taken out of context, are simply confounding. Some pieces demand a familiarity with classical texts and poetry, even a command of ancient Greek and Latin, that must surely have left many dumbfounded, even in literate New England. The *Osborne Observer* and *Spy* published extracts from a Latin oration delivered at the 1790 Harvard commencement without translation. While graduates of college and grammar school graduates might have appreciated the opportunity to recall their vocabulary lessons, most readers weren't so fortunate. Even when editors weren't quite so ostentatious as to include a dead tongue, they often arrived at a level of obscurantism that seems to have reached almost competitive levels. A particular passion was to ridicule the pretensions and petty vanities of city folk. One article, describing a character named "Beau," was littered with references to Linnaeus's categories of the animal kingdom, "Mrs' Milliquet's paduasoy," and oblique references to Bostonian social clubs. "He is literally made up of marechal powder, cravat and bootees," the article hooted, and "the tailor and the shoemaker, the perfumer, and the laundress, must all fit in council, before a beau can take any public steps. He has as many, & as outre names, as an Indian sachem or a Spanish grandee."[8] Perhaps the inside jokes and digressions were an essential part of the form; a pastor in Merrimack County didn't need to know about Fanny Williams or the Jocky Club, except that they served as signifiers of urban extravagance and conceit. Such excoriations were frequent insertions on page 4, and presumably experienced editors kept some on file, along with poetry and sermons, for slow news weeks.

Prurience, as it always has, held limitless attraction. The *Spy*, shrewdly recognizing that its readers could subsist on a diet of bovine ingenuity and ludicrous effeminates for only so long, ran with that headiest of concoctions: lust and murder.

> A Florentine nobleman, having lately some cause to suspect his wife's fidelity with a young Irishman upon his travels, reported to his family that he was going upon business into the country, for a few days. The lovers unfortunately fell victims to the deception, and were that same night detected by the husband who was let into his mansion by a confidential servant. The lady was first alarmed by his foot upon the stairs, jumping from the bed, ran to a closet window, from which she threw herself into an area. The gallant being entirely unprepared for defence, was instantly run through the body. The lady, however was rather worse off, for having broken her thigh in the fall, a mortification took place, and she died in four days: the gallant is in a fair way of recovery.[9]

Stories like this were no doubt sensational, but they could also have a tragic and sometimes even sympathetic air. It was the lovers who were "unfortunate" to be caught out in the ruse, and the lady was taken by a mortification. Readers were not being asked to condemn either the lady or her lover; indeed, the story itself had a melancholic, romantic note. Editors, usually thundering moralists, were sometimes capable of these moments of nuance, which perhaps reached readers of a more wistful disposition. They could shed a tear at the needless death, while quietly thrilling at the operatic exoticism of swashbuckling travelers and jealous Florentine noblemen.

While the Irish gallant's misadventures seem to prove that popular tastes are, in many fields, impervious to fashion, readers could hardly be expected to tolerate their weekly helping of sex and violence without atonement close at hand. Religion played a large part in the composition of period newspapers, which served as a sort of notice board for local congregations, as well as acting as a means of long-distance communication between churches. If this juxtaposition of titillation and redemption bothered anyone, the ministers didn't let it get in the way of utilizing the press. Most of the shorter religious articles provided notification of services or recorded recent meetings. "The Ecclesiastical Convention of New Hampshire met in this town on Wednesday," the

Courier reported. "It was pleasing to the pious, the friends of religion, morality and order, to see a greater number than usual of the Reverend Clergy of the State assembled on this occasion. At 3 o'clock, P.M. they repaired to the Meeting House, where a Sermon as delivered by the Rev. ISRAEL EVANS."[10] Reprinted sermons could be a valuable source of revenue or sometimes came with a subsidy, and advertisements of the following sort were common, with the newspaper proprietor a source of religious texts as well journalistic ones: "Mr. Woodman's Sermon, For SALE, at this OFFICE. A variety of Pamphlets, also for sale,"[11] or "Just received, and for sale at this office, A SERMON, Preached at Putney, at the Funeral of the Rev. J. Goodhue—By Wm. Wells."[12] Letters of thanks were also a regular occurrence and were often a thinly veiled promotion for some pamphlet or future religious gathering, underscoring the commercial aspect to religious life in America. One letter, related to the sermon of one Reverend Buckminster that celebrated the life of the late George Washington and "delivered in this town, on Saturday last," informed readers that "this discourse, should be in the possession, of every citizen in America; a few cents could not be better laid out in the purchase of so admirable a sermon; and it is impossible that time could be better employed than in perusing and practicing the precepts so pleasingly inculcated."[13]

Newspapers also provided transcripts of sermons. Most of these were concerned with scriptural interpretation, local events, sometimes, through the prism of allegory, politics, and national affairs. Religious speakers were intensely invested in current events, which both inspired their themes and attracted comment; indeed, some of the most politicized content to be found in the pages of some newspapers came in the form of spiritual tract. For many, the birth of a new nation offered a rare chance at a metaphysical revolution. The interests of Providence seemed to have coincided with those of the Union, and thus rarely could these reprinted sermons be perceived as entirely apolitical, even when they did not communicate a partisan bias. On occasion, however, the connections between church and state were explicit in the extreme, as when the *Oracle of the Day* recorded, "The Honorable Legislature of the State of New Hampshire, have appointed the Rev. Mr. Goddard, of Swanzy, to deliver an Election Sermon in June next." The *Courier* noted, "The Election Sermon was delivered on Thursday, by the Rev. Mr. Payson, of Rindge; Text, Eccle[s]iastes ix. 18. Wisdom is better than weapons of war; but one sinner destroyeth much good.—Genuinely patriotic and purely American."[14] The final phrase is surely the most telling, drawing the explicit connection between nationality and sanctity.

Often, preachers used the histrionic language of the late eighteenth century to treat contemporary political issues. In a Thanksgiving sermon, of over two pages of small-set typeface (it was common, and presumably commercially desirable, to serialize sermons over multiple issues), the pastor of Medford, Massachusetts, contextualized recent American history in the divine narrative. The sermon started in general terms, declaring that "at certain periods of time, through the several ages and among the different nations of the world, God breaks forth in signal and remarkable dispensations for the relief of the righteous, or for the punishment of the wicked. His providence is seen justifying its own procedure in vindicating and delivering oppressed innocence, or in precipitating prosperous guilt from its lofty seats." Such rhetoric was common enough both in the pulpit and on the page, but it was followed by language far more overt in its political messaging. "Of all our political blessings for which we ought on this day, make our grateful acknowledgements to the Divine Goodness, our federal government is the greatest, the chief, and in fact, the basis of the whole . . . ," Osgood exhorted, before becoming more precise in his historical meaning:

> The federal government was no sooner organized, than it speedily rescued us from this eminently hazardous situation. It gave fresh vigor to each of the state governments; awed into submission the factious through all the states; restored the course of justice, and thereby established peace and good order among the citizens at large. It recovered the sinking credit of the nation, together with that of the respective states; and gave such a spring to commerce, agriculture, manufactures, and all those useful arts which supply the necessaries and conveniences of life, that they flourish to a degree incomparably beyond what had ever been known in this country before.[15]

Alexander Hamilton could not have put it more plainly in his reports on credit and manufacturing. Osgood went on to rail against the "Democratic Societies," the "engine of party," and the "ambitious few," warning of the dangers of mob rule and would-be American Jacobins. "Were the councils of hell united to invent expedients for depriving men of the little portion of good they are destined to enjoy on earth," he concludes, "the only measure they need to adopt for this purpose, would be, to introduce factions into the bosom of the country. Faction begets disorder, force, rancorous passions, anarchy, tyranny, blood and slaughter. May the God of order and peace preserve us from such dreadful calamities! And to him shall glory be forever."[16] It can be difficult, in newspaper clippings such as these, to tell where the preacher ends and the politician begins.

Some of these sermons were locally sourced, but many came from outside the state. Surprisingly, denominations that were generally out of favor in New England had their material published apparently without objection in the New Hampshire press, and these predictably came from farther afield. The papers' taste for the foreign seems to have extended into matters spiritual, as when the *Concord Herald* ran a piece under the heading "Roman Catholic Sermon." The glowing language betrays no sign of disapproval, noting, "On Sunday, the 4th inst. the Rev. Mr. Chibot, Superior General of the Clergy in St. Domingo, who came to this place with the fleet from Cape Francois, delivered an elegant and affecting discourse to his emigrated flock, in the Catholic Church." The paper saw fit to include a full translation of the sermon. There was also room for discourse, and even criticism, between religious figures and members of the public. Andrew Murphy argues that the achievement of "religious toleration" in the seventeenth century was something accomplished in the main by pre-Enlightenment Christians rather than eighteenth-century philosophes. This tradition can be seen in evidence in newspapers that, despite sometimes exhibiting definite religious affiliations, published sermons and scriptural analyses from a variety of denominations. For the most part, these correspondences were carried out with a scholarly air and gentlemanly deportment. In response to one religious essay, a correspondent to the *Federal Observer* wrote: "I neither question, contest or vie with the abilities, the political knowledge, or information of the author—They are doubtless great. Opposition grounded as mine is, will rather increase, than diminish his fame in these respects—I oppose him only in his assumed character of a Religious Teacher." Responding to the anticipated objection that the good governance and the church are naturally aligned, he retorted, "I only remark here that Jesus Christ gave no hint, of such a connexion between his church and the State. . . . Are not politics natural topics for political ministers?—ministers of the gospel are quite out of the question here." Not all disputes were conducted with such equanimity. Sometimes rebuttals took the form of paragraph-by-paragraph analyses, which placed the original text alongside the commentary. An extracted sermon in the *Oracle of the Day* claimed, "Power, honor, popularity, and even Hell itself, have been ransacked in vain, for language and malice to blast these associations. But they stand on the unshaken ground of the State and Federal Constitutions, and cannot fall unless the Constitutions themselves fall—which will never take place, till the all grasping arm of Tyranny, shall banish Liberty from these unhappy climes." Set against this was a correspondent of the paper, who declared, "How the Prophet can conceive of ransacking honor to find language and malice, we are at a loss to determine. But it is certain that he possessed neither the spirit of rhetoric nor of prophecy: for the Democratic Societies have already gone the way of all the earth.—Dust thou art and unto dust shalt thou return."[17] Such battles could rage on for weeks at a time.

In general, sermons by known preachers and clergymen were treated with respect, if not necessarily with acquiescence. Another type of religious writing in newspapers was written commentary on Bible passages, often produced by laypeople. The unwritten rules that tended to govern responses to religious speech in formal settings did not apply to these missives. "I SAW a piece in your paper under the signature of *Alcander*, representing the great parent of the Universe to be *the author of sin*; that being the case, the great god must of consequence be the first sinner," one irate reader wrote in, "and as all sinners must be punished, and God is the ruler and governor of all things, from whence is he to receive his punishment? Or with what propriety can he inflict punishment on any of the human race for sin? Awful! Horrid idea this!" The correspondent did not mince words with the implications for the mysterious Alcander, expressing that they "should not think strange if the Almighty God should instantly strike those of such a pernicious principle dead, and send them to an eternal state of misery."[18] Three other correspondents replied to Alcander's incendiary tract in the *Gazette*. However, it should be emphasized that such articles were in the minority. For the most part, the religious content in newspapers formed part of an ongoing process of mutual discourse. It is difficult to conceive that the work of newspapers did not serve the purpose of broadening the reach and influence of local churches. Indeed, some printers evidently thought of themselves as adjunct to the holy and often liked to pen lengthy epistles on their own place in the spiritual as well as temporal spheres. "THE Divine Ruler of the Universe evinced his affection for man in a particular manner, when led him to the thoughts of that noble invention, the PRINTING PRESS," one such article began. "A retrospective glance at former ages, will soon expose the clouds of darkness and bigotry, which over shadowed the whole world: The disadvantages that the ancients labored under, will obviously appear even to a common observer; but when the PRESS arose, like the Sun after a thick fog, the dark mists vanished from before it, and by degrees the whole world became illuminated by its splendor." It can be difficult to read some of these paeans and not see how they might not have been received as at least self-aggrandizing, if not downright blasphemous. "Under the influence of printing, RELIGION reared its sacred head; and, by its means has become widely extended. The - may be very properly stiled, 'The Nurse of Protestantism'; for without its aid, it could never have been established. The BIBLE, that library of Divine knowledge, would have been of little use, and few, very few indeed, would have ever become the possessors of the inestimable treasure if the PRESS had not lent her aid."[19] Yet, judging by the editorial columns of papers throughout the state, the sentiment was broadly tolerated, perhaps even accepted. This belief in the use of print to bring enlightenment to the public as a crusade was perhaps a comfort to printers struggling to make ends meet.

There was an essential duality about the role and identity of the editor in the eighteenth century. "Despite shortcoming and difficulties," Jeffrey Smith notes, "writers proudly claimed central roles in what they perceived to be the Enlightenment's general expansion and refinement of men's minds. . . . The pedagogic pretensions of periodical writers fit

the Enlightenment's view of mankind's potential." When Daniel Fowle
began publishing the *New Hampshire Gazette* in 1756, he told his readers that he would supply them with "Extracts from the best Authors
on Points of the most useful Knowledge, moral, religious or political
Essays, and other such Speculations as may have a Tendency to improve
the Mind, afford and Help to Trade, Manufactures, Husbandry, and
other useful Arts, and promote the public Welfare in any Respect." On
the other hand, there was scant pretension that the newspaper was to
act as a definitive repository of events; rather, the editor presented the
information that had come to hand from other sources (most frequently,
as shall be seen, other papers), unverified and often uncommented upon.
Frequently, no attempt at all was made to disguise foreign authorship,
as was often made clear by the language used. One article, datelined
from London, began: "The Americans, as our readers will see by the
resolution of Congress inserted in this paper, have laid an embargo on
ships in their ports. Letters from thence state, that notwithstanding this
measure, the general wish is, that they maintain their neutrality, but that
a step of this kind was necessary as a measure of retaliation, to hasten
the settlement of the indemnity that may be due to them for injuries
their commerce has sustained by capture and detention of their vessels
by the English cruisers."[20] In this piece, like thousands of others, the
editorial "voice" is that of the London journalist, writing about Americans as a foreign people, which seems not to have bothered the editor of
the *Oracle*. Therefore, for the most part, the idea of a coherent political
persona for a newspaper (which is frequently taken for granted now)
had yet to be developed. It is, in a peculiar sense, a postmodern exercise:
a collage of the possibly true, in which the burden of credulity is placed
on the reader. Indeed, the recurring introduction to a news item, "The
following is an authentic account," acknowledged both the third-person
narrative voice and the flexible nature of journalistic authenticity. This
is not quite to say that the eighteenth-century editor had no sense of
integrity, but rather that he probably did not view himself as a servant of
the public in the manner that emerged with the advent of muckraking.[21]

Editors could be disarmingly candid about this "cut-and-paste"
approach. "A SUITABLE part of the MINERVA shall be appropriated to

the purpose of political information," Josiah Dunham informed readers of the *Eagle*. "It shall contain a journal of the proceedings of Congress, and of the Legislatures of New Hampshire and Vermont; together with a register of marriages, deaths, &c." Almost every newspaper of the period published editorial requests for political gossip, polemics, anecdotes (both humorous and exemplary), poetry, and community notices. How many of such contributions were rejected is unknown, but the avidity with which they were sought suggests that they were badly needed, and the caliber of many of those printed suggests that most editors had little scope for discrimination when it came to quality. Dunham made plain to his readers that he would be relying on "the assistance of the literati of every description. Original communications will be eagerly sought, and judicious selections from the latest European publications of this kind; together with extracts, useful and pleasing; sentimental and pathetic. Particular attention will be given to the variety of tastes; and it shall be the object of the Editor to serve up a favorite dish for every palate."[22] The need for variety as well as quantity was a driving force in these calls for contributions. They were also a means of engaging customers: a reader might extend their subscription in hopes of seeing their joke published. As a by-product, the public gained a new outlet for their creative impulses, with what might be generously called mixed results.

Among the most popular form of amateur contribution was poetry. Verse, doubtless because of the pleasing way that its short lines filled column inches, was a particularly welcome form of contribution, and subscribers supplied verses in a dizzying variety of forms, which were usually characterized by a greater degree of ambition than craft.

POETRY (ORIGINAL)—ACROSTICS

HEZEKIAH

Hear the sick monarch wail in mournful lays.
"Ev'n in my bloom, hast thou cut short my days!
"Zion! No more I view thy beauteous walls,
"Each succour fails me! Death relentless calls"
"Kind hope is fled!" But lo ISAIAH comes!
In his mild eye, celestial mercy blooms.
Adieu, vain fears! Awake, my grateful lays!
Heav'n hears my fervent vows, & shall live to praise!

EZEKIEL

> Enwrapt, though saw'st by Chebar's sacred stream,
> Zion's immortal CAR, and flaming Cherubim!
> Emblem of HIM, whom raptur'd John records,
> King o'er all kings! Imperial *Lord* of lords!
> Infolded in the Cherub's wings, thy foul
> Exults! But veils in mystery the whole,
> Led by the VISION, and inspiring ROLL![23]

Acrostics were popular, as were topical and satirical poems, limericks, faux-nursery rhymes, and reworked lyrics to popular tunes. Odes to Washington, and later Adams, were produced to fit the meter of songs like "God Save the King" and "Yankee Doodle," and the patriotic verses were clearly written with public performance in mind, as evidenced by phonetic spelling and frequently irregular composition. When local troubadours were unable to supply the necessary material, the work of famous English poets was deployed to fill the void. Poets who went on to great acclaim often escaped the notice of American papers. In spite of his famous volume of 1798, *Lyrical Ballads*, Samuel Taylor Coleridge received one reference in the New Hampshire press of the 1790s, and William Wordsworth was entirely absent, despite writing the most important verse regarding the French Revolution in the English language. Devon's Peter Pindar (John Wolcot), on the other hand, a poet with a sharper, more immediate style than either Coleridge or Wordsworth, appeared one hundred times in the Federalist-era New Hampshire press. Frequently, however, newspapermen seemed to show a preference for established, often dead, poets. Milton, that beloved favorite of New England Puritans, appeared two hundred times, although mostly in anecdote and biography, with only fifteen of his actual poems being reproduced. Shakespeare was referenced seventy-nine times, with six of his poems reproduced. When it came to selecting poets, both readers and editors seemed to prefer known quantities, but with new poets critical reputation had a relatively minor impact on who did and did not feature.

Poems were also a means by which the newspaper editor could address the reader. "It has been a practice, in many places of the United

States, for some years past . . . ," the *Farmer's Weekly Museum* explained, "at the commencement of an anniversary, to convey to their customers a small poem by way of congratulation for a happy year." While these tended to be brief, cheerful ephemera, they were a modest means of the newspaper communicating with the reader outside of their traditional authorial voice. "In some of these annual effusions we discern much pleasantry, and in a few, much good poetry." While such "jocularities" were frequently meant only as passing amusements, they were also a small opportunity for the editor to flex his creative muscles.[24]

Newspapers also had an altogether more solemn obligation to fulfill. Obituaries were not hugely common, probably due to the relatively small scale of town life in New Hampshire and a finite number of people available to appear in them. They were less frequent than poems, for example, or shipping manifests. Nonetheless, they are plentiful enough (2,243 of them from 1790 to 1800) as to constitute an important feature of newspapers of the period. The first sort of obituaries are little more than notifications of a biological event. "DIED," the *Oracle of the Day* barked, "Mrs. MARY RAYNES, Aged 44, wife of Mr *Nath'l Raynes*, of that town—In this town, Mr. EDWARD PARK, Aged 25." "Died," the *New Hampshire Gazette* mentioned in passing between two articles, "since our last, Mr. Benjamin Newmarch Cutt, aged 21 years." Others, while still jarringly unsentimental, were somewhat more descriptive. "Died, at Charleston, S.C., Mr. Thomas Wadsworth, Esq. merchant formerly of Boston—also, on Sunday, the 29th Sept Mrs. Jane Wadsworth, relict of Thomas Wadsworth, Esq. who died about a fortnight before; both of the prevailing fever, at his seat on Long Island, Jonathan N. Havens, Member of Congress."[25] Notices like these often crammed in multiple cadavers, implying a rather less sentimental and rather more matter-of-fact attitude toward mourning than would become the norm in nineteenth-century papers.

Many obituaries, however, did contain a palpable sense of grief and loss and were moving in their devotion. These were frequently not written by the editor but rather were submitted by friends and family members, and therefore tended to be rather more personal and heartfelt. In a piece on the death of a Jonathan Chadbourn, who had died at the age of forty-seven, a relative had written: "In his life, were conspicuous the endearing characters of a dutiful son, the most affectionate husband, an indulgent parent, a kind master and faithful friend, with a mind enlarged with the most liberal sentiments, and a heart fraught with benevolence; his diffusive goodness and active charity endeared him to society when living, and make his death long regretted."[26] Articles such as these were not just reports of a death but tributes to a loved one and a part of the grieving process for those they left behind. One correspondent, however, took a more jaundiced view of the role of the newspaper obituary. "Domestic occurrences form a very essential, important and agreeable part of a newspaper," he explained. "A *death*, if it is a wife, will make husbands envy the widower; wives and widows pity the deceased, and hurt at the husband's good fortune, exclaim against the monster for not shewing a proper degree of sorrow on the occasion; while one of them, perhaps, marries him a month after."[27] While we can only speculate as to the plight of the contributor's unlucky wife, the article does hint at a broader role for notifications of death; in a society in which widows and widowers seldom remained single for long, the appearance of a newly eligible entrant to the marriage market was a locally newsworthy event.

Not all obituaries concerned local bereavements, and the more exotic notices normally contained the sort of biography that might now be associated with newspaper coverage of obituaries. Many notables from farther afield received biographies, as did some Old World celebrities. The more elaborate examples would even be embellished with poetry or other literary devices: "Yet manly, generous, noble, candid, kind / In manners gentle, tho' resolv'd in mind," read one tribute to a prominent candlemaker.[28] Nor were they all either baldly descriptive or reverently elegiac. Some were voyeuristic in their examination of the idiosyncrasies and flaws of the deceased, reinforcing the proposition that there are few generalizations that can be safely made concerning late-eighteenth-century newspapers. Some even have an uncomfortable freak-show tone that would be seldom found in later obituaries of private citizens. "Mr. Bartlett, a superannuated carpenter of the navy; though in perfect health, he confined himself to his room for 23 years," went a piece in the *Sentinel*. "He wore nothing during this period but a morning gown, he did not make use of either fire or candles, never read or amused himself in any manner, and would suffer no person to see him except his relations where he lived." In addition to his peculiar habits, the unfortunate Mr. Bartlett's grooming was not spared either. "Neither his hair or nails were cut, or his face shaved for the above time; before he died his hair reached the floor, and was so matted together, from not being combed that it was as hard and firm as a board; his nails were about one inch longer than his fingers, curved like a parrot's bill."[29] Bartlett, it can only be assumed, had at least one enemy with enough time to pen this dubious eulogy. Obituaries of these sort were not by any means common, but they did crop up from time to time, presumably to the ghoulish delight of their readers. Some of these exhibits of human oddity were written in better humor and instead focused on the unlikely achievements of the untutored or unfortunate. They are written in the same fashion as articles detailing the exploits of the Pumping Cow, in their attempt to provoke wonder and curiosity. One such piece, titled "Negro Tom," a memorial to the "famous African Calculator," is illustrative for a variety of regional and racial mores that it exposes. Little of Tom's background is shared, other than the name of his owner and that Tom was "brought to this Country at the age of 14, and was sold as a slave with many of his unfortunate Countrymen," the wording of which at least hints at a degree of sympathy on the part of the author. If the article is scant on biographical details, it is lavish in its praise of Tom's talents.

This man was a prodigy. Though could neither read nor write, he had perfectly acquired the art of enumeration. The power of recollection and the strength of memory were so complete in him, that he could multiply seven into itself, that product and the product, so produced, by seven, 57 seven times. He could [recite] the numbers of months, days, weeks, hours, minutes and seconds in any period of time that any person chose to mention, allowing in his calculations for all the leap years that happened in that time; and would give the number of yards, feet, inches and barley-corns in any given distance, say the diameter of the earth's orbit; and in every calculation he would produce the true answer in less time than ninety-nine men in an hundred would take with their pens.

The article continued at length, citing a litany of other astonishing examples of his skill. It eventually concluded that "had his opportunities of improvement been equal to those of thousands of his fellow men, neither the Royal Society of London, the Academy of Sciences at Paris, nor even a NEWTON himself, need have been ashamed to acknowledge him a Brother in Science."[30] When it is observed that this article was published under an Exeter, New Hampshire, dateline, the context becomes more interesting. Unlike most obituary notices that came from afar, this one was written by the editor of the *New Hampshire Gazetteer* (probably Henry Ranlet) and was presumably from fragments of intelligence gathered about the savant. Though in the minority, these oddly touching biographies often were some of an editor's best work.

Though less common than obituaries, happier announcements of engagement and marriage also appeared in newspapers. They were often little more than announcements, a sparse declaration of a legally sanctioned union. The *Eagle* of Hanover was typical when it declared, "MARRIED—At Kittery, Rev. Jonas Hartwell to Miss Sally Smallcorn."[31] For the most part, marital notices followed this formula, except for occasionally adding in the phrase "the agreeable" before the name of the bride, as with "the agreeable Miss Emma Cullham."[32] The usual practice for editors was to condense all the matrimony notices into one contiguous paragraph, which can often tell us as much about the expanding reach and circulation as it does about the thriving institution of marriage. A single article in the *Oracle of the Day* managed to list all the marriages that had taken place in Providence, Rhode Island; Bridgewater, Reading, Quincy, Salem, Haverhill, and Boston, Massachusetts; and Livermore, Maine. Twenty marriages were summarily dispensed with in 204 words.

The more detailed articles about marriage frequently dwelled on the duration of the courtship. Presumably an extended period of wooing attested to both the authenticity of the relationship and, perhaps optimistically, the chastity of the couple. "MARRIED—At Pembroke," the *Mirrour* noted, "on the 13th inst. by the Rev. Mr. Coley, after a courtship of almost 12 years, Mr. SAMUEL EMERY, to Miss POLLY M'CONNEL."[33] Extremities of age also attracted special interest. "MARRIED—At Gloucester (Mass), Mr. Elisha Harrendon, aged 83, to Mrs. Eleanor Lushure, aged 88, being his 8th wife.... In England, Mr. B. Wilkinson, age 20, to Mrs. Frith, a blooming widow of 60."[34] Only very rarely was wedded bliss afforded any of the florid prose used in the case of the deceased. When adornment was added (and it was done so in fewer than one in fifty incidences), it was usually in the form of a trite couplet. "Long may their Glass of Matrimony run / To count the happiest years beneath the sun!"[35] On at least one occasion, the printer took the opportunity to announce his own marriage. "News! News! Lately married by the Rev. Professor Smith, Mr Moses David, Editor and Printer of the Dartmouth Gazette, to Miss Nancy Fuller." While these were happy tidings, the note that followed suggested that the young union had already experienced its first quarrel: "APOLOGY—The above important article of domestic intelligence should have appeared some weeks ago, but the press of foreign news would not allow its place. But the Printer would now inform his good customers, that he is firmly and substantially—MARRIED."[36] One only hopes, for his sake, that the apology was accepted. Sometimes, the nuptials were celebrated with a burst of verse, in the style of the following:

> Fair Columbia's rural plains,
> Do far greater bliss display,
> Than grand Peru's rich domains,
> Therefore raise the jocund lay.
> This is Peggy's wedding-day,
> Sing and dance the time away.[37]

For the most part, however, no embellishment was provided, and marriage notices acted in the service of public information rather than romance. Even when poems or notes of congratulation appeared, they were usually much briefer than obituary notices.

One of the most important, if least celebrated, roles of the Federalist-era newspaper was to act as a widely accessible public record of legislation. These accounts of the legislative process were produced by private citizens or, if it concerned the federal government, occasionally by someone in the employ of a Philadelphia newspaper.[38] Legislative content differed from general news content in a number of important ways. First, it frequently overrode the typical format of a newspaper. When a particularly momentous federal law was enacted (and of course, in the

1790s, many were), newspapers might dedicate half, or more, of their pages to it, and advertisements might be the only items to survive the cull. In an age in which news items ran anywhere between three lines and a few paragraphs, legislative items were the longest passages of sustained prose to be found in newspapers. Legislation was usually reproduced wholesale, without comment or abridgement. In contrast, most news content either was written with an eyewitness, anecdotal tone or betrayed an unambiguous bias in its depiction of events. As domestic political reporting became swamped in partisan mudslinging and outright libel, legislative insertions were as close as the reader would get to a firsthand account of what was going on in the wider world, and the solemnity of its deployment reflects that. When the First Bank of the United States was created, the *New Hampshire Gazette* dedicated practically an entire issue to it, including not only the full text of the legislation but also the preamble taken from the *Congressional Record* as well as extracts of speeches given by congressmen. The full enumerated powers and regulations of the First Bank of the United States, in the exact language of the bill itself, take up two pages, half of the entire newspaper. Sometimes, these would be so long as to overspill the newspaper entirely. "To give detail of the Secretary's report," the *Gazette* announced with regard to Hamilton's report on public finance, "would more than fill the bounds of a newspaper—but when we can obtain a copy, it shall be inserted in full in the *Gazette*."[39] Legislative articles not only contained the law in full, but usually finished with the official codified language to be found at the end of all of such documents, usually without comment: "For which the faith of the United States is hereby pledged. FREDERICK A. MUHLENBERG, *Speaker of the House of Representatives*, JOHN ADAMS, *Vice President of the United States, and President of the Senate*. Approved, February the 25th, 1791. GEORGE WASHINGTON, *President of the United States*. Deposited among the rolls in the Office of the SECRETARY OF STATE. THOMAS JEFFERSON, *Secretary of State*."[40] This extremely comprehensive approach meant that, in effect, a collector of newspapers could keep on file a fairly comprehensive record of major legislation.

There are a few ways to explain this unswerving attention to legal detail. Cynically, it might be suggested that such bills were heaven-sent opportunities for editors to take a weeklong vacation. When a long document of undeniable importance came to hand, the perennial need to fill pages would temporarily abate (indeed, some acts were printed over the course of multiple issues). The next week's issue would, in turn, be packed with correspondence from readers reacting to the bill. Peter Stallybrass wrote that the most important legacy of the rise of print was the resultant "incitement to writing by hand," and judging by the contents of newspapers this seems to have been the case.[41] In the weeks following the passage of a piece of landmark legislation, the contents of newspapers published across the nation become noticeably homogeneous, a contrast from the usual picture of local variation. Some editors were spared the tiresome business of even formatting the pages; the layout, as well as the content, would sometimes be lifted directly from another publication. There is, however, a more generous, and probably more plausible, explanation. While newspaper editors seemed to cater to a broad spectrum of tastes, legislative content was the best way that they could fulfill a civic duty to their constituents, who otherwise would not have had access to such information. It was not only the affairs of the United States Congress that filled pages. Courts, both supreme and circuit, provided judicial content for the papers. Lacking access to official documents, these reports tended to be shorter, and less rigidly formal, but nonetheless provided the public remote access to their courts of law. Some of the court cases recorded were not particularly notable or exciting, and so suggest an appetite for legal coverage of any kind. Or perhaps newspapers were doing what was perceived to be their public duty, by relaying the happenings of the courthouse to the far corners of the state. One report from the Dover Superior Court was written in typical style: "Yesterday morning came on before the Superior Court sitting in this town, the trial of JAMES WEYMOUTH, of Lee—for the crime as stated in the indictment, of wilfully passing (with intent to defraud the public) four *Counterfeit dollars, and one ten dollar Salem Bank Bill.* After a full and impartial hearing, the jury returned a verdict—GUILTY."[42] This reporting of local events extended from the courthouse to state or even town politics. In 1800 the election of the New Hampshire state governor was more widely reported than the president of the United States, and the upper house of the state government, not the federal, was the assumed meaning of the appellation *senate*.

The newspapers of the early national period did more than inform the public of current events. When Josiah Dunham promised a "dish for every palate" in the *Eagle*, he was acknowledging that different readers would come to his newspaper needing different things. The farmer might be waiting on the latest set of market prices, the party member the news from Congress, or the immigrant news about the old country. In just four pages, a newspaper had to serve a host of constituencies, each with their own tastes, interests, and biases. In addition to factual information, the newspaper had other needs to supply. Poems, riddles, and ribald stories brought pathos, humor, and entertainment into the homes of people with scant access to the world at large, and not only reinforced an incipient sense of political and religious community, but much more fundamentally connected people to one another. "Anxiety about political identity acquired even greater potency because of the transformation and democratization of public life in the eighteenth-century Atlantic world," Marcus Daniel contends. "The expansion of the newspaper press (fuelled by the growing appetite for commercial and political information) reinforced this development but also reconstituted it at a more abstract level, connecting private readers and citizens through the impersonal medium of print."[43] The most salient feature of these newspapers was their preoccupation with the human element, with anecdote and portraiture. Not everyone in eighteenth-century America lived in remote isolation, of course, but for those that did, these spores of otherness that landed on their porch were a window into a world of princes, presidents, and pirates.

The window, crucially, could be opened. The lines between reader and journalist were, in the first years of the American republic, so fluid as to be essentially meaningless. Unlike later journalistic forms, where the contributions of subscribers might be confined to the letters page or a comment section "below the line," the reader was present throughout. With each letter, each piece of rumor and hearsay, each gripe or grievance, an individual might leave a small but indelible impression on their community. More than that, these acts of participation were a means of expressing a new level of investment in the American project. If becoming and remaining informed was the duty of good citizen, adding to the sum of public discourse was a cherished privilege. By providing a forum for such civil acts, printers and editors were not just stewards of this commonwealth of ideas but instrumental in allowing the American belief in the sovereignty of personal opinion to take hold. A boon for democracy, no doubt; what it meant for the tone of American political discourse was, as we shall see, quite another matter.

CHAPTER FOUR

"WE HAVE IT BY A RELIABLE GENTLEMAN IN THAT PLACE"

Finding the News

The last mail gives a fresh supply of Foreign News: the latest
informs of an intended, ripening REVOLUTION in Ireland, and
that 20,000 United Irishmen were assembled in readiness to
advocate and effect her independence—This intelligence was bro't
by a late arrival at Boston, 50 days from Dublin, and is corrobo-
rated by a later arrival at New York.

—*Concord New Star*, July 4, 1797

Newspaper editors relied on numerous sources for their
domestic news. They exchanged papers with printers from both neighboring towns and other parts of the country, cribbing stories and columns. They might receive a letter from a member of the public, whose
identity was sometimes explicit and sometimes hidden behind the veil
of a pseudonym. Sometimes, it was merely a matter of talking to people: catching rumors from a merchant on market day or the scuttlebutt

from travelers spending the night at a local inn. Every now and then, and when they could get away with it, they just made it up.

When it came to news of the wider world, dispatches might reach the hands of the editor in similar fashion, but it was necessarily channeled through a single source: a ship crossing the ocean. America was, even after it achieved its hard-won independence, extremely reliant on the regular arrival of vessels from both the Old World and the Caribbean. It was on these links that Americans depended not only for dispatches but also for key staple and luxury goods, finished manufactures, and the cash that was generated from the stream of exports flowing in the other direction. The gravity of this is reflected by the growth and power of America's port cities, New York, Philadelphia, Boston, Baltimore, and Charleston. Even the relatively modest shipping trade done in Portsmouth made it the most important town in New Hampshire. This did not just make these cities rich; it placed them at the center of early American culture. For a people who still largely faced out toward the Atlantic, a direct connection to Europe, and especially Britain, conferred a patina of cosmopolitanism on these coastal communities to which other Americans were, by turns, deferential and resentful. This cachet reflected the fact that many Americans, even those who were proud of their sovereignty and revolutionary heritage, still looked eastward to Britain, France, and the other established imperial powers as the locus of world civilization. Although this was beginning to gradually change, the process was a slow one. While Richard Merritt's content analysis of six newspapers of the colonial period found that from 1735 to 1775, they took an "increasing interest in things and events American," they continued to be mainly preoccupied with English and international affairs.[1]

This interest continued into the early national period. There are more than 11,000 articles containing incidences of the word *London* published in New Hampshire from 1790 to 1800. Of these, 3,263 had a London dateline, meaning that the story had first originated in a London newspaper. Approximately 1,700 newspaper issues were put out in New Hampshire in the same period,[2] meaning that on average nearly 2 stories per issue came from the London press alone. While much of the news to reach America from the London press was not British,

London (and to a much lesser extent Portsmouth, United Kingdom) acted as America's conduit to the wider world. As the work of Michael Durey amply demonstrates, it was not only newspapers and broadsides passing between the Old World and the New. Radicals and intellectuals traveled between the ports of the Atlantic, bringing with them not only printed matter but ideology as well. That they were attracted to the United States as a refuge owed, as Durey points out, to the availability of American journalism in Britain. These men, and the few well-heeled American tourists who might travel to Europe, were an ancillary source of news. Printers in port towns also frequently cultivated relationships with seamen, who could be an invaluable source of foreign news. In addition to necessarily being current on maritime affairs, they naturally kept abreast of trade, weather, and war. However, such oral testimony could also present challenges, especially with regard to chronology. A sailor's account might be more current than the most recently arrived newspapers, but this could be difficult to verify. "We have not an article of European real news, through any channel, later than heretofore communicated," the *Courier of New Hampshire* explained. "Judging from the latitude and longitude in which the vessel from Bremen was spoken with by Captain Tilton ... we have reason to think our information from Europe to be later."[3] In spite of this uncertainty, men like Captain Tilton were invaluable sources of news, particularly about places without newspapers of their own. However, for regular intelligence gathering, American newspapers lacked either the resources or the reach to support anything resembling a foreign news bureau, and so stories clipped directly from the pages of the British press had to suffice.

The English newspapers that arrived on American shores were not evenly distributed across the Eastern Seaboard. Commerce and climate both played a part in this. The ports of northern New England maintained a far busier trade with Great Britain than those of the southern United States. Thanks, in part, to the mid-Atlantic Gulf Stream, many captains found it expeditious to make the journey from England to harbors likes Portsmouth, New Hampshire, and Portland, in what is now Maine.[4] Language, too, played a role. While most editors dealt, whether through choice or necessity, only in news that arrived in English, some were able to translate stories, mainly from either French or German. Those that then copied those translations in their own papers could include sources inaccessible to monoglots, even if they themselves would have been incapable of reading the originals.[5] For the most part, however, news about continental Europe was taken from, and filtered through, the prism of the London press. It is unsurprising, then, that many Americans, particularly in the North, took such a dim view of the French Revolution when one of their chief sources of information was France's primary antagonist.

While London generally supplied a high proportion of the foreign intelligence, the *London Gazette* in particular remained the paramount source of British news in the United States. Nearly 200 articles were published under a *Gazette* dateline in New Hampshire in the 1790s, but that is to ignore the 775 articles that appeared from "a London paper," most of which were either copies of, or copies of copies of, *Gazette* articles. By comparison, the *Gazette of the United States*, the most important Federalist paper in the country, received 170 datelines in the New Hampshire press. This made a newspaper printed more than three thousand miles away one of the most important in America. It was the *Gazette* that broke the news of the storming of the Bastille to the English-speaking world[6] and acted as the primary source for reports on the Napoleonic Wars. This had profound implications for American readers. While not propagandist in purpose, the *Gazette* was the official organ of the British government, primarily given over to the publication of state and judicial notices, as well the issuance of royal proclamations. While it was a printed source of news, it was not a newspaper in the conventional sense. It was produced not by editors but by government officials and published under a royal crest under the heading "published by authority."[7] Newly independent Americans might resent the mouthpiece of the British Empire supplying their foreign news, but the *Gazette* remained one of the most trusted and widely available publications throughout the anglophone Atlantic world.

The *Gazette* was not the only English publication to have an impact on American shores. The London *Times* (founded in 1785 under its original, less succinct, name of the *Daily Universal Register*) quickly became another major source of news for American editors. Unlike the *Gazette*, it was a privately run enterprise, and one that regularly fell in and out of favor with both Parliament and the Crown. As a result, the *Times* was a source not just of news but of editorial opinion and commentary as well, and these were often reprinted in the pages of American newspapers. Compared to the drier dispatches of the *Gazette*, *Times* pieces tended to be rather more assertive, even belligerent. "General Washington, say the London Times, will be unpantheonized for his wise and manly address to his countrymen," the *Farmer's Weekly Museum* related. "It is to be regretted that the President could not, with prudence, remind the Americans of their origin, their ancient ties. . . . To caution them against France, and the corruptions and treasons of foreign intercourse and partiality, seems all he could hope to do with success!"[8] No doubt because of entries such as these, the *Times* found far more favor in Federalist New England than it did elsewhere and was reprinted with great avidity.

While all newspapers arrived by ship, the means by which they got on and off those ships varied. Some were simply carried by individual travelers, who stowed copies of papers with them as they boarded in Bristol, Liverpool, or Portsmouth. A steadier supply of news was carried by the "packet boats" that plied the Atlantic waters with increasing frequency in the eighteenth century. These small vessels bore letters, official communiqués, and, inevitably, newspapers. More than a thousand newspaper articles published in New Hampshire in the Federalist period were brought over by these means. These packet-boat services were both a wellspring of news from the outside world and of vital importance to Americans themselves. They provided not only a means of doing business with the Old World but also a speedier means of communication with other coastal Americans. The schooner *Sally* made constant trips between Portsmouth, New Hampshire, and Newburyport, Massachusetts, offering "freight or passage" in addition to carrying letters and papers.[9] Packets not just advertised in newspapers but also drove commercial activity and consequently generated further advertising revenue. Appleton & Barrett, a general store of Amherst, posted an advertisement for a "fresh assortment of European goods" that had "just arrived by the packet from Liverpool."[10] Such services, consequently, were a means of acquiring news, customers, and money.

Most printers did not have the luxury of regularly arriving packets.

Inland newspapermen were dependent on not only the vagaries of the Atlantic crossing but also the nascent intra-American communications network of the early republic. While they might arrange for British newspapers to be delivered directly to them, such arrangements were rare; the difficulties of communicating with and paying British merchants were exacerbated when overland post further complicated matters. Most of the time, they either made deals with coastal printers to have newspapers and dispatches forwarded to them or simply relied on transcribing what they read in the port-town papers. While such an approach was often a necessity if any foreign news was to appear at all, it did present a number of unfortunate limitations. First, it meant that these papers were reliant on the American paper faithfully copying the European dispatch. Some editors clearly signaled when they were presenting verbatim copies, as when the *New Hampshire Gazette* headed columns with "The following paragraph is copied from a London paper."[11] It was not always so apparent who was doing the writing at any given time; some editors simply reproduced the London stories verbatim, while others threw in asides and marginalia. In such cases, it could be difficult to discern what was original and what had been added on; in most cases, the terminal editor simply reproduced the whole thing. The next major problem was that the second editor down the chain would be exposed only to the news that the first editor had chosen to reproduce from the packet. Short of simply bootlegging issues of the *Gazette*, American printers obviously could not include every story contained within; therefore, which stories spread and which didn't was at the discretion of the printer who received the London paper in the first place. The situation seldom ended there. A printer in Concord, depending on publications in Boston and Portsmouth for his foreign news, might then be read by his fellows in Hanover, Walpole, or Brattleboro. Any news that *he* omitted would then not be available farther out west. And thus, relayed from town to town, news of the outside world was warped and attenuated with every subsequent publication.

However, these conditions were, in the early years of the American republic, in a state of flux. Peace between Britain and the United States meant that by the middle of the 1790s, the Atlantic was once again teeming with merchant vessels. In 1792, 4,430 tons of shipping arrived in New England from Bristol alone (quadruple what it had been prior to the revolution), with 5,500 reaching the middle states. After a financial crisis of 1793 decimated Bristol's mercantile capital, the burgeoning docks of Liverpool stepped in, and trade intensified yet further.[12] This had two important consequences. Most obviously, it meant that British trading vessels were arriving in American ports, bearing goods, people, and news, with ever-increasing regularity. More subtly, but no less important, the interests of the two countries remained bound up in ties of profit, language, and print. In some respects, Americans interacted more with Britons than they had in colonial times, and this fed a hunger for news on both sides of the ocean. Of course, for many merchants, the coasts of Britain and America were not the only stop on the journey. Ships engaged with the slave trade, or its products, also set anchor on the coasts of Africa and in the Caribbean. While this extended the journey considerably, it also meant that news from these regions was finding its way into the pages of American newspapers. Articles from Jamaica, St. Kitts, and Trinidad all began appearing with greater frequency as the decade progressed.[13] Seventy-six articles from or about Jamaica appeared in the New Hampshire press of 1790, compared to 205 in 1799. Such articles were a combination of advertisements for goods and ships, tales of naval operations, and stories about British colonial politics and slave uprisings. For New England merchants, most of whom benefited directly or indirectly from West Indies trade, such dispatches were as vital as those from London or New York.

This burgeoning maritime traffic increased not only the amount of news reaching American shores but also the speed with which it arrived. In 1790 it took news from its first appearance in a London paper just over seventy-four days to appear in the Portsmouth press. In 1800 this time had fallen to sixty-three days.[14] This cannot be explained by ships simply moving faster (they were, but not fast enough to account for the whole difference); the *Mayflower* took sixty-six days to sail from old England to New England in 1620.[15] Transatlantic voyages by the end of the eighteenth century, traveling directly in well-maintained vessels, with fair winds and in the right season, could expect to take six weeks.[16] Of course, not all crossings took place under such favorable conditions.

These newspapers weren't just traveling from one port to another; they had to be taken from a printer's office in London, passed onto a ship, and then upon their arrival in Portsmouth be delivered to the printer there. The increasing speed of communication between London and New Hampshire, therefore, was the result of a combination of increasingly quick and frequent travel both on land and on sea, as well as increasingly sophisticated networks of distribution and exchange. Finally, with newspapers being published more frequently, the likelihood of one going to print soon after a packet of news arrived increased.

Whether news from England took eleven weeks to arrive or nine, the fact remained that Americans existed at a temporal remove from the rest of the world. The *Farmer's Weekly Museum* ran a satirical piece on the subject that first appeared in the *Minerva*: "What news! What news! Cries the merchant, as he enters the Coffee-house, has this vessel brought any

FIGURE I. MEAN TRANSMISSION TIME OF NEWS FROM LONDON TO NEW HAMPSHIRE TOWNS (WEIGHTED)

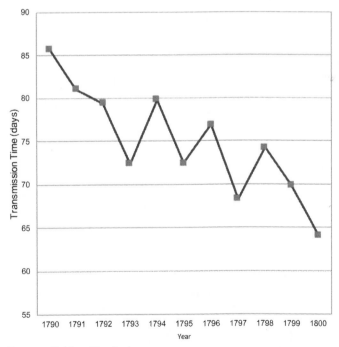

Data compiled from NewsBank.

news? What late paper has she brought, and what news from the Rhine? Has the fleet sailed? How was flour in London? How was rice in Harve? Will there be peace this winter? Has the sedition bill passed? All these questions are rung in one's ears, before a man can fairly turn around." Before long, the Democrat, the flour shipper, the speculator, and the West India trader were all clamoring around for the latest. "O! Such hurry— such bussle! Stocks have risen a penny in Philadelphia. Now see the brokers running from street to street. Stand clear, or you will be jostled off the foot way."[17] The thirst for information was not simple curiosity; possessing the latest news, especially if it was gotten before one's rivals, could be a source of profit or political advantage. Yet, as the author's jaded, mocking tone suggested, there was more than a little absurdity in men unwilling to wait another hour for news two months old. Certainly, for the unscrupulous financial operators, there might be money in knowing things before others, but for ordinary people, would knowing of the fall of Austria sixty-five or sixty-six days after the fact matter all that much?

While such considerations did not trouble readers overmuch, in spite of their protestations it mattered to printers quite a great deal. Editors were at constant pains to emphasize the "lateness" of their news. The word *lateness* in this context had a positive rather than negative con-notation; it meant that the news had only just arrived, usually on the day of press, and by implication was being included in this newspaper before others in the vicinity. "LATE NEWS FROM ENGLAND," a lead story in the *Oracle* read. "Yesterday arrived in this port the Snow Mary, Sam-uel Tripe, master, in 56 days from Liverpool—Capt. Tripe informs us." Such trumpeting could make a newspaper seem like a vital source of breaking news rather than a stale record of past events. Even no news could be presented as an update. "The Papers received by the last Mail contain no late News of Importance," the *Mirrour* informed its readers, although it assured them that "we have endeavored to extract the most material for this Day's Repast."[18] Editors might bemoan the more sharp-elbowed members of the community agitating for the latest intelligence, but they also did everything they could to supply the demand.

Of course, once one newspaper in town printed a story, rival editors were free to appropriate it for their own publication. Given that most papers printed on different days, this practice was reasonably common. The *Oracle of the Day*, for example, printed a Saturday edition,[19] while the *New Hampshire Gazette* was published on a Tuesday.[20] News that arrived in town on a Thursday or a Friday was, therefore, more likely to appear first in the *Oracle* than the *Gazette*, while the *Gazette* would have the advantage when it came to Sunday or Monday news. In such circumstances, stories were commonly appropriated. As the number of newspapers increased, so too did the sharing. In 1790 just four articles with a London dateline were copied from one Portsmouth newspaper to another; in 1800 twenty-five such articles were copied. The time it took for these copied articles to appear also fell, from a week in 1790 to two or three days in 1800.

The speed with which New Hampshire editors got the news depended in large part on their geographic location. Portsmouth editors enjoyed the readiest access not only to overseas news but also to the best roads, most consistent stream of coach traffic, and closest proximity to Boston. Printers in other towns had to wait rather longer, and their subscribers longer still, for their newspapers to be delivered. The Concord papers had, in 1791, to wait an extra week for the London news to arrive; on average they got it eighty-six days after the original date of publication. Once a foreign story hit the mainland United States, its rate of travel slowed considerably. A distance of only forty miles could add six or seven days onto the journey of a news story. The average rate of movement for a story from Portsmouth to Concord was about seven miles a day (which is not to say that the courier was literally traveling seven miles a day, but given stops, delays, and rest days, this was the mean). By comparison, news moving from London to Portsmouth traveled at about forty-four miles per day. Those who lived farther inland might wait weeks, or even months, to learn of a foreign event that had become common knowledge along the seaboard. The *New Hampshire Recorder*, based in Keene, a small town in the western part of the state, ran a report of a meeting that took place on June 24, 1790, on December 9, some five and a half months later.[21] Such lapses became more and more frequent the farther west one went.

Networks of subscribers to newspapers did not neatly confine themselves to state boundaries. A paucity of Vermont newspapers meant that residents of that state often had to reply on newspapers from New Hampshire, Massachusetts, and New York. Within New Hampshire itself, many people subscribed to nearby out-of-state newspapers. One notable example was the *Essex Journal & New Hampshire Packet*. This paper, published in Newburyport, Essex County, Massachusetts, was, as the name suggests, aimed at an audience of readers in both northeastern Massachusetts and southeastern New Hampshire. Inland merchants were solicitous of any maritime news, which a Newburyport-based paper would be sure to provide, and it also provided New Hampshire readers a window into the political milieu of their southerly neighbors.

News from the outside world did not take one path to get to printers and their readers. An editor might have a direct contact with a ship's captain, a merchant, or even an English printer and thus receive the news directly. They might subscribe to one of the big-city publications, having the *Columbian Centinel* delivered from Boston or the *Gazette of the United States* from Philadelphia. Even when they didn't subscribe, sometimes materials came to hand by serendipity. "The loan of a Boston Centinel of last Saturday, from a Gentleman in town," an article on an English naval battle in the *Concord Herald* began, "has enabled the Editor to present his readers with the following articles of intelligence." They might exchange news with friendly editors in the next town or, as described earlier, filch from their competitors. It was also common practice to cross-reference newspapers from different locations. "We copy the following from the *Boston Commercial Gazette*," the editor of the *Federal Observer* noted, "although the Philadelphia papers received by the last mails make no mention of it." The copy that followed read: "The following article is copied from a Hand-bill, printed at New York.... *A gentleman arrived last night from Philadelphia informs.*"[22] Who was to be believed, the Philadelphia newspapers that didn't print the story or the copy of a New York handbill in a Boston paper based on the testimony of a gentleman from Philadelphia? Word-of-mouth stories were frequently published on the vouchsafe of "reliable gentlemen." All editors relied on a mixture of all of these sources, but as various conditions changed, such as the ease and speed of travel, the advent of the Post Office Department, and the increasing reach of subscription networks, so too the extent to which they could rely on differing channels of information.

To further complicate matters, it could be difficult to tell how many iterations a story had passed through on its way into a newspaper. It was impossible, of course, for an editor in Hanover, New Hampshire, to know how a story in a London newspaper had been sourced; some of them, in turn, had come from local English newspapers or were based on reporting done in French, Dutch, German, or Spanish. Things did not necessarily become any clearer when the story hit American shores. Most stories did not come straight from the pages of a newspaper printed in London but rather arrived from another American publication that had copied it from a London paper. Of course, an editor might realize, if he was copying a copy, that it was perfectly possible that the copy he was copying was, in fact, based on a copy. An article that appeared in the *Concord Mirrour*, which appeared under a dateline from the *Columbian Centinel*, began: "By an arrival at Portland, from Rotterdam, the Editor has received the papers printed in that city as late as June 17, which are 17 days later than before received. They being printed in the Dutch language, the translation was difficult to be procured." The story had gone through four different copies, and one translation, before reaching Concord. Even when stories acknowledged this, they often shed little light on the issue. One article in the *New Hampshire Gazette*, with a New York dateline, begins, "On Saturday last, we were informed from Philadelphia." As to whether the (unnamed) New York newspaper got it from a Philadelphia paper, a correspondent, or hearsay, both the reader and the editor could only speculate. Most of the time, however, even such tenuous hints were absent. Sometimes, provenance was alluded to but in ways that raised more questions than were answered. "Intelligence has been received at Philadelphia," the *New Hampshire Spy* confided in its readers, "from a channel that can admit of no dispute."[23] Rather than being second- or thirdhand, in some cases a news story might be sixth- or seventh-hand, having bounced around from newspaper to newspaper. The appearance of stories from, for example, Georgia in the New Hampshire newspapers did not necessarily indicate that printers in the most northerly of the states were subscribers to newspapers in the most southerly; rather, they read someone, who read someone, who read someone, who did.

In 1790 the three greatest external conduits of foreign news to New Hampshire were the presses of Boston, Philadelphia, and New York. Between them, they supplied ninety-nine articles with a London dateline to the New Hampshire press, 47 percent of the total that appeared that year. By comparison, seventy articles were sourced directly by New Hampshire editors through their networks of contacts and correspondents. Fifteen articles were copies taken between New Hampshire editors (all of which, unsurprisingly, came from Portsmouth), and the remaining forty came from other towns outside of New Hampshire.[24] This meant that while editors had a wide base of sources to draw from in theory, with London datelined articles from twenty different towns appearing in the New Hampshire papers, in practice they relied on either their own news gathering or the printers of America's three biggest cities, with more than three-quarters of their foreign news coming from these sources. Thus, the influence and power of the larger city newspapers not only touched their own readers but also emanated out into the milieu of places like New Hampshire; a reader in Keene did not need to subscribe to a Boston newspaper to be reading news from Boston.

Certain big-city papers were particularly relied on by New Hampshire editors looking to fill pages. The *Columbian Centinel*, published and edited by Benjamin Russell, was the most important paper to come out of Boston and was comfortably New England's most widely read paper. Over seven hundred articles from the *Centinel* were reprinted in New Hampshire in the 1790s.[25] Solidly Federalist and conservative, *Centinel* articles had little trouble finding appreciative audiences among both New Hampshire editors and readers, while also being a steady source of English political correspondence. The other major Federalist newspaper, the *Gazette of the United States*, was established in New York before moving to Philadelphia in 1791. The quasi-official organ of the Federalist Party (it received private funding from Alexander Hamilton), the *Gazette* published articles, sometimes written under pseudonyms, by leading figures within the party; John Adams published his political thesis statement, the *Discourses on Davila*, there. Editor John Fenno was himself an important Federalist writer and thinker, before being replaced by none other than Joseph Dennie. Some 176 articles in the New Hampshire press were credited to the *Gazette*. From New York came a variety of newspapers, including the *Daily Advertiser*, the *Price Courant*, and Greenleaf's *New York Journal and Public Register*.

Not all of these big-city newspapers were as sympathetic to the outlook of New England Federalists. In the early 1790s, the Democrat-Republicans, seeking a print outlet of their own, established the *National Gazette* in direct opposition to the *Gazette of the United States*. The *National Gazette*, which published from October 1791 to October 1793, was credited only twenty-nine times across the whole of New Hampshire (the *Gazette of the United States*, on just a year and a half more, received six times as many datelines). Most New Hampshire editors were not willing to be associated with a well-known Jeffersonian publication. Its editor, Philip Freneau, became something of a byword among the New Hampshire correspondents for rabble-rousing and demagoguery. Letters defending John Adams were addressed to "Mr Freneau," who became totemic of the democratic tendency in the early American press. After the *National Gazette* folded, a new bogeyman appeared, in the form of Benjamin Franklin Bache's *Philadelphia Aurora*. If Freneau was distrusted, then Bache was despised. Many Federalist editors warned darkly of the potential pitfalls presented by large party-funded papers (so long as they weren't Federalist). "It is asserted as a fact," the *Rising Sun* of Keene alerted its readers, "that the late French minister, Fauchet, was a subscriber for a thousand of Bache's Aurora. The price of this paper is eight dollars per annum. Of course, Mr Bache's yearly income from the French minister must be 8000 dollars." Accusations of foreign interference in the American media were, it seems, a tradition that started early. "We have a right to doubt the truth of this assertion," the *Sun* admitted. "But if true, we shall find no difficulty in accounting for the illiberal abuse which is daily emitted from that press, against the President, and other influential characters in the United States." An article in the Concord-based *Courier of New Hampshire* offered a brief history of "Jacobinical" interference in the press. Newspapers had, according to the author, been made a "system of calumny and obloquy" against not only the government but also the very fabric of the United States. "One of the first newspapers devoted to this system was the National Gazette, printed at Philadelphia. . . . The Aurora of Philadelphia, the Argus of New York[,] the Chronicle of Boston, and a number of other inferior papers in various parts of the country, were soon enlisted into the same service." The primary purposes of these papers were, as the article would have it, to produce "streams of abuse and falsehood, mis-representation and slander . . . which have been circulated with incredible industry."[26] Needless to say, these papers were not as widely used by New Hampshire Federalist printers as the *Columbian Centinel* and *Gazette of the United States*.

The 1790s witnessed an explosion in the quantity of foreign news being reported in American newspapers. In 1795, 375 articles originating in London newspapers were printed in New Hampshire, more than double the 173 articles printed in 1792. By 1800, this number had risen again, with 533 London news stories appearing. While this can be partly attributed to increasing amounts of news coverage overall, other contextual factors contributed to this rapid growth. Mass public interest in the French Revolution was the primary driving force behind this shift. In 1790, 585 articles mentioning France appeared in the New Hampshire press, rising to 2,016 in 1795. As the "dawn" of the Revolution receded and the bloodshed began, accounts of the rioting, executions, and terror flooded the American press, such stories being rather more popular than those about the deliberations of the French National Constituent Assembly. "By an ingenious mechanical process," the *Mirrour* informed its readers with a gleeful licentiousness, "down dropped the Guillotine, the Head was at once chopped off, and the Blood flowed, when the Company in general, and particularly the ladies, eagerly and joyfully steeped their Handkerchiefs in it." The subsequent wars that engulfed Europe were also covered extensively, and with a similar eye for carnage. "The battle which took place yesterday upon the Nidda was smart and bloody," one report in the Keene *Sentinel* noted. "There were several charges with the bayonet, as well as of the cavalry."[27] In an era before the advent of the war correspondent, readers had to make do with eyewitness accounts or the testimony of soldiers.

As the volume of foreign news increased, so too did the number of routes that it took into New Hampshire. While the papers of Boston, Philadelphia, and New York continued to be important sources, contributing 70, 48, and 53 London articles, respectively, other sources rose in prominence. New Hampshire editors were increasingly coming to depend on one another, whether through active cooperation, such as the sharing of letters, or copying. Fifty-nine articles with a London dateline that made their first American appearance in a Portsmouth paper were reprinted in papers across the state, more than either Philadelphia or New York. Editors in other New Hampshire towns were also increasingly contributing to the shared pool of knowledge about the outside world. New Hampshire newspapers reprinted London-sourced articles from Concord (230), Hanover (2), Walpole (7), and Amherst (10). By such exchanges, news began traveling not only to the state but within it. However, the most important development was a growing network of small-town papers that extended beyond the state. By the mid-1790s, stories from newspapers all over America were finding their way into the pages of small-town and country newspapers, even along the fringes of the republic. Articles from papers in Elizabethtown in Maryland, Augusta in Georgia, and Charleston in South Carolina all appeared in the pages of the New Hampshire press. Closer to home, New England papers outside of Boston also came to another important source of New Hampshire printers' foreign intelligence. Newburyport, Massachusetts, provided 17 London news articles in 1795 and 29 in 1796. News also came, albeit in smaller quantities, from the West, with Vermont papers in Rutland, Windsor, and Brattleboro supplying a few articles a year each.

This trend toward increasing diversity in the sources of news on which New Hampshire editors could draw continued into the end of the decade. By 1799 30 percent of all London datelined news appearing in New Hampshire came from towns outside of the state other than Boston, Philadelphia, and New York, and another 33 percent came from within New Hampshire itself. While the big-city papers continued to be an important stream of news for papers (37 percent) across the country, they became just one set of voices, albeit prominent ones, in an increasingly turbulent and competitive media marketplace. In 1800 articles with a London dateline were copied from newspapers in thirty-six different towns, spread across eleven different states, as well as the Maine territory (still, at that time, a part of Massachusetts). What this meant in practical terms is that getting foreign news became easier for readers. In 1790 the New Hampshire newspaper reader was required, if they wished to read every foreign news article circulated in the state, to read nearly every article in every paper. The number of articles that nearly or completely reproduced the information available in another New Hampshire publication was only 9 percent; the remainder was available in only one newspaper. By 1797, however, the proportion of shared news had risen to 22 percent. While this might have represented a redundancy for people who subscribed to more than one paper, for most people it meant that they were more likely to get access to the major stories of the day.

The growing network of newspapers that saw reports, stories, and rumors being shared by papers throughout America was a product of not just the greater reach that publications could boast, but also the increasing speed with which they were traveling across the country. In

FIGURE 2. SOURCE OF LONDON NEWS, 1790–1800

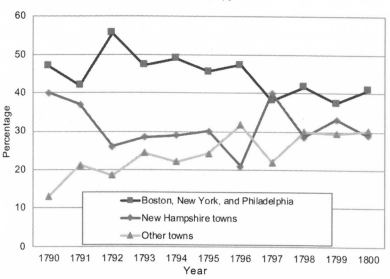

Data compiled from NewsBank.

1790 a news story published in Boston took an average of nine days to reappear in the Portsmouth newspapers; by 1800 this had fallen to five days. These lengths of time did not necessarily reflect how long it took a horseman to go from one place to another, but rather how frequently a post rider might make the journey and, most crucially of all, how many stops they might make along the way. Samuel Beane, a Boston post rider advertising delivery of newspapers from "Boston, Concord, Exeter or Portsmouth" would be making stops in no fewer than sixteen towns, villages, and hamlets along the way.[28] Such detours could cumulatively add days onto such a route. Boston, of course, at least had the benefit of proximity and regular traffic between it and New Hampshire towns, and from late 1792 an official U.S. postal route joined it and Portsmouth.[29] In the 1790s, the time taken for news to travel from New York fell from twenty-two days to twelve days. Within the state, the change was even more pronounced. The average time taken for stories from Philadelphia to be printed in the Concord press was forty-seven days in 1790; by 1800 the time lapse had fallen to eighteen days. When the first newspaper in Hanover, the mostly northwesterly town to get one, was established in 1793, readers there would wait an average of thirty-three days of Philadelphia news to appear in their paper; by 1800 the delay was cut down to twenty days. All across the state, a greater proliferation of news was arriving with greater rapidity, whether brought into port on coastal sloops, passed from traveler to traveler, or carried along the emerging network of carriage routes. The overall average time it took for Boston stories to be reprinted in New Hampshire newspapers generally fell from eighteen days in 1790 to seven days in 1800.

This increasing immediacy did not just manifest with news from the big cities. The speed of exchange between newspapers within the state also underwent an acceleration. News stories originating in Portsmouth took nineteen days to appear in the Concord newspapers in 1790 and only five in 1800. The forty miles from Portsmouth to Concord no longer seemed quite such a world away. Once again, the establishment of a post office played a large part in this change. In a piece simply titled "Post-Office," the *New Hampshire Gazette* of Portsmouth laid out the new arrangements:

The Mails, from November 1st to May 1st, are arrived to, and be dispatched from this office as follows: The mail from Boston will arrive every Tuesday and Friday at 11 o'clock A.M., and will leave this Office at 1 o'clock P.M. on said days. The Mail from Portland is to arrive on said days, at 10 o'clock, A.M. and will leave this office as soon after the arrival of the Boston Post as the Mails can be sorted and properly arranged. The Post from Concord and Hanover is to arrive at Mondays, at 5 o'clock P.M. and to leave this Office on Tuesdays, and 12 o'clock at noon.[30]

The long-term consequences of the introduction of these regular services, in concert with less formalized modes of newspaper delivery, will be discussed in much greater detail in the next chapter, but their immediate effect was to cap the amount of time one might reasonably expect a letter, or a newspaper, to arrive at its destination. If one could not make private arrangements, the weekly post was always an option. The almost spiritual significance of this lifeline was captured in a poem published in the *Farmer's Weekly Museum*: "The Post comes in—The Newspaper is read—The World is contemplated at a distance."[31] The introduction of such regular deliveries provided a source of solace and comfort for the isolated.

FIGURE 3. TRANSMISSION TIME FROM PORTSMOUTH TO OTHER NEW HAMPSHIRE TOWNS

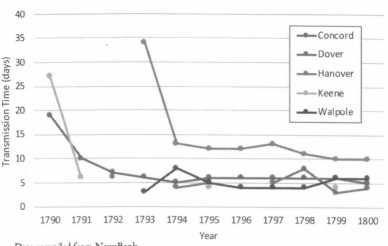

Data compiled from NewsBank.

Another advantage of getting news from closer to home was that a printer was far more likely to have personal contact with the source. These relationships between friendly editors, built up over time, at least gave the printer a degree of assurance that the "reliable gentleman" supplying their news was, in fact, both reliable and a gentleman. These contacts could even be a means of people in other towns perusing copies of a newspaper. "The Printer of the Courier has a file of the *New Hampshire Gazette*, from the first of January 1797. Any person wishing to examine ... may be gratified by applying at the Post Office in Concord."[32] By providing access to the public to these archives, the proprietor of the *Courier* was not only performing a public service but also giving people an incentive to visit his shop.

The task of filling newspapers columns became, in the 1790s, simultaneously easier and more complicated. For most of their history up to this point, the fundamental challenge that most American newspaper printer-editors faced was one of information scarcity. For newspapers in big commercial centers, at the nexus of networks of commerce and culture, the problem wasn't so bad. The regular arrivals of ships and stagecoaches were just a part of this. Centers of governments created legislation and gossip. As Trish Loughlan has observed, events "like Washington's death in 1799 travelled through the republic at a relatively quick pace, but not because there were sophisticated or reliable print networks to do the job. In fact, 'hours of even days before the first locally printed newspaper accounts appeared,' most people had already heard the news through commercial or political networks, passed mouth to mouth and by private letter." Immigrants brought not only news with them but also diverse opinions and ideologies. Universities and learned societies held symposia, published proceedings, and gave prizes. And, of course, the cities themselves, with their crimes, fires, and other assorted trials and inconveniences, generated a steady supply of news. For those on the fringes, news could be a rare and precious commodity. For the most part, a feast-or-famine dynamic of abundance and dearth prevailed, with news coming in large chunks, followed by periods of relative silence. "We are left, by the latest foreign prints," the *New Hampshire Gazetteer* sighed with exasperation, "to wander in the wilds of conjecture as to European news and politics."[33] The factors that underpinned this cycle will be explored in depth in the next chapter, but for most provincial editors of the colonial and revolutionary periods, information was something to be stockpiled in expectations of hard times. It was circumstances such as these that made editors reprint the same poem three or four times over the course of a year or the proceedings of state governments hundreds of miles away.

In the early years of the American republic, this began to change. As more sources of news and information became available in places like New Hampshire, editors were seldom faced with the serious threat of not having enough to publish. Not only was news from Europe, the Caribbean, and the larger American cities arriving in greater quantities than ever before, but the movement of information within the state reached hitherto unprecedented levels as well. In 1790 Portsmouth, Concord, and Keene were the only towns in New Hampshire to have regularly published newspapers. By 1800 these towns had been joined by Walpole, Hanover, Dover, and Amherst. The rise of the country newspaper created a virtuous circle. With more newspapers, there was more news, or, more precisely, more newsprint in circulation. Previously, a resident of Portsmouth would have had an easier time learning of debates in the House of Commons than they would of goings-on in their own state. As communications within the interior grew easier, and printing spread, they might read of the results of the Dartmouth College Lottery (winning number 5834)[34] or the proceedings of the circuit court in Concord.[35] Mundane as such things might be, they gradually inculcated a wider sense of community and commonality between the relatively scattered and isolated people of the American hinterlands.

However, this variety of news fundamentally changed the job of the newspaper editor. Whereas previously their task had been to stretch thin material out over four pages, the new abundance meant that, increasingly, editors were forced to edit. Faced with a choice of what to or to not include, the personal preferences, biases, and attachments of the editor came to matter more. Whereas earlier on newspapers had generally taken a relaxed approach toward the sources that they elected to reprint from, starting in around the mid-1790s they increasingly came to identify themselves in more politicized names. Bland appellations like the *New Hampshire Gazette* or the *Oracle of the Day* were joined by more overtly partisan titles such as the *Federal Observer* or the *Republican Gazette*. The *Mirrour* was transformed into the *Federal Mirrour*, before making an about-face as the *Republican Gazetteer*. The greater availability of political writing from different parts of the United States, as well the ability to choose from positive and negative coverage of the French Revolution, meant that rural newspapers were able to be tailored toward specific audiences and ideologies in ways that would have been much more difficult a generation earlier. "We publish the following observations to counteract an injurious effect which the electioneering remarks in one of our late papers may have made upon the minds of the public," the editor of the *Farmer's Weekly Museum* wrote in 1800. "Which were inserted partly to avoid the imputation of partiality, and, partly, we are sufficiently sincere to acknowledge, through imperception of their intention and origin."[36] That the *Museum* had been fooled by a piece of Republican satire was undoubtedly a source of embarrassment, but it was the origins of the piece that were most disturbing. To have printed something that came from an opposition, rather than a Federalist, paper would have been a meaningless distinction ten years earlier; by the election of 1800, it was a faux pas that merited a printed apology.

Big-city newspapers like the *Columbian Centinel* of Boston or the *Aurora* of Philadelphia undoubtedly had the largest readerships and the greatest reach of the early American newspapers. However, these were far from being the only sources of news in the early United States. Newspapers across America drew from a wide array of sources. These included the major urban presses, as well as foreign newspapers and oral testimony, but they also made use of an ever-expanding network of weekly and biweekly small-town and village publications. This cross-pollination of print meant that the newspapers of New Hampshire became inflected with the voices, opinions, and prejudices of an unprecedented range of writers, professional and amateur. The implications of this for American political culture will be explored in chapters 7 and 8, but it had longer-term consequences, too. At the very moment that the project of American nation building began, as precarious and fractious as it proved to be, Americans were writing to and reading each other more than they ever had previously. These discourses were not always pleasant or productive, but if anything resembling an American identity was forming, they were a contributing factor in its emergence. When readers in New Hampshire read articles containing passages such as the following, it is not hard to see this process in action: "In a great nation the mind of the individual seems raised a grade or two, and the virtue and talents of men seem exalted. The American union, if kept entire, will confirm this theory—it contains within itself the seeds of its own improvement: it will call forth all the energy of the human character. A nation so numerous, spreading over such a pace & so wonderfully prosperous, will excite and reward the highest efforts of genius and virtue." This glorious "horizon of light" contained only "one cloud . . . charged with tempest, and darkness, and desolation." "The separation of the states would blast our hopes," the article warned. "It is the only risk we run as a nation."[37] The predominantly Federalist editors of New Hampshire viewed themselves as key agents in this process; the republic, if it was to survive, had to be a republic of letters. The extent to which the burgeoning newspaper industry was a force for unity in that tempestuous and fragile new union was quite another question.

CHAPTER FIVE

CLIMATE, COMMERCE, AND COACHES

Delivering the News

All the News is frozen up—the Boston post has not arrived—and we have nothing but a poor cold collation to serve up for our customers this week.

—*Concord Herald*, January 25, 1792

Commerce and communication were utterly contingent on the physical environment of early America. The patterns of both were at the mercy of geography and climate to such an extent that it is impossible to divorce the movement of goods or ideas from the vicissitudes of the weather. "The mail due yesterday had not arrived at the publication of this day's Gazette," Portsmouth's *New Hampshire Gazette* informed its readers, "owing to the almost impracticableness of passing, the weather being extreme cold, and the roads wholly blocked up with snow."[1] Such notices were commonplace throughout the New England press of the late eighteenth century. Any analysis of the systems of information that circulated around the early United States needs to acknowledge the central importance of these environmental factors. It also needs to accommodate the human responses to these challenges, the systems established to overcome the obstacles presented by granite, ice, and mud. This chapter will look at the material conditions of travel and transportation in Federalist-era New Hampshire. Our chief source of knowledge about these journeys comes from the newspapers themselves, in the form of advertisements: for postal routes, stagecoaches, and post riders. Locating the movement of the news in a broader context of rural commercial culture requires an understanding of the climatic, economic, and social imperatives that informed the ways in which people bought and sold information.

If news frequently took circuitous, and occasionally absurd, routes to make it into the hands of small-town printers, the most precarious leg of its journey from event to story to popular knowledge was usually the last. Getting newspapers to a customer base dotted over a hinterland spanning dozens of miles presented a daunting logistical challenge. While most urban publishers could rely on their readers either collecting their papers in person or being conveniently concentrated in tightly packed neighborhoods, printers with a rural market needed to reach remote farmsteads, woodland cabins, and the tiny fishing villages strewn along the rugged New England coast. And while the nascent federal postal service was a reasonable (not to mention economical) means of sending newspapers over relatively long distances to larger communities, it was patently ill-suited to this sort of distribution. In order for newspapers to reach customers in anything resembling a timely fashion, printers were forced to rely on their own means of delivery.

In his study of access to information by rural people in northern New Hampshire and Vermont, Gilmore distinguishes between zones of "full access" (areas with basically unfettered access to printed material through a bookstore or printing shop), "partial access" (containing people who lived more than a day's travel away from a vendor and who had to mainly rely on post riders and peddlers for their books and newspapers), and "minimal access" (which were not even served by post riders or regular traveling merchants). Writing of the "Upper Valley" region (the northernmost and least urbanized quarter of New Hampshire), he estimates that by 1800, about a third of the region's population still had minimal access, meaning that the remainder had either direct or indirect access to printed material. Given the relatively sparse population of the Upper Valley compared to the rest of the state, the large majority of New Hampshire residents had at least partial access to a regular supply of publications. While Gilmore notes that in the early 1790s, approximately one-third of Upper Valley residents had newspaper subscriptions, this was rapidly changing: "The deep penetration of newspapers in north-western New England took place with astonishing rapidity, in just thirty years, 1785–1815."[2]

Printers found inventive means to reach these thinly dispersed markets. Between them the various papers of Concord (the *Herald*, *Courier*, and *Mirrour*) could boast subscribers in thirty-three different towns, villages, and hamlets, in a radius that spanned from eastern Vermont and the Canadian border to the Maine coast and southern Connecticut.[3] Many of these locations listed only one or two subscribers, making the expense and effort of incorporating them into delivery routes all the more remarkable. Nor did such routes form pleasingly elliptic circuits; wooded, mountainous New England meant that courier itineraries zigzagged across the landscape, circumnavigating impassable terrain and making detours to far-flung patrons, over some of the craggiest, least forgiving paths in the young nation, if such meager provision were even available. It is perhaps unsurprising that so many papers miscarried, a fact that the *Farmer's Weekly Museum* bemoaned when it noted, "By every mail, we receive complaints, that our papers are not duly received, and many aver, that for three, four or six months, they cannot find those papers, regularly addressed to them."[4]

The constant need of men willing, or sufficiently desperate, to do such arduous and unrewarding work is evinced in the pages of the papers themselves. "WANTED—A man to undertake riding as a POST, a circuit of about three days from this office," read one typical plea in the *Political and Sentimental Repository*. Post riders were a necessary means of filling in the gaps left by the expansive but patchy apparatus of the new postal system, private contractors hired out by printers to reach their less handily placed clients. These individuals had to be both skilled horsemen and willing to work for meager and sporadic pay. George Barstow, a contemporary historian and journalist, observed, "Even an ordinary stage was an accommodation, which, at that time, was scarcely to be seen in our principal cities; and a humble post-rider, journeying leisurely along the seaboard, and occasionally, diverging a few miles into the country, for a considerable time performed the whole mail service of this state." The post riders themselves became more than mere bearers of the news but a vital instrument in the social and cultural life of rural American society. Many even took out advertisements in the papers they delivered, keen to promote the secondary services by which many of them supplemented their income. One notice, taken out by a Nathaniel Wilcocks, informed the public that he had undertaken "to ride as a Post from Concord to Claremont," passing through "the towns of Hopkinton, Warner, Sutton, Fishersfield, Wendall, and Newport." Wilcocks promised, "All persons who wish to furnish themselves with The Concord Herald, may be supplied at a reasonable price. People living off the road, and in the adjacent towns, may have their papers left at some places on the road for their conveniency, where they can join in small neighborhoods and send for them—and care will be taken that they are punctually delivered at the places agreed on." More than just promoting his own services, Wilcocks also advertised that an associate, John Lathrop, had "commenced riding as a Post, from Concord to Dartmouth College, and from thence to Haverhill," suggesting a degree of partnership or at least cooperation between individual riders. Lathrop would "carry The Concord Herald, and supply those persons on his route who have a desire of taking the same," and Wilcocks assured readers, "Any person having letters to convey, or business to transact, on either of said routs, may depend to on the care and fidelity of the Postriders to serve them for a reasonable reward."[5] Post riders, therefore, became the pulse of countryside communication; if the postal routes could be thought of as the arteries of information, then the riders acted as capillaries, expanding the reach of both dispatches and correspondence to most Americans. Without the steady custom that newspapers provided, it is doubtful whether such men would have been able to ply their trade and might never have drawn previously isolated Americans into the broader political and cultural conversation.

Post riders were more than mere delivery boys in another important sense: they served as business agents, in some senses franchisees, of the printer, responsible for the collection of payments and living on the proceeds. "OZIAS SILSBY, POST-RIDER," read one insertion, "BEGS leave to inform his Customers, that the third six months (from his commencing riding) will expire the first of November next:—He therefore requests ALL, who are indebted to him for papers, to settle up their arrears by that time, which alone will enable him to continue his route."[6] The triangular interdependence of printers, rider, and the public was frequently invoked by those encouraging prompt payment. The notion of a public sphere, although not articulated as such, was not a theoretical construct but an active and vital component of the post rider's professional identity.[7] They were, or at least styled themselves, public servants. Sometimes, post riders would pick up their quills and contribute directly to the pages of the newspaper they delivered, appealing directly to their customers. One piece was headlined, "THOMAS SMITH, Postrider's Good Natured Invitation to his Customers," makes for a typical example. "IN spite of windy, rainy, scorching, and freezing days, and a crippled frame," Smith began, deploying just a touch of pathos, "you well know what for years that I have regularly left you Walpole papers, for your own amusement in the evening, and for the instruction of your families at all leisure hours." The strategy of presenting one's self as not a mere carrier of papers but the bringer of education and entertainment was a common one among post riders. "I have cheerfully made a weekly jaunt over the hills you inhabit," he continues, "because I did not doubt that the good and true men of Newhampshire were willing to pay the Post, who brought them so many new and curious things. Many of you have paid my bills at sight—this raises my spirits, and makes me jog on to your doors merrily. But some, when they see me unclasp my pocket book, will run and hide behind the loom or bed; the sight of an accompt is so terrifying." The mention of a "loom" is also an oblique insight into the occupations and class of many of his patrons, who could be weavers just as well as lawyers, and once again situated Smith and his fellows as public servants. "These folks that are so easily frightened are now informed, that they must muster up a little courage, and not shrink for such a trifle, as the dun of a Postrider."[8] If the lightness of tone was calculated to mask a more serious financial anxiety, it also communicates the sense that Smith truly felt himself an itinerant member of the communities through which he passed on a weekly basis.

Of all the challenges faced by these couriers, the most elementary, in both senses of the word, was the weather. In the month of February, it took news from London eighty-nine days to reach New Hampshire. In June the same process took an average of sixty-five days.[9] For the time it took for news to travel to fluctuate so greatly indicates the extent to which early American networks of communication and transportation were forever at the mercy of the climate. Nor was it simply the snows of winter that delayed these movements. The wet, muddy springs that characterized the months of April and May in New England further allayed the circulation of news. It is telling, perhaps, that news traveled at the same speed in May as it did in December.

New Hampshire today experiences climatic variance both topographically and chronologically. Summers, particularly in the Atlantic Southeast of the state, are warm and humid. Winters are severely, sometimes even preposterously, cold. In January temperatures regularly dip below ten degrees Fahrenheit, and average annual snowfall ranges from sixty to one hundred inches.[10] This is, historically, relatively mild. The global climate in the seventeenth and eighteenth centuries has been characterized as a "little ice age,"[11] leading not only to cold of even greater extremes but to all manner of other effects as well. One account, written in May, gives an impression of the chill, reporting that "yesterday, and the day before, hail and snow squalls, with piercing northerly winds . . . ice was frozen to a considerable thickness . . . and vegetation appears shrouded, in its infancy, in melancholy mourning."[12] Such bitter cold, the article explained, was disrupting the migration of birds, the cycle of the growing season, and the movements of animals, all vital considerations for hunters and woodsmen.

Local publications were understandably preoccupied with weather, and rural papers with their constituents of farmers, woodsmen, and landowners were even more acutely conscious of its effects. In an era before scientifically precise meteorological measurements could be taken on a consistent basis, most papers relied on anecdotal, usually reader-created, accounts of conditions on the ground. These reports sometimes seem motivated less by a journalistic spirit than a perverse competitive-ness as to whose weather was the most wretched. "I observed some time since in your paper the account of the snow lying fifteen feet deep on the sunny side," an oddly triumphal letter to the *Repository* stated, "and thirty feet deep on the other side of the White-Hills." The lengths to which newspaper correspondents went, often in bracing or even dan-gerous conditions, to collect measurements can be startling. They also show the extent to which weather persisted in memory or perhaps in the notebooks of the more assiduous. "You may also add," the letter continued, "that in Banington in July last, that the FROST on the sunny side of the hills near Bow-Pond, lay near ten inches deep—about five miles below said pond in said town in a deep hollow between two high hills there was a HALE near six feet deep—at the same time there was SNOW seen at the N.W. Part of town five feet ten inches deep."[13] Prior to the advent of day-to-day forecasting, such reports served more as a record than a useful guide; newspapers' weather reports would, under the best possible conditions, always be at least a week out of date by the time they reached readers. That did not, however, seem to dampen the appetite for such content; the New Hampshire press of the 1790s produced some 763 articles about snow. In the winter months, scarcely a week passed without most newspapers mentioning it at least once.

Sometimes extreme cold directly interfered with manufacturing, and printers were not immune. The natural rhythms of rural and village life and labor, which were in large part shaped around the vicissitudes of heat and cold, could grind to a halt under sufficiently severe frigidity. "People who were on their way to and from market have lain weather-bound for several days," the *Concord Mirrour* croaked. "The most hardy have shrunk from their enterprises, and joined the general chorus, *Ah! Bless my heart, how cold it is!*" A printer, obligated to produce his paper on a weekly basis, could not afford to "lay weather-bound." Even manu-facturing could be jeopardized by extreme conditions, as large cast-iron machines became painful to handle and ink froze in its barrels. Readers of the *New Hampshire and Vermont Magazine* were informed in October 1797 that due to the "extreme cold weather," the entire business of the paper had had to move establishments and was now located in "the office to the upper part of the house owned by Mrs Ebenezer Gray," where they were assured "the business will be continued." Unless a printer had the means to set by a store of materials in the fall, the supplies necessary to the operation of a press could become expensive or even unavailable, as foundries and paper mills ground to a halt. The business of the paper could also be impeded by the pecuniary implications of the season. As the general current of trade ebbed, so did the specie essential to the printer's livelihood. As the printer of the *Mirrour* explained in an article titled "Scarcity of Money," "It seems to be unusually scarce at present, if we judge by the lamentations of the busy part of the world. Almost every thing that we have to sell is sold for exportation in the fall and winter. The returns in cash or goods are not made till the following summer. This accounts for the greater scarcity of cash in the winter season."[14] As the supply of money contracted, so too did the printer's ability to invest, replace, and maintain. While he might trade and barter with locals for his day-to-day necessities, he also required printing stock and ink, which were mostly imported from England, a costly investment even disregarding the season in which they were shipped, and credit could be extended only so far.

If manufacturing was complicated by adverse weather conditions, then distribution and delivery could be rendered next to impossible. No matter what route or means were taken, eighteenth-century methods of transportation were subject to the elements. The boats and small ships that moved goods and information along the seaboard were regularly thwarted, or even destroyed, by the harsh weather, as the following report typifies:

> Thursday last arrived here one of the packets that plies between this place and Boston. She sailed from Boston on the 5th March for this port, with a valuable freight on board, but meeting with a heavy gale put into Cape Ann and came to anchor, but the wind blowing so high, could not ride the gale out, was oblige to put away to sea without cables

or anchors, the vessel being very much strained, leaked, all hands (being three) to the pump two nights and two days with only a few raisins and biscuit in their pockets to support them, finding they could no longer tend to the pump, all of them being frozen, the Captain first threw his own goods over to preserve those on freight, finding the water still gaining on them, were for the preservation of their lives and the freight below oblige to clear the deck to light the vessel; remained several days in a distressing situation, the wind blowing a mere hurricane, the vessel loaded with ice, & they covered near two inches thick, when the gale abated. . . . The Captain has frozen both of his hands very much, and one of his feet. Mr. Hiram Coffin has frozen both of his feet, and it is feared he will loose them.[15]

If coastal means of travel and transmission occasionally met with misfortune and vessels struggled with the ice storms and rocky inlets of the New England seaboard, the vehicles used in overland travel were often scarcely fit for the purpose. With bare wheels, no suspension mechanism (the elliptical spring was not invented until 1804 and not commonplace until much later), and the most primitive of steering mechanisms, it is a wonder that any post coaches traversed the American wilderness at all. Indeed, many did not; coaches overturning on Americas highways were such a problem as to be considered basically routine.[16] Besides the technical limitations of these vehicles, the roads they traversed in the late eighteenth century were barely worthy of the name. The first hard-surfaced road in the United States, built by the Philadelphia and Lancaster Turn Pike Company and completed in 1795, ran 62 miles from Lancaster to Philadelphia. This, like most of 175 farther miles that would be built over the next forty years, was an essentially private enterprise, paid for by customer tolls.[17] Few places benefited from such lavish provision, and local citizens were constantly lobbying for such conveniences. "NOTICE is hereby given," ran the Eagle, "that Elisha Paine and Jonathan Freeman, Esquires, and others, have petitioned the General Court, representing the great want of a public road from Dartmouth College in Hanover, to Merrimack-River in Salisbury, &c, and praying, that grant be made to them, their heirs and assigns, of the exclusive right of laying out, making and maintaining in repair, a Turn-Pike Road." Most of the time, the best one could hope for were corduroy roads, consisting of lines of felled trees, although even such modest improvements were a welcome change to what preceded them. In New Hampshire, the commercial hub of Portsmouth was linked to Boston, the only road in the state of sufficient quality to support a traffic of coaches carrying both human and commercial traffic. Beyond the extreme southeastern corner of the state, however, travelers were to rely on "bridle paths or cart trails that wound over ledges, around stumps, and through brooks."[18] Even these austere routes were available only in the vicinity of villages.

Winter was not the only season to present difficulties in this regard. A wet spring or summer could turn a narrow forest trail into a strip of churned mud, and with no central authority responsible for maintaining smaller roads, that was how they normally remained until baked by the summer sun into an unforgiving crust. Travelers would frequently post notices and requests in newspapers as to their repair, although these seem mostly to have gone unheeded, as suggested by a short notice that read, "There is a deep run in the road—a carriage or a load of lumber will almost turn over every time they pass; it can't be avoided—five minutes work would repair it; but 'tis not the usual time to mend roads in the spring."[19]

When presented with these conditions, some travelers trudged (or squelched) on, others found longer but more passable alternatives, and some gave up altogether. Extreme rainfall, while not as prevalent a problem in New England as in other parts of the United States, still had the capacity to wash out roads and fields, damage both crops and carriages, and ultimately hamstring the workings of the rural economy. The press of 1790s New England abounds with vivid and terrifying accounts of pelting rainstorms. "We are informed that great mischief was done in various parts of this State, to the inhabitants, on Monday last, by storms of hail and rain," read one article simply headlined "HAIL STORM." There is a note of relish in the account of the destruction wrought. "The hail was so violent, as to demolish glass, and destroy the fruits of the earth in a surprising degree. The orchards are in a great measure stripped, the fields of corn nearly ruined, and the harvest of English grain scarcely worth gathering." Such a maelstrom would wreak havoc on business of all types, the printer's and the post rider's included, and the preoccupation with weather no doubt reflected the interests of the men who compiled them as much as those who read them. "The size of the hail-stones was very large; a lad picked up three, after the rain, which succeeded the hail, was over, which together weighed three ounces. In short, the wind, rain and hail, probably have never been equalled in that part of the country."[20] Journalists and correspondents naturally wrote more about rain during the wet spring months, the very time at which the spread of news slowed. It is surely not too much of a conjecture to suppose that desperate editors, strapped for fresh news arriving from the outside world during these slack months, turned to local weather reports as a means of filling column inches.

If the movement of commerce and knowledge turned with the seasons, then all three were bound inextricably together in early American culture, particularly the culture of village and rural life. Not only did the difficulties of travel make nonessential jaunts infeasible for all but the most leisured individuals, but when journeys were undertaken, they were also made to serve a variety of different purposes. If one knew of a neighbor or relative traveling to a particular place, an informal economy of favors existed: travelers might carry cash, bills, letters, newspapers, books, and any number of other printed or written sundries. Where even a private post rider was unavailable, most Americans were forced to rely on other members of the community or even the kindness of strangers. These modest, separately inconsequential acts, taken together, made up the economies of money, information, and goods on which newspaper printers relied.

If these interlocking local economies, carried out in barter or cash, credit or favors, provided the necessary context for a viable printing business, they also provided perhaps the printer's most important source of newspaper revenue: advertisements. Given the delays and unreliability in the collection of subscription dues, most newspapers relied on carrying advertisements taken out by businesses and individuals to make ends meet.[21] And just like everything else in the life of the printer, these fluctuated, in a fairly predictable manner, with the seasons. New Hampshire papers took on 43 percent more advertisements in November than they did in February.[22] As economic life slowed down, and cash reserves dwindled, so too did the numbers of shops willing to take out paid advertisements in papers. In such a fallow period, papers would fill the empty space with the usual time-less material they kept on hand: poetry, sermons, and short essays, most of which had little to no contemporary relevance. What couldn't be as easily compensated for, however, was the shortfall left in a paper's account books. Coupled with rising material prices and difficulty of delivery, it isn't surprising that many newspapers were forced to close in the first few months of the year. "The Editor of the *Federal Gazette and Daily Advertiser*," read one typical example, "having tried, at a very considerable expense, the experiment of a daily paper, finds himself under the necessity of abandoning it for want of sufficient encourage-ment." The author's disappointment is palpable, and he is unable to conceal a quantity of self-pity, when he continues that he had "fondly flattered himself, and his friends had strengthened the delusion, that a publication of this kind, conducted on true Federal principles, and supported by unremitting industry, could not fail of success. Experi-ence, however, had convinced both himself and them of their error."[23] Commerce, and by extension advertising revenue, would typically recover in the literal and figurative thaw of early summer, before reach-ing its apex in the period of late fall and early winter, with a scramble to conduct business, and clear stock, before the snows set in. The rhythm of planting and harvesting, as well as the arrivals and departures of ships, informed that of the newspapers.

The commercial impetus behind the movement of most information in early America and the speed and course of that information were inextricably bound. As the volume of commercial content in newspa-pers increased, so did the alacrity with which the news spread.

As people did more business, the more they exchanged and desired the latest intelligence; equally, though, as people consumed more infor-mation, they conducted more business. Knowledge is the lifeblood of investment, trade, and speculation, and people who participate in the greater human discourse are far more able, and likely, to engage in long-range moneymaking pursuits than those living in isolation and ignorance. As historian Ian Steele explained, "If commerce were crucial to these improvements in communications, the improvements would, in turn, change the methods and expectations of those doing

FIGURE 4. ADVERTS PER MONTH COMPARED TO AVERAGE
TRANSMISSION TIME, 1790–1800

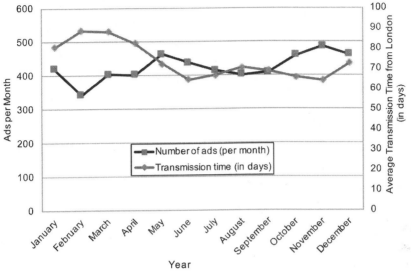

Data compiled from NewsBank.

business."[24] As the resulting trade was carried out, whether on foot, horseback, or carriage, rumor and dispatch moved with it. In those months in which the most business was done, news traveled farther, and faster. One did not lead neatly to the other, but rather the two phenomena, the movements of money and information, existed in a happy symbiosis.

Newspaper advertisements do not just provide a window into the quotidian side of small-town life; they are also a vital component of the form and construction of early American newspapers and represent important vectors of culture in their own right. After news articles, advertisements were the most common content of the weekly provincial paper, with 56,132 appearing in New Hampshire in the 1790s alone.[25] They also give a unique insight into human geography of the communities to which they marketed. Businesses were understandably keen to make their location as unambiguous as possible. As helpful aids like building numbers and zip codes had not yet been devised, business owners were forced to be descriptive, in a way that assumed both local knowledge and a small scale of urban life. As such, proprietors frequently had to use informal language in directing their customers, as when Samuel Bowles promoted his place of business as being "at his Shop in *Daniel-Street*, a little below the State-House, *Portsmouth*." The repeated sense that many of these advertisements convey is that the relationship between the buying public and merchants, tradesmen, and artisans was grounded in a level of social familiarity and exchange that went much deeper than simple commercial transaction. The fostering of such relationships was not just a social but also a commercial necessity, as some level of trust and even friendship was, as Peter Mathias has explained, an essential component of the otherwise uncertain world of eighteenth-century business. It was through ads like the following that such men were able to assert their presence and importance in the public sphere. One auction notice invited "Country Traders, Shopkeepers, and others in town and country" to the sale of a "general assortment of GOODS, suitable for the season, in large or small lots." The language of retail was generally mixed with that of civic duty. "Constant attendance will be given," wrote Abraham Isaac, author of the advertisement, "and the smallest favours gratefully acknowledged by the Public's humble servant." Many who took out advertisements in the papers operated out of their own homes and sold sundry goods that came to hand more by accident than design. Frequently, these notices were intended to be one-offs, normally with someone (not necessarily a recognized merchant) looking to shift some excess supply of cloth, tobacco, Bibles, or flutes. The range of people who might feasibly take out newspaper advertisements was much broader than it would later become, thanks in large part to low costs and low demand. Sometimes, advertisements were not directly preoccupied with the selling of goods or services, acting rather as community notices or even as a means of handling antisocial behavior. "The Person who took a dozen of large purple and white SHAWLS from a shop in Market-Street, on Monday last, is desired to return them immediately, and NO questions will be asked," one insertion read, before warning that "otherwise, they may depend on being exposed."[26] By carrying notices like these, the newspaper helped fill in a number of important social roles, some of which went unfilled in the sparsely populated America of the eighteenth century: town crier, constable, and moral arbiter.

As time passed, the advertisements changed in both character and source. Given the local readership of most papers, it is perhaps unsurprising that ads taken out by businesses and individuals within New Hampshire made up 90 percent of the total commercial content. In fact, given the quantity of newspaper content that came from outside of the state, the advertisements were by a considerable margin the most local thing about the newspapers; they were often the items in the newspaper most directly relevant to the daily lives of their readers. They were authored by fellow townsfolk, neighbors, even friends, rather than by journalists or correspondents in remote London. In addition to alerting readers to the availability of goods before the corporatist efficiency of retail had taken hold and made everything available all of the time, it offered a dash of local color and gossip. When people read that Samuel Larkin was selling off his entire stock at a discount, they learned, or at least could infer, more than purely commercial information.[27]

Advertisements and price listings also made up the bulk of exchange between newspapers within New Hampshire. While foreign and national news flowed in from the metropolitan centers, notices of prices, harvests, and real estate passed through the network of villages, taverns, and settlements that spanned from the prosperous coastal inlets to the rustic backwoods. Citizens of the town of Hanover, home of Dartmouth College, but for most of the 1790s not home to an active newspaper, took out twenty-one advertisements in the Portsmouth papers, more than a hundred miles away.[28] That they did so suggests that not only did they want people in Portsmouth to see their notice, but they knew that people back in Hanover read the Portsmouth papers, too. The necessity of ordering goods remotely was, for many rural inhabitants of New Hampshire, opened up exclusively through the newspaper. If advertisements made newspapers a fiscal possibility, they also provided the social impetus that made their existence necessary to people throughout the state. Not only were the people of Hanover reading the Portsmouth paper; they were also participating in its creation.

The advent of the Post Office Department also had a noticeable effect on the sources of advertisements. While colonial Americans had access to postal services, such provisions were quickly dwarfed in the early national period. Just prior to the revolution, there were approximately four and a half post offices per one hundred thousand inhabitants. A half century later, there were seventy-two per one hundred thousand. Not only did this expand the potential network of communication, but it also subsidized it. "The rates established in 1792 called for a charge of 1 cent for newspapers sent up to 100 miles and 1.5 cents if sent further, which represented substantial savings to a publisher who had been paying private carriers," according to Paul Starr. In the years that preceded the postal service's establishment, most of the ads came from either the state capital, Concord, or Portsmouth. This reflected the greater reach and influence of these political and mercantile centers, as well as their position at the heart of the nascent state infrastructure. The postal system blew apart this dominance in short order. In the years from 1790 to 1794, the representation of Concord in statewide advertisements fell from 55 to 32 percent, as people from across the state gained the ability to easily access the editors of the papers they read. "The extraordinary significance of the post in American public life," writes David Henkin, "from the 1790s at least until the 1830s lay precisely in this special relationship to the periodical press, whose rhythms it mirrored and reinforced."[29] Even people from outside of New Hampshire began buying up commercial space in the papers; in the two years after the creation of the postal service, out-of-state ads shot up by 70 percent. As the significance of the localized weekly press became more apparent, businessmen and merchants in major American cities even began promoting themselves in papers they likely hadn't even heard of just a few years before. By 1795, 16 percent of the commercial content of New Hampshire papers was taken up, and paid for, by entrepreneurs in New York, Boston, and Philadelphia. The blossoming of the market benefited businesses in both the city and the countryside.

As this frenzy of commercial activity created the circulatory system necessary for the transfer and dissemination of information, the ads themselves also became an integral part of American printed, and popular, culture. Early American advertisements reveal as much about contemporary understandings of mass communication as they do about the advent of mass consumerism; they also hint at the first forays into the quintessential modern art form: marketing. Promotions for what might be called luxury goods were often exhibited, by the standards of the day, in the most ostentatious content in the entire newspaper. In an age in which graphic content was, if present at all, usually confined to a corner of the front page, a small number of purveyors of "fancy goods" inserted symbols and engraved logos into some of their entries, clearly intending for these symbols to guide consumers to their shop by a hanging street sign. The sort of luxuries sold in such establishments was aimed at the upper classes and, rather more so than other commercial blandishments, at women; they thus tended to rely on vivid description to stoke the imagination. "A beautiful assortment of LADIES' fancy Hats and Bonnets, with straw trimmings, bands and tassels . . . ," one such gushing notice read. "Elegant assortment of book and Jaconet Muslins, sprig'd muslins of all kinds, strip'd and sprig'd do; Book muslin Handkercheifs of all kinds. A large assortment of sigur'd Muslinets and Dimities; Ladies' and Gentlemens' best Beaver Hats." While the market revolution that would seize America was still in its nascent stages, advertisements such as this were clearly designed to attract the disposable incomes of fashion-conscious and affluent elites. The relatively standardized and recognizable spelling and syntax of the news and legislative columns are elusive in many advertisements; they were usually reprinted, without editing, correction, or comment, by the more consistently literate newspapermen who published, and relied on, them. Exoticism was also appealed to when it came to the selling of luxuries, and seldom did advertisers miss an opportunity to trumpet the origins of their wares. Justin and Elias Lyman, of Hartford, Vermont, took the opportunity to notify the public that they had "on hand a quantity of the best of ROCK SALT, which they wish to exchange by the cask, one bushel for one and half bushels of the like Wheat." Often, apparently incongruous goods were lumped in together. The same commercial for rock salt also listed a "large supply of English, East and West India Goods," including "Crockery and Glass Ware, Nails and Nail Rods, Crown Glass, Russia Iron, blister'd and English Steel . . . English Beaver HATS."[30] Hartford, Vermont, while only five miles away from Hanover (where this ad was taken out), lay across the Connecticut River, with an eight-hour round-trip over a winding, boggy path, hardly a journey one would wish to make while carrying a load of rock salt and steel. If one could not ford, or find a ferry over the river, then the journey to Bellows Falls (north of Walpole) to take the toll bridge turned the journey on foot into a matter of days rather than hours. When businesses such as these took the time and expense to advertise in out-of-town papers, they could not have done so expecting to attract passing customers. A degree of logistical investment, be it a wagon or a riverboat, would have been necessary to make these sorts of intercommunity transactions a realistic possibility. This is precisely what happened. The net freight earnings of the U.S. carrying trade rose from $5.9 million in 1790 to $26.2 million in 1800.[31] As trade increased, so did the circulation of information around it. Allan Pred explained the phenomenon in systematic terms when he wrote, "Pretelegraphic long-distance trade was almost always the outcome of information acquisition (through the press, mails, or business travels). . . . In particular, when trade was undertaken at the initiative of a purchasing importer, retailer, wholesaler, or industrial unit, the actual commodity of the shipment had to be preceded by some knowledge of an information exchange with the supply source." Pred argued, correctly, that the interaction between the movements of money and knowledge wasn't one way. "Economic historians usually are justified in describing American regional or urban growth between 1790 and 1840 primarily in terms of trade. Yet such trade was as much the outcome of information flows as it was the generator of them."[32] The multiplier effect of information on commerce was mirrored by the way in which the flow of commerce carried information. While the information revolution was not the sole cause of nineteenth-century American capitalism, it was a necessary precondition of it.

Not all items on the New Hampshire newspaper subscriber's shopping list demanded such grandiloquence as the "fancy goods." While the availability of stylish goods obviously preoccupied the larger ads, newspapers were also a part of an agrarian economy that had little need for glamour or persuasion. The following is typical of thousands of examples:

GRAIN.

WHEAT, RYE & CORN,

FOR SALE AT THE STORE OF

ALLEN & BOND.

- Subscribers for Washington's Political Legacies, are requested to call at the above place, and receive their books
- A few copies on hand for sale[33]

This advertisement leaves rather more questions than it answers. It offers no clue with regard to the street, town, or even state in which the business is located. The *Sentinel*, published in Keene, was widely circulated throughout southwestern New Hampshire and had its readers and correspondents in Brattleboro, Vermont, and Springfield, Massachusetts. The reader is also left guessing as to the price of the goods offered (pricing was often left to the imagination, and when it was referred to, descriptive terms like *cheap* were preferred) and ignorant of the quantity or quality of the goods available. Advertisements such as these, in contrast to those for luxury goods, were produced with a narrow audience in mind, intended for customers with a preexisting relationship with the business, and perhaps even with the proprietor. Wheat, rye, and corn are not impulse purchases and are normally procured in volume, on a regular basis. Advertisements such as these, therefore, had no need to fire the imagination with seductive adjectives or exotic pedigree. They existed to inform a receptive commercial constituency, and the very opacity of its terse language and composition to outsiders underlines for us the tight-knit, personal nature of much of early American economic life.

Advertising for such staples was sometimes taken out by buyers rather than the sellers. Ebenezer Duston put out a request "for the use of the Workmen on Concord Bridge" for "Pork, salt or Wheat, Veal, Indian corn, Lamb, and Mutton, Butter, for which the Cash, and a generous price, will be given."[34] Such advertisements were surprisingly commonplace; in an age of ubiquitous and relentless marketing, it is hard to imagine a time in which consumers had a need to seek out retailers or wholesalers for specific goods. If such goods were not being offered in the newspaper, then an individual had to take it upon themselves (at personal expense) to request them. This demonstrates the central importance of the paper in rural economic life, as the primary point of entry for members of the public into the larger world of goods and trade. Newspaper editors themselves did not hesitate to use their own pages to procure needed sundries, as when George Hough, editor of the *Courier of New Hampshire*, notified that he wanted "Wheat, Rye, Corn and Oats—Also, cash," from his customers. That he added cash to his list of requests, seemingly as an afterthought, is suggestive of both the dearth of specie in the local economy and his pressing need for food; it is therefore not surprising that he published this request in late December. At least in this case, the reader had some notion of from whom the request came. Other such request ads offered no clear indication as to whom the advertiser might be, beyond a name (often abbreviated):

SHEEP SKINS.
Wanted immediately, a quantity of GOOD

TANNED SHEEP SKINS,
The grain of which must be whole and the
Skins tolerably free from holes.

NATH. LADD
N.B. Oak-tanned Skins will be much preferred[35]

Who was Nathaniel Ladd? Where did he live? How might someone with sheep skins, tanned or otherwise, reach him? What was he willing to offer in exchange? Notices such as these either assumed a huge amount of local knowledge or required the printer to act as an unofficial intermediary. As the one person in a community with access to such knowledge, printers frequently had to act as go-betweens, making new connections between subscribers possible, facilitating trade, and fostering new business relationships. While they would not be directly remunerated for fulfilling this role, it helped in driving both subscriptions and advertising revenue.

Government policy, at both the state and the federal levels, changed the way people did business. In the years following the establishment of the federal postal system, both government controlled and privately operated postal infrastructure proliferated. From 1790 to 1800, the number of post offices in the United States grew from 75 to 903. Over the same time period, 1,875 miles of post routes grew to 20,817, and total postal revenues shot from $37,900 to $280,800 per annum.[36] Most of these services were conducted on a contractual basis by individuals, and rather than creating a whole new class of information couriers, the main effect of the law was to regulate and standardize many of the existing ad hoc provisions already in place. "The kinship of the post office and the press," Kielbowicz had written, "dates from the very beginnings of American journalism when postmasters founded most of the early newspapers. In fact the postal law enacted in the 1790s simply codified custom that had evolved during the colonial period." As such, postal agents still relied on the newspapers to promote their services and to communicate with their customers both actual and potential. "THE Proprietors of the MAIL STAGES from Springfield to Hanover take this method to inform the Public that they propose running their STAGES twice a week, under the following regulations viz. Beginning on the twelfth of August." Announcements like these reflected the gray area between government service and commercial enterprise that most of these ventures occupied. "The STAGE will leave Springfield on Tuesdays, and Fridays, at eleven o'clock A.M. Dine at Northampton, Lodge at Greenfield, proceed on to Brattleborough on Wednesdays and Saturdays, where they meet the Hanover STAGE, and exchange passengers and return to Greenfield on Wednesday and Saturday nights & proceed to Springfield on Mondays and Thursdays." These notices hinted at a network of onward services and sometimes provided the itineraries of other routes. "Hanover STAGE Leaves that place on Tuesdays and Fridays, in the morning, Dine at Charleston, Lodge at Westminster proceed to Brattleborough where they meet Springfield STAGE and exchange passengers; the Hanover STAGE will return to Westminster on Wednesday and Saturday nights—on Monday, and Thursdays proceed to Hanover Fare, for passengers, 3d per mile, with 14lb, gratis; one hundred and fifty weight the same as a passenger; genteel Carriages and careful Drivers will be provided."[37] The emergence and subsequent boom of these services in the middle part of the 1790s revolutionized the ways in which the public in general, but printers and editors specifically, could access and transmit information.[38] The owners of such carriages had already, for a fee, agreed to carry printed materials, but these arrangements became gradually more formalized.

The fine details of routes and offices were normally handled at a state or even local level. In 1791 the New Hampshire Legislature had, prior the creation of the federal postal agency, passed a statute creating "four routes of post, to be thereafter appointed to ride in and through the interior of the state."[39] The riders were commissioned to operate the routes on a fortnightly basis, traveling alternately clockwise and counterclockwise through the countryside. The men operating these routes were paid a subsidy of between nine and twelve pounds,[40] and the law also fixed postal rates for both letters and newspapers. Post offices were created at nine different locations scattered across the state.[41] In keeping with the quasi-governmental nature of the work, the appointed postmasters who ran these offices (most of them printers) were not paid from the public purse but rather granted a surcharge of two pence on any posted materials they handled. Most of these services were, as before, already being conducted on a private basis, and many of them were now simply undertaken under contract from the state or federal authorities. Nor did they replace the privately contracted post riders in the employee of printers; the two systems coexisted, side by side, overlapping in some areas and diverging in others. The early American postal system could be shambolic, but the huge increase in the use of its services suggests it was preferable to having no system at all.

These developments in both public and private infrastructure had various implications. The explosion of the stagecoach industry spawned a number of subsidiaries, some of which are visible in the advertisements of the time. The demand for sturdy long-distance horses, capable of traversing semiwilderness tracks and trails, increased rapidly. From 1793 onward, the steady increase in advertisements like that for "Three good Horses, from 5 to 9 years old, suitable for a Stage" is indicative of the demand.[42] Services also began using newspapers to appeal to newly mobile travelers. Mail roads and coach routes also entered into the other aspects of commercial life, as proximity to a well-used route could be used by advertisers of real estate as an attractive feature. "A Bargain—TO BE SOLD," one such advertisement read, "If applied for in one Month, The Mansion House of the Subscriber, which is situated on as pleasant a spot of Land as any in the town, and is excellently calculated for a public Stage House, for the entertainment of travellers from the country or elsewhere." The trickle-down effect of this small revolution in transportation and communication touched many and even provided new opportunities for those engaged in less salubrious livelihoods. An article titled "10 Dollars Reward" reported the theft of "a black superfine Broad Cloth Coat and pocket-book, of red morocco leather; Containing valuable papers of no service to any person, but the subscriber—viz. R. Yeaton, junr. Note of hand for 1700 Dollars, and mortgage on a Bake-house and land situate in Buck-street, Portsmouth, in favor of the subscriber." The newspaper provided a forum for the injured party to recover their property or, at the very least, air their grievance. "The person who took the Coat out of the basket will please to consider, altho' the crime of Robbery has been already committed by him or them, they may have nevertheless shown generosity by not destroying the papers in the pocket-book, but he or they may leave them in some public house or road where they may be picked up and returned—All Tavern keepers in the road between Salem and Portsmouth will oblige the subscriber to enquire about it, and their trouble will be generously paid by N. ROUSSELET."[43] Not only does such a notice reflect the way many would turn to the newspaper as a means of resolving such crises, but there is also a sense of the manifold uses the new communication structure was being put to and the perhaps ill-founded trust placed in it. Sometimes the stage drivers themselves, perhaps unsurprisingly given their precarious employment, were uncovered as the culprits in such cases. A small local scandal of 1794 found a few unscrupulous carriers were found to be pocketing their fees before depositing their burdens in the nearest stream or ditch. One such felon was discovered to have helped himself to at least $2,100 of his patrons' cash and goods.[44]

These stagecoach services blossomed in the second half of the 1790s, and their routes and schedules were published in the very newspapers they carried. In 1792 only two services existed, running twice weekly from Portsmouth to Portland and Boston. The Portland service departed at 6:00 a.m. on a Monday morning and was *scheduled* to arrive in Portsmouth at 10:00 the following evening, a two-day trip for a journey of 50 miles, if conditions were favorable. Boston, by comparison, took twenty-eight hours for a journey of 60 miles, demonstrating that it wasn't only distance but also roads and landscape that would determine journey times. By the end of the decade, however, New Hampshire residents had a wide array of coach services on which to ride or send their mail. The Boston and Portsmouth services had both been cut to a single day and ran every day, barring Sunday. By 1800 practically any town of note in New Hampshire had at least a weekly coach running to Boston, as well as many other out-of-state locations: Kennebunkport, Maine; Newburyport, Massachusetts; and Brattleboro, Vermont, were all available locations to travelers every other day (with the return journeys being made on the alternating days). A weekly route was even created connecting Hanover to Hartford, Connecticut, a three-day excursion that covered 150 miles, following the general course of the Connecticut River. And of course, from these destinations, both travelers and newspapers were able to make onward trips to practically anywhere in the nation. The upshot of these developments for printers and editors was that, in practical terms, using the mail stage in 1792, a letter written in Portsmouth could be expected to take an average of ninety-seven hours to arrive at the Boston post office. By 1800 that average had fallen to thirty-five hours. This effect is even more profound when we consider that this both got news to the printer more quickly as well as expedited the subsequent delivery of the newspaper.

These routes did more than create and expedite connections between newspaper editors and correspondents; they also helped bring the news to towns that had hitherto been cut off from the flow of information. Small New Hampshire towns like Marlborough, a community without a newspaper or post office, suddenly found itself as a stopping point on various stage routes. The infusion of commerce and news that these carriages brought not only could have a transformative effect on the residents' knowledge of the wider world, but also encouraged them to contribute to and advertise in newspapers themselves. To take Marlborough as an example, only one piece of correspondence from the town appears in the papers prior to 1794, the year in which coach services began stopping there. From that point, letters and advertisements from Marlborough began appearing in nearby newspapers on a roughly bimonthly basis. This same trend was in evidence at wagon-station towns across the state, including Charlestown, Hampton Falls, and Dunstable.

As people who had been previously removed from the possibilities of mass communication were hooked into the network, their first use of the medium was as a means of doing business. Most of the advertisements that began to appear from the newly connected towns were related to the buying and selling of real estate. One such, for a farm, described a plot "lying in Marlborough, containing four hundred acres, or thereabouts, well calculated to make 3 good Farms. There are two good houses, &c. on said Farm, viz. One 2 story House, 30 feet square; a BARN, 51 by 30 feet; with Sheds, Out houses, &c. The other, House, is 34 by 29 feet, finished in the best manner; a Barn, 40 by 28 feet." Such descriptions went into an exacting degree of detail, which seems somewhat excessive until we consider the challenges of marketing real estate without the benefit of photography or illustration. "There are two good Wells near the beforementioned houses," the farm advertisement continued, "which never have been dry. Also, three good orchards, well situated 3 Farms, containing about 100 trees each, mostly grafts of excellent fruit, Pears, Plumbs, Peaches, Quinces, &c. Also, two Pews in Marlborough Meeting House, which would be sold with or without said Farms." Other notices dealt with the prosaic events of rural existence. "Taken up by the Subscriber, on or about the 15th, A dark, brown COW," one such missive read, "with a lined back, supposed to be about 7 or 8 years old.— Any person proving property, and paying charges, may have her again." For editors with column inches to fill, however, the drama of village life also proved a rich vein of human interest news. "On Saturday last," ran a short piece in the *Journal*, "a Barn belonging to Major Richard Roberts, of Marlborough, was consumed by fire, together with about twenty tons of hay therein—it is said to have been set on fire by Mrs. Roberts, who for some time past has been much deranged in her mind."[45] Stories like this, which were reprinted in multiple newspapers, became a part of the cultural fabric. Just as Marlborough was learning about Boston, Boston was learning about Marlborough. America, slowly, was getting smaller.

These expanding networks permitted other types of social engagement. Wedding and mortuary notices began to be taken out by readers farther afield, giving such life events a platform that had previously been unavailable. While such pieces were often celebratory or mournful (as appropriate), many got right down to business, as with this typical notice from the *Gazette*: "ALL persons indebted to, or that have any demands against the estate of Ensign Jeremiah Blake, late of Hampton-Falls, yeoman, deceased, are requested to exhibit the same for settlement to Jeremiah Blake, executor of the last will and testament of the deceased." The proliferation and spread of communication had implications for familial as well as commercial relationships. New opportunities for civic organization and improvement in small towns were opened up, too. Projects that would once have required an in-person meeting, whether in the town square, tavern, or church, could now be orchestrated remotely. "The Court House in Charlestown has long been a subject of complaint, but like other things which concern everybody, receives no attention," one letter to the *Museum* bemoaned, and asked why "a building scarce large enough for a jail should so long answer the purposes of a prison, and a place to administer justice, excites the wonder of strangers and of most of the inhabitants of this county; few individuals would suffer the inconveniences which the public endure in that little dirty room—The surrounding filth, and the crowd which are obliged to attend court, render the place disgusting and very unhealthy." The correspondents were not ambiguous about their motivations for writing when they concluded, "It is hoped that our representatives at the next session of the General Court, will raise money to build a new Court house; the sum which individuals will pay will be too trifling to be compared with the present inconvenience."[46] That the people of Charlestown would post such a request in a Walpole newspaper, some eleven miles away, strongly indicates a collective understanding that their fellow townsfolk had access to the *Farmer's Weekly Museum*, or at least spoke to people who did.

These concurrent developments in travel, communication, and commercial life, shaped by environmental forces and human expediency, touched almost every aspect of life in the American hinterlands. In the newly minted United States, with revolution and turmoil still fresh in the memory, the circulation of political and ideological currents to those on the periphery was an essential catalyst in the still nascent formation of a national identity. The arrival of weekly reports of goings-on in Congress in places like Hampton Falls and Dunstable made engagement in the emerging political culture possible in ways that could never have emerged otherwise. Equally crucially, those very same rural Americans, by contributing to the paper in the nearest town, were adding their own voices to the American conversation. "The public sphere was no longer patrimonial in the sense of being more or less congruent with the relatively small numbers of people who lived in close physical proximity to the seats of power," Richard John has written. "Instead, it now became disembodied, stretching far beyond specific localities to enlist the minds and hearts of millions of people." This accords with Jurgen Habermas's own placement of this phenomenon. "It is no coincidence that these concepts of the public sphere and public opinion," he wrote, "arose for the first time only in the eighteenth century. It was at that time that the distinction of 'opinion' from 'opinion publique' and 'public opinion' came about." The party politics of the Federalist and Jeffersonian eras were forged in the heat of this transformation. When Simon Newman wrote that "a well-to-do merchant's wife in Delaware could have read of a Federalist celebration in Albany," or that "on the Kentucky frontier a settler could read about the popular protests against the Jay Treaty in Charleston," these small but numerous events of connection had telling and important effects on Americans.[47] They simply would not have been possible without the web of mail riders, stagecoaches, and newspapers that increasingly came to crisscross not only New Hampshire but the entire United States in the 1790s.

Just as important, if not quite so immediately visible, were the social consequences of this newly accessible communication. The ability to read and post notifications of important life events, to advertise goods and services, and to engage more fully in the spheres of religious, civil, and cultural life helped to close the spaces between people scattered sparsely across a landscape of farms, woods, and mountains. Perhaps most significant of all, information, ideas, culture, and identity were not being broadcast from the top down but exchanged. The media that served these audiences was created for, and to a certain extent by, them. "The advantages of a country paper were conceived to be of too much importance not to merit attention," the editor of the *Amherst Village Messenger* told his readers, explaining that "by reason of its comparative cheapness at the press, and its smaller expense of carriage, news politics, and the world, are made more accessible to the people at large." If the editor had any doubts as to the value of his work, he does not betray it in this piece. "Patriotism, therefore, will cheerfully enlist itself, as a promoter of this means of information. Owing to the unfrequency of advertisements, it contains a greater proportion of news and entertainment; and better consolidated." And, as is so often the case, the author eventually turns to a gentle prodding of his subscribers. "The country-man will, at the end of the year, more willingly pay the price for a paper, nearly the whole of which will be in some degree useful to him, than to pay double the money for a paper issuing from the Metropolis, two thirds of which can be of no possible service to him, and was not originally designed for his use. . . . [A] country paper, for the use of the Yeomanry, is capable of being made superior to a paper calculated for the city."[48] While William Bigelow, editor of the *Messenger*, was surely engaged in a good deal of self-congratulation, he hit on an important truth. While the initial impact of the profusion of communication and publishing networks would have the immediate impact of putting foreign and metropolitan material in the hands of country readers, the longer-term consequence would have to be that the newspapers themselves, even what constituted the news, would have to change. A year before Bigelow wrote his editorial, the *Messenger* received a letter from a correspondent who styled himself "A Farmer," from which he seems to have drawn substantial inspiration:

> One of your subscribers is pleased with the idea of having a Country Paper. He hopes that it will not be called a country paper merely from the circumstance of its not being edited in a seaport, but from its being

calculated for the genius of the country in opposition to that of the metropolis. I have for some time past been a subscriber for the *Centinel*, and it provokes me to the quick, to think how much money I have expended for a paper, so large a part of which has been entirely useless to me ... than if it had been as much *blank paper*. The entries at the custom house and the management of the theatre are wholly foreign to my business. Of what importance to me that the *Rival Queens* is to be acted this evening, and that Mr Hodgkinson will appear in the character of Alexander; or that Mr Duport teaches dancing in its highest refinement? The greater part of the paper ceases to be useful immediately upon its leaving the precincts of Boston.... For the employments of the village are different from those of the town, and the views of the husbandman from those of the merchant.... It is impossible that a paper appropriated to one, should be adapted to the wants of the other.[49]

This was the ultimate significance of the arrival of the news in hamlets and backwoods. Week-old copies of the *Columbian Centinel* would not long suffice for men like the nameless farmer, and in demanding publications that filled their needs, they helped to create a culture around themselves. What that culture was, and what the implications were to be for the future of American politics, is the subject of what follows.

CHAPTER SIX

"THE LAY PREACHER"

Making the News

Nothing need be said on the part of the Editor to prove the utility of periodical publications; their usefulness is acknowledged by every civilised nation—Monthly publications are established in most of the U. States; even the State of New Hampshire supports a publication of this kind.

—*Independent Gazetteer*, September 14, 1793

The printers and editors of New Hampshire relied, as many of their fellows did around the country, on reprinting news from other sources. This was not, however, all that they did. While the majority of newspaper content, taking in advertisements, poems, foreign articles, and assorted miscellany, consisted of copies, the men who produced small-town weekly newspapers did write. Sometimes they did so of necessity; there were column inches to be filled. They did, however, sometimes profess a higher sense of mission. "Every man who feels interested in his own fate . . . should apply to the NEWSPAPER, the faithful re-gifter of the transaction of the day," an editorial in the *New Hampshire Gazetteer* explained. "Its pages testify concerning public men and public measures." Their roles included, the editor explained, holding the powerful to account and recording events for posterity and to "sound the alarm" when liberty was endangered. "Impartial every Editor ought to be," the editorial continued, "for, if patronized by the people much is entrusted to him; self interest, if no other motive, stimulates, and must induce the Editor," as the "destruction of the free press" would spell the end of his profession. Whether motivated by republican virtue or enlightened selfishness, printers and editors turned their pens to one cause or another on a regular basis. When they did so, they were primarily addressing their own readers. In his New Year's message to his readers, *Oracle of the Day* printer Charles Pierce felt "every possible impression of gratitude" to his "patrons and supporters," only somewhat undermined by his subsequent harangue about late subscription dues.[1] The first loyalty of the printer had to be to the subscribers and advertisers who paid their bills. However, just as they harvested the newspapers of editors both within and without New Hampshire, they too found larger audiences throughout the broader sphere of American print. Just as an article from a paper in Georgia might occasionally appear in the New Hampshire papers, the work of New Hampshire editors traveled in the contrary direction.

The extent to which New Hampshire newspapers were read by people outside of the state is difficult to exactly ascertain. Clues to the extent to which their work was circulated, passed on, and reprinted, however, can be found in looking at the places and amounts in which their work was being reprinted. In 1790, 29 percent of news published inside of New Hampshire was reprinted outside of the state; by 1800, this had risen to 44 percent.[2] The reprints, as might be expected, were most tightly concentrated in the North. Twenty-eight percent of the reprinted articles appeared in Massachusetts, 11 percent in Connecticut, and 6 percent in Vermont; altogether New England made up 47 percent of all the reprints. However, articles found their way all over the country. Newspapers in every state, including the new additions of Kentucky and Tennessee, as well as the District of Columbia, included articles first published in New Hampshire. Six percent of the reprints occurred in South Carolina, with the states south of the Mason-Dixon line making up 10 percent of the total. Just as the volume of reprints increased over time, so too did their reach. The number of southern towns that published New Hampshire news quadrupled from 1790 to 1800.

As this was taking place, the channels along which this news was traveling continued to take shape. Just as news traveling into New Hampshire was moving faster and faster, so too did news emanating from the state. In 1790 stories appearing in Portsmouth newspapers took an average of ten days to appear in Boston and eighteen days to appear in Philadelphia. By 1800 this time lag had fallen to just four days for both cities. Towns along the coast continued to receive the news much more quickly than their inland counterparts. In 1800 news from Portsmouth took a week to reach Greenfield, a town in western Massachusetts one hundred overland miles away; it also took a week for news to get to the port of Georgetown, South Carolina, a town more than eight hundred miles away. The relative speed of communication along the seaboard created what was in effect an interlinked set of subnetworks in the early United States.

Eighteenth-century America was a maritime society, in which the important cities were ports and day-to-day lives were influenced by happenings on the streets of London and Paris.[3] In terms of information time, Portsmouth, New Hampshire, was not much farther removed from London than it was from Kentucky, particularly in the very first years of the republic. Coastal trade routes were among the most important commercial enterprises in the young nation, and they were expanding rapidly throughout the Federalist era. The quantity of tonnage freighted in coastwise and internal trade rose from 103,775 tonnes in 1790 to 272,592 tonnes in 1800. This activity strengthened and expanded American transportation infrastructure, as coastal shipping services and overland routes developed to meet the demand.[4] News might leave Portsmouth by sail and arrive at Providence, then Baltimore, then Charleston, where the news would be taken up by editors in those towns. Once those newspapers were printed, they would find their way through their respective region. The editor of the *Augusta Chronicle* in Georgia, or the Tennessee

Gazette in Nashville, was highly unlikely to see the original copy of the *New Hampshire Spy* that had been put on the schooner at Portsmouth, but they might get a copy of the *Charleston Daily Advertiser* that carried the story. Due to this, as well as the long-distance overland travel and the challenging Appalachian terrain, stories were taking three to four weeks to reach Kentucky and Tennessee even in 1800, at a time when the entire Eastern Seaboard was getting the news in less than a week. As the geographical dimensions of the American frontier were being rolled back, the flow of information slowly began to follow behind.

These regional pockets of information dissemination, with news radiating out from port towns to the hinterland, could be found up and down the Atlantic Coast; indeed, Portsmouth served such a purpose for the rest of New Hampshire. What this meant for the readers of American newspapers was that content was being shared by more and more printers and that a convergence was taking place in what was appearing from one paper to the next. To take New Hampshire as an example, in 1790, 32 percent of the news published in the state with a London dateline had not been published elsewhere in the United States before; by 1800, this had fallen to 17 percent. This phenomenon, which was taking place all over the country, meant that while Americans were seeing more and more of the same news as one another, they were also learning more about one another, too. It wasn't just that people in Georgia were being exposed to events in New Hampshire; they were getting to know the opinions and ideas of New Hampshire writers, too. This was not a process that necessarily led to a blossoming of empathy and fellow feeling, as readers often did not care for what their fellow Americans were thinking and writing. However, it did have the important effect of giving writers, even in relatively obscure places like New Hampshire, a hitherto unimaginable audience.

These early national journalists of the 1790s shared some common ground with the pamphleteers of earlier generations. They were often political, if not extremely partisan, and explicitly wrote in support of an agenda. On the other hand, they wrote to a regular schedule, which often meant that they dealt with a much broader range of issues than their predecessors or were forced to address the same issues in increasingly ingenious ways. They also identified themselves in a variety of ways. While some used their names or initials, most preferred pseudonymity. This took many forms. Many authors preferred a classical name with either mythological or republican connotations—Apollo or Cicero, for example. This trend had started in the years preceding the American Revolution, and during the war many opted for the names of those Roman heroes who, once martial glory had been achieved, returned to their simple lives as farmers and citizens.[5] Some Americans thought of the break from Britain not as a break from their common history but as a resumption of the self-government they thought characterized the Athenian democracy or the Roman senate. Using not just the political ideals of these societies but also their nomenclature and architecture, an American aesthetic might emerge that was not merely a poor imitation of the English. Classical names remained popular after the revolution, but their context and implied meaning changed. The influential *Federalist Papers* were written under the pseudonym Publius, although this name was only one of a series that Alexander Hamilton adopted and discarded throughout his career as an essayist, and the various names adopted, "Metellus," "Catullus," "Tully," "Horatius," "Camillus," "Titus Manlius," were all chosen for specific effect depending on the arguments being made.[6] According to Eran Shalev, by this time they "served less as stylistic gestures, but emerged more as vehicles through which substantive political ideas could be expressed." This change represented the need for journalists of differing political persuasions to distinguish themselves from one another. Federalists, proponents of a strong and dynamic government, might adopt the names of Roman heroes like Marc Anthony and August Caesar, who had championed the power of the state. Republicans, conversely, preferred republican martyrs like Cato and Brutus, who had died, in one way or another, in the defense of constitutional government. However, as Shalev has pointed out, "Federalists also used names such as Publius and Fabius, two eminent Romans who easily could have embodied anti-imperial notions, while Republicans summoned ancients such as Agrippa, the powerful deputy of Augustus, the first of the Roman emperors." Some names, such as the rebel-slave Spartacus, were rejected by both sides.[7]

Others, perhaps wishing to distinguish themselves from such high-falutin pretension, preferred a caricatured "down-home" rustic name. Some alternated, as when John Adams wrote under the sonorous Novanglus on some occasions, and at others preferred to go by Humphrey Ploughjogger, when he affected the style of an honest, if grammatically maladroit, farmer. Another route was to take a comic name that made some allusion to one's character or politics. The polemicist William Cobbett wrote under the name Peter Porcupine while in the United States, and he was just as prickly as his alias. Different causes account for the popularity of pseudonymity in this period. Names themselves could be used to create an almost subliminal context for audiences. In an age before illustrative materials were present in newspapers (cartoons were absent from all but a handful of 1790s papers), journalists needed to use all the resources at their disposal to portray an authorial image, and a well-chosen pseudonym could be helpfully evocative. Some sociological interpretations of the role of the journalist place less emphasis on "authorship," which is to say the production of "text," and more on the concept of "performance."[8] The curated public persona of the journalist was an essential part of the reader's experience. More practically, it was an age of imperfect freedoms for editors on both sides of the Atlantic. The advent of the Alien and Sedition Acts of 1798 highlighted how vulnerable many journalists remained, although it must be noted that normally assumed names did little to protect editors from the grasping arm of the law.

While these were common practices among the contributors to newspapers, editors themselves often felt no need to provide an identification at all when writing. James Thomson Callender, the highly influential Philadelphia editor and journalist, would become infamous as the man who sought to expose Jefferson's relationship with Sally Hemmings, but he had in fact been writing prolifically, albeit anonymously, for a decade. While he might have done so in the knowledge that most of his immediate subscribers would know him by name, newspapers traveled much farther than their initial audience of the local library and tavern. Therefore, the work of these editors became synonymous not with themselves or some nom de plume but rather with the title of their publication.

Readers across America came to associate certain writing styles or political positions with certain newspapers, while often having very little idea as to who was responsible for the text. When other newspapers appropriated editorials, they could do either of two things. They could run the piece completely uncredited, a practice that was far more common in the early days. Alternatively, they could head such an article as being "from" such and such a paper. In the early years of the 1790s, this was most commonly done to herald a piece from a foreign newspaper, most commonly the *London Gazette*. As time passed, it became an ever more common practice for editors to credit the work of their American colleagues in their own pages. In some cases, the minimal approach would be to simply include the city of publication in the dateline.[9] Articles credited from papers with an avowed link to a particular party or faction, like the *Gazette of the United States* or the *National Gazette*, carried with them a packet of implicit meanings to the politically aware reader.

New Hampshire, despite being both geographically and culturally peripheral, produced a number of editors and correspondents who were reprinted and read fairly widely in the United States. However, in the early national period, nobody in the state came close to matching Joseph Dennie in terms of national influence, readership, and notoriety. Dennie, whose background is sketched in chapter 2, was the editor of the *Farmer's Weekly Museum*, based in Walpole, for the second half of the 1790s. Unlike most editors, he was not responsible for the printing of the paper, a task that fell to the long-suffering David Carlisle. Without the pressures of business or manufacturing to occupy his time, Dennie was able to turn his energies (such as they were) to not only editing the paper but, more important, penning editorials and treaties, many under the pseudonym of the Lay Preacher.

Dennie produced articles on a variety of subjects, some of which could be described broadly as human interest, but often took the form of allegory or treatise. There were epistles on the virtues, drawbacks, and etiquette of smoking;[10] an ongoing war on April Fool's Day;[11] and an advice column on the removal of all curtains to increase exposure to healthful sunlight.[12] One article, headlined "TO THE LOVERS OF CIDER," was typical of this portion of his work. "What would you give to destroy the whole race of Caterpillars?—Give?—I would give more than I'll say—but it is impossible. I have tried experiments, until I am tired," Dennie wrote, implying his familiarity with the craft of cider making when there is little reason to suppose that he had ever done so much as climb a tree. "Yes, you have tried flaming tow and lamp oil; you have shot their nests to pieces, with your musket, and pulled them down with your long forked poles; and all this you have done on rainy days, when the caterpillars were mostly within their nests—and you have found, to your mortification that they would often repair their nests the next day, or if you decreased the number for the present season, they were, after all your pains, as numerous as the next."[13] It is hard to imagine being entertained or amused by writing like this (indeed, it is hard to imagine that anyone ever was), but Dennie's light folksy style fitted well into the parish-noticeboard tone of most small weekly newspapers, as did the comic imagery of countryfolk blasting away at apple trees with their muskets. This article alone was reprinted in Philadelphia (twice); Brattleboro, Vermont; Norwich and Windham, Connecticut (twice); Boston and Greenfield, Massachusetts; Keene, New Hampshire; Portland, Maine; and Hudson, New York, which suggests either that he was extremely well liked or that the caterpillar scourge of the late 1790s has been underemphasized in the historical record.

In his famous and widely circulated Lay Preacher series, Dennie often adopted a religious tone quite distinct from his rustic material and the equal of anything in the King James Bible for sonority and solemnity. As with so much journalism of the day, it took for granted in its allusions a deep and intensive familiarity with scripture that can leave the contemporary reader flummoxed. A formula often employed was the relation of an Old Testament story, typically in a style so overwrought as to seem a parody, to make a contemporary point. Taking on Genesis in a Lay Preacher of 1799, he concluded after much ornate verbiage, taking in some rather spurious references to Macbeth and Milton, that "we all know, from the context, how well Jacob behaved under this stinging disappointment. After a concise, but pointed remonstrance to his uncle, he calms the tumult of desire, and for the love of his betrothed, promised Laban to set out, like the shepherd swain of Lycidas, 'tomorrow to fresh field and pastures new.'" It is hard to imagine a more distant piece, in terms of content or style, from "To the Lovers of Cider," yet the two were written almost exactly a year apart from one another. "This is an excellent moral to be drawn from the story," Dennie concluded, "and, if among my readers of any of the more ardent and unsuspicious suffer from a Laban, and love like Jacob, let them copy the resignation of a patient man, and wait seven years longer for gratification, rather than be enraged, or dejected for a month, or even a day."[14] Dennie, despite producing hundreds of these carefully composed and well-supported tracts, demonstrated almost no personal spirituality or faith in his private correspondence. Once again, his earnest religiosity in print was frequently in stark contrast to his languid indifference among his confidants. This is not to say that Dennie was irreligious, or even impious, but his personal papers from this period give little indication of his devotion. Often, the subtext of the religious Lay Preacher pieces was political or else explicitly framed current affairs in religious terms. Good government and Christianity were symbiotic in Dennie's political philosophy, or at least that which he shared with the public. "The infamous philosophy and morals, introduced by the French missionaries of vice and profligacy, excite the abhorrence of some, the derisions of others, and neglect and contempt in all," Dennie exhorted in one column. "We still hold fast that religious liberty, with which the founder of Christianity hath made us free; we still adhere to the 'form of found words,' presented to us in our Bibles and Liturgies. We are not entangled with the yoke of that bondage, which a Helvetius or a Rousseau would impose . . . and under God, we have nothing to fear from Frenchmen without, or traitors within, while Adams promulgates salutary law among a rejoicing people."[15] Dennie was hardly alone in invoking biblical precedent in matters temporal, to claim that "Jefferson is only a cypher on our national page," while invoking the authority of the "supreme magistrate" (an ambiguous phrase that Dennie often toyed with) is to leave no doubt as to the position of Providence in party politics.

When Dennie turned his pen directly to matters of war and state, he retained his idiosyncratic style, but with a good deal more bile than his homilies on early rising or biblical commentaries.[16] "TO men of the complexion of Condorcet and his associates," he elaborately opined, "most of the miseries of France may be ascribed. Full of paradox, recent from wire drawing in the schools, and with mind all begrimmed from the Cyclops' cave of metaphysics, behold a Sieyes in the form of a politician, drafting, *currente colano*, three hundred constitutions in a day, and not one of them fit for the use, but delusive as a mountbanke's bill, and bloody, and the habilments of Banquo." In passages such as these, it is clear that Dennie is unabashedly writing for an extremely narrow audience of college-educated, classically versed gentlemen—individuals, in other words, much like himself. "Of this dangerous, deistical and Utopian school, a great personage from Virginia, is a favored pupil. His Gallic masters stroke his head and pronounce him promising. Those who sit on the same form cheerfully and reverently allow him to be the head of his class." Much of Dennie's writing in this vain doesn't merely require a familiarity with Latin tags, but also demands a working knowledge of the wider American newspaper scene, as when he concludes that "in allusion to the well marshalled words of a great orator, him they worship; him they emulate; his 'Notes' they go over all the time they can spare, from the 'Aurora' of the morning, or Talleyrand's letter at night. The man has talents, but they are of dangerous and delusive kind," a statement with little meaning unless one understood the *Aurora* to be a Democratic-Republican newspaper.[17] Dennie frequently invoked France in general, and the French Revolution in particular, as the source of all that was malignant and unsavory. "I am persuaded thou wilt think with me that all the evils," he confided to his readers, "all the atrocities of the French revolution originated in a false, impious and captious philosophy."[18] Dennie was certainly neither the first nor the last American commentator to find an external phenomenon and attribute to it a plethora of domestic problems, but he was responsible for a disproportionately large proportion of the anti-French propaganda that emerged from New Hampshire in the 1790s.

Dennie also unleashed his acid pen against fellow editors, frequently accusing them of calumny and double-dealing. Casting aspersions as to patriotism and suspected Jacobinism was a common tactic among Federalist newspapermen of the era, but Dennie raised the practice to

an art form. "A small paper," Dennie noted, "called the Bee, of New London, which began tolerably, but has since dwindled to most downright
democracy and French principles, contains a proposal for printing a
literary paper, to be baptised the Honeycomb." Dennie's snobbery here
is given full vent: "Mr C. Holt, printer and democrat, gives us a fine
specimen of the learning of his publican tribe. . . . The illiterate state
of a democrat's brain is well understood. We know that of genius they
never exhibit a spark, but really supposed that they would not stumble
over easy words of three syllables. As we are concerned for these people, we wish to take some little pains in their education, and cheerfully
recommend certain elementary treatises, such as Mrs. Barbauld's Lessons for Children two years of age."[19] While no more venomous than
hundreds of other salvos to be found in American papers of the day,
this piece is noteworthy for a particular breach of etiquette. By specifying Charles Holt, the Connecticut publisher, by name, Dennie was
engaging in a level of ad hominem attack uncommon in an age when
many writers preferred formulations such as "the editor of that organ"
or "the printer." Dennie's name is practically invisible in the papers of the
1790s. His name appears in a list of Harvard graduates that appeared in
a handful of newspapers in 1790. The only time his name achieved any
national notice was in his short-lived bid for the House of Representatives in 1798, in a short article that was published by papers in New
York City, Philadelphia, and Charleston. "Joseph Dennie, Esq. of New-
Hampshire, is in nomination to represent a district of that state in the
next Congress," the article read. "This young gentleman, to a sound and
penetrative discernment in political science, adds a brilliancy of imagination, a facility of expression, and a general knowledge of literature,
which cannot fail to insure him a distinguished station in the national
literature." His literary deftness was, in and of itself, a qualification, as
was his political record at the *Museum*. "Being editor of 'The Farmers'
Weekly Museum,' he has long been in the habit of diffusing political
enigmas, and in vindicating the federal government against the aspersions of internal and external enemies."[20] Dennie also achieved some
national notice for writing a biography of George Washington in 1800,[21]
but by this point he was already on his way out of New Hampshire and

taking up a position as Timothy Pickering's personal secretary.[22] There are no mentions of Dennie whatsoever in American newspapers of the decade that focus on, or are much interested in, his editorship of the *Farmer's Museum*; indeed, the subject is raised only in connection to his political ambitions or appointments. By undertaking personal, named smears on fellow printers and editors, Dennie was at the least pushing the bounds of propriety, if not overstepping them entirely.

If Joseph Dennie had lived in an era of syndication deals and royalties, he might have made a small fortune. Unusually, for a time in which editors delighted in the commercial failure, or even imprisonment, of their fellows, his outpourings were highly regarded. Fellow Federalist editors published articles complementary to Dennie. William Cobbett wrote in his *Porcupine's Gazette* of "the many beautiful passages, which have made their appearance in the FARMER'S WEEKLY MUSEUM.... The writer does infinite honor to his country." If it was not common practice to credit a fellow editor, it was rare indeed to praise them while doing so, as with this introductory comment in the *Salem Gazette*: "in the neat, elegant and classical paper, called *The Farmer's Weekly Museum*." According to the editor of the *Rising Sun*, Dennie could "boast that it is superior to most of the Gazettes of the Union, in matters of taste and criticism." "It is presumed, and we believe from good grounds," the article continued, "that a gentleman, whom genius and acquirements have almost unparalleledly distinguished, is a stated contributor to this reservoir of amusement and instruction ... proof sufficient to the justice of the above tribute and the celebrity of The Lay Preacher." Examples such as these demonstrate the clannishness that many American editors felt. While the warmth with which sympathetic editors wrote of one another pales in comparison to the invective spewed at their perceived enemies, it demonstrated the increasingly comradely feelings among editors of like political stripes. Indeed, historians have also noted the extraordinary reach of Dennie's prose. Andrew Peabody wrote in the late nineteenth century, "The *Museum* obtained a circulation extending from Maine to Georgia, and as far west as Ohio, filling weekly a large extra mail-bag." Clifford Shipton, publisher Isaiah Thomas's biographer, estimated that the *Museum's* circulation was about two thousand.

Newspapers were, at the time, the most common and important means of long-distance information transmission, and so while a circulation like this was impressive from a small-town paper, it was not altogether unheard of; Frank Luther Mott has estimated that about 90 percent of all mail in the early United States was made up of newspapers.[23]

Dennie was a prig, an egotist, and a dissembler and demonstrates the distance that often existed between printed newspaper content and private opinion. The following letter, written to his mother during his editorship of the *Museum*, is typical of his correspondence. Gone is the florid prose of his Lay Preacher columns; his writings to trusted confidants were inflected by a patina of lordly indifference designed to mask a petty fury, which makes his usual compliments to his countrymen seem a trifle insincere. "In my Editorial capacity, I am obliged to the nauseous task of flattering republicans," although there is scant evidence of any such flattery toward republicans in his published works, he continues, "but, at bottom, I am a malcontent, and consider it a serious evil to have been born among the Indians & Yankees of New England." Dennie imagined for himself an alternate life, had the War of Independence gone another way. "Had it been for the *selfish* patriotism of that hoary traitor, [Samuel] Adams," he told his friend, "I might now, perhaps, in a Literary Diplomatic, or lucrative Situation been in the service of my rightful King, and instead of shivering in the bleakness of the United States, felt the genial sunshine of the court."[24] While Dennie would not admit to such Tory predilections in print, his fervent, one might almost say obsequious, Anglophilia was evident in many of his columns. While an abiding affection for Old England can be detected among many Federalist editors, particularly of the Northeast, Dennie's devotion must have been an occasional source of discomfort even to Hamiltonian readers. Take, for example, his hagiographic portrait of the former British chancellor Charles Townshend, in a column of 1799. "He was the delight and ornament of Parliament, and the charm of every private society. To please universally was the object of his life. . . . No man can read this vivid detail of the charms of versatility, without acknowledging its mighty operation in adorning and smoothing life."[25] Considering how widely reviled were the Townshend Acts, and how inextricably in the popular mythos of the young country they were bound up with the War of Independence, Dennie's public admiration of the man seems all the more remarkable.

Dennie, who never in his life met a stranger he could not look down on, had no genuine commitment to egalitarianism or to the republic. While he lacked the fortitude to criticize as august a figure as John Adams in this letter to his friend Jeremiah Mason, his sarcasm was barely concealed, and it is telling from his other letters that he held neither Adams nor Washington in any high regard. "I have arrayed myself in sables and prattled history with Belknap. I have lounged at the sofa of Philencia and have darted Federalism at her French spouse. But, Jere, I find this mode of wearing away life intolerable." Dennie's weariness can, at times, feel affected, as when he writes, "On Sunday morning I almost arranged to ride to Portsmouth in the middle of the week. But among many great little events which agitate this puddle called Boston, the arrival of John Adams is one. People here tell me it is wise to make my rustic bow to the great man, & I must dine with the king to-morow & drink some dozen of such perplexed toasts as the bungling creatures here give."[26]

Dennie neither published nor printed the newspaper that he edited. Editors who were able to get widely reprinted tended to be those who could afford the time to work on their writing uninterrupted. Dennie was the only New Hampshire editor to regularly receive attention outside of the state and was for a period a standby of editors in New England (and some beyond) looking to fill column inches. Dennie could not always be relied on to provide even that. Unusually for a man of his profession, Dennie possessed what we might generously call an artistic temperament. His irritation at being asked to produce weekly commentaries would sometimes spill over into the editorial pages. "We are pledged to furnish Criticism once a fortnight," he groaned, "and it must not be understood that the Lay Preacher, like a regular clergyman, is holden to officiate weekly. His range of topics is not wide, and he reserves to himself the right of judging what his sermons can be composed, with most credit to himself and most benefit to the reader. Under the disadvantages of a solitary situation, a limited subject, a body of no Herculean vigor, and an

invention often checked and always tardy . . . The Lay Preacher has stipulated to officiate occasionally, and next week those who please, may read
another of his productions." Dennie's churlishness can be attributed to a
few different factors, beyond his natural disposition. He did not consider
himself a hack, someone who might be expected to turn out a contrac-
tually designated number of column inches a week. He rather thought
himself an essayist, able to write prodigiously when inspired, but under
no obligation when the muse deserted him. His falling out with Carlisle
after a mere three years only raises the question of how the proprietor
was able to tolerate him that long. Unlike most of his contemporaries
and rivals in the small country papers, he had an eye on posterity. "Should
he impose upon himself the periodical drudgery of literature," Dennie
explained, writing as ever in the third person, "his sermons would resemble the flatness of Daniel Burgress, or the rant of Whitfield, and judges
of composition would suppose him either purblind . . . or dozing like
a stupid secretary."[27] At times, he seemed to be disillusioned with the
very concept of news itself. "In America," he opined, "the impertinent
eagerness for news should be scolded, or laughed in to moderation. The
country gentleman, at peace on his farm, asks for translations from the
Paris Monieur, absurdly anxious for the welfare of Frenchmen, skipping
over the carcass of their king and country." Dennie made it clear, in terms
that would please Thoreau, that current events were of no real concern
to the serious man. "Devote not life to hearing and telling new things," he
continued. "If ye have business, mind it; are you masters of families, stay
at home. . . . Action, not tattle, is the business of life."[28] An odd sentiment
indeed for a newspaperman. Dennie's contempt for jobbing writers can
seem a trifle odd, given the large quantities of frequently turgid prose
he had turned out over the previous few years. By 1799 he seems to have
thought the *Museum* increasingly beneath him, and this feeling is
reflected more and more in his latter-day articles for the paper.

Thanks in large part to its distinctive name, and its reputation, newspapers clearly headed articles taken from the *Farmer's Weekly Museum*,
making its influence easy to trace. Numbers were low in 1794–95 (9 articles reprinted in 1794, 60 in 1795), and in 1793 the paper was too obscure
to achieve much notice, suggesting a rising notoriety over these early

years with Dennie assuming editorial control. Then the paper entered its zenith from 1796 to 1798 (in the peak year, 1797, 507 of the articles were reprinted outside of New Hampshire), before going into decline and eventually out of existence altogether.[29]

In 1800, months after the newspaper had ceased publication, articles from it were still surfacing in the pages of out-of-state newspapers. Dennie's articles were most commonly reprinted, unsurprisingly, in Boston and Philadelphia. Both cities had multiple daily newspapers and were well connected in terms of transportation links and communication times, and both were home to editors naturally well disposed to Dennie, both stylistically and politically. In 1796 editors in Boston and Philadelphia printed 43 and 39 Dennie stories, respectively, about a quarter of the national total. By 1798 these two cities made up less than fifth of all reprints. As with news generally, Dennie's articles were reaching wider and wider audiences spread across an expanding network. Indeed, he seems to have found respective audiences outside of the major cities. In 1796 more of his articles were reprinted in towns like New Bedford and Brookfield, Massachusetts, and Providence, Rhode Island, than in New York City. His work was particularly popular in Connecticut (with Hartford and Windham taking 90 and 52 articles, respectively) and also reached a large southern audience, with editors in Augusta, Georgia, and Charleston, South Carolina, both enthusiastic vectors of his outpourings. In those inchoate times of nascent regional partisanship, an apparently Democratic-Republican or Federalist city or state would still have a receptive audience on the other side of the divide.

The Postal Service Act made provision for newspaper exchanges between editors. Section 21 stipulated "That every printer of newspapers may send one paper to each and every other printer of newspapers within the United States, free of postage, under such regulations, as the Postmaster General shall provide."[30] It must be emphasized that these were decidedly informal relationships.[31] Publishers were not obliged to share their editions with rivals free of charge. This was a particular problem for the press on the geographic fringes. Not only did they find themselves at a great remove spatially, but they often had less to offer the better-connected editors of the big urban dailies. The system, therefore, frequently broke down. Dennie even suspected foul play was at work, as he wrote an article headlined "Something Rotten in the Post Office Establishment" in 1798. "Of the various papers, transmitted by different printers in the United States," Dennie informed his readers, "many of the most valuable never reach us, and we are often at a loss for necessary information, nor from the absence of attention and punctuality in our brother printers, but from the villainy of democratic deputy post masters, or the supine inattention, or wilful connivance, of the principal himself." Dennie believed there was a calculated plot to cut off his supply of papers. "The politics of the Farmer's Museum are well known," he concluded, "and it will soon be made a very serious question, whether our papers are not wilfully withheld, suppressed, or destroyed, by those, who are averse from the dissemination of Federal principles."[32] How much further Dennie took these suspicions is unknown.

Editors frequently had to rely on third- or fourth-hand information from more local publications. Rather, these networks were made up of social and commercial acquaintances, or frequently formed through happenstance. Nonetheless, the daily papers in the big cities seemed to grow in share when content was scarce. When the quantity of *Museum* content dried up, so did the geographic dispersal of locations. By the point of the newspaper's decline in 1799 and 1800, New England communities, places like Warren, Rhode Island, and Leominster, Massachusetts, made up the bulk of the reprint locations. During the highest concentration of this content, the share held by a variety of secondary and tertiary news towns grew, and the picture fragments significantly. It is evident from an editorial published in mid-1797 that the *Museum* had subscribers in all U.S. states but Georgia, Tennessee, and Kentucky.[33] While this reach was quite extensive for a publication like the *Museum*, it was by no means an aberration. Many American editors, some of whom hailed from the geographic periphery of the country (for example, Matthew Lyon of Vermont), gained a measure of fame and notoriety. At a time when ideology was becoming an increasingly important aspect not just of American politics but of cultural life as well, men who were capable of pithily capturing the spirit of either party's ethos were likely to achieve widespread recognition.

Some of Dennie's pieces traveled less well. His articles in praise of the Alien and Sedition Acts were taken up with enthusiasm in New Hampshire, Connecticut, and New Jersey but were either ignored or printed alongside vehement rebuttals in Vermont, New York, and the South. The reasons for these differences can be put down to a combination of physical distance and regional politics. While the paper's position was generally antislavery, in that it would occasionally publish letters and copied articles critical of the institution, Dennie himself never seems to have authored a word on the subject during his time at the *Museum*, although what he chose to publish was hardly a reliable guide to his private opinions, if he had any on the subject. Dennie's strong Francophobic feelings were received very well among his New England audience, but it is notable that he gained almost no traction whatsoever in Virginia and North Carolina. The one major urban area with a strong newspaper industry that Dennie failed to make an equivalent impact on was New York City. It was not that his articles were not arriving; plenty of newspapers in New York State, as well as in neighboring Connecticut and New Jersey, were publishing his material. Many major New York papers, like the *Commercial Advertiser* (née *Minerva*), the *Herald*, or the *Spectator*, did not carry him, whereas McLean & Lang's *Gazette* and Johnson's *Diary and Mercantile Advertiser* published his articles fairly frequently. Personal taste accounted for some of this, but partisan preference was also an important factor. The *Gazette of the United States*, a staunchly Federalist Philadelphia publication that Dennie would later edit, ran his editorials more than 50 times from 1796 to 1799. Another famously pro-British paper based in the temporary capital, Cobbett's *Porcupine's Gazette*, frequently ran Dennie's work. In contrast to these Federalist organs, their Democrat-Republican competitors were much less interested in Dennie's writing. For perhaps the most famous Republican paper of the mid- to late 1790s, Benjamin Franklin Bache's *Aurora*, our digitized archives show no attribution of any of Dennie's work.[34] We know that Bache, and his successor, William Duane, were aware of Dennie, because they had no shortage of unkind things to say about him. "The Editor of the *Farmer's Weekly Museum*," one *Aurora* piece ran, "appears to set even the exemplary execration Fenno drew down on himself, and the very foundations of our government at nought . . . one of the most execrable and daring attacks on the principle of elective representation that we recalled to have seen."[35] Dennie's writing seems to have had an understandably divisive effect, and the degree to which Republican journalists loathed him can only have delighted Federalist editors all the more.

The extent of Dennie's reach becomes all the more remarkable in the context of New Hampshire's position in the national newspaper scene. From 1797 to 1798, 1,305 articles relating to the state were published in the rest of the United States. There were eleven newspapers operating in the state at the time, spread across five towns. Of these the largest, Portsmouth, was home to three newspapers, the *Gazette*, the *Oracle of the Day*, and the *Federal Observer*. During the same period, there are 713 separate instances of newspapers outside of the state reprinting articles from Dennie and the *Museum*. Put another way, Dennie's work had a greater impact on the American press than the rest of the state's editors combined in those two years. New Hampshire was on the periphery of both national journalism and politics, and its newspapers printed far more news of the outside world than that from within its own borders. Dennie stands alone in achieving anything like national recognition, albeit through pseudonym, as a New Hampshire editor in the 1790s.

Dennie, while not a figure of primary national importance, was for a time an influential journalist and writer. His work could be found not only in the papers of America's major cities but also throughout New England, the Hudson Valley, the mid-Atlantic, and even in the coastal regions of the South down to northern Georgia. Outside the residents of Walpole and its environs, the editors of friendly papers, and his political acquaintances, his name would have been known to only a fraction of Americans. Dennie's name did not appear once in the paper during his time as editor. This was not a universal practice. George Hough, who ran the *Courier of New Hampshire* in Concord, frequently signed his name and printed correspondence addressed directly to him in his paper.[36] One is tempted to suppose that so proud a man as Dennie was not particularly desirous of having his name associated with such a backwater operation; he certainly had no qualms about having his name

widely known later, in the more literary stage of his career. It was the
Farmer's Weekly Museum, and the Lay Preacher, not Joseph Dennie, that
carried the cachet. However, it is only with Dennie that the *Museum*
had anything like this level of success. Indeed, no other paper in New
Hampshire could compare to the national reach of the *Museum* at its
height. American readers were developing a kind of brand conscious-
ness in news that we today take for granted. Not only could they express
their consumer choice through their newspaper selection, but those
newspapers refracted the choices available to readers all over the country as well. The reader of the Federalist newspaper in Philadelphia, the
Gazette of the United States, by opting for that instead of the Republican
National Gazette, was actually tapping into a whole range of identifiable
news brands.

The regular reader of the *Gazette* would come to recognize papers
like the *Museum*, having never even picked up a copy. The dateline
would also carry with it a number of identifiable but somewhat nebulous ideological connotations. Readers could expect a view of the world
tinged by a strong Anglophilia and equally fervent Francophobia. There
would be general approbation of the Hamiltonian program, a strong but
not entirely unreserved support of central administration and financial
development. Outside of the explicitly political articles, however, in the
articles on country life, the passing of the seasons, or the homilies on
Christian family life, there is a looser cultural conservatism that somewhat confounds stereotypes of the partisan dichotomy of the 1790s.
The rustic style and content of many *Museum* columns were a complete
affectation, in that the dandified Dennie could no more handle a plow
than shoe a horse, or do much else described in his many pastoral allego-
ries. His audience, however, had no way of knowing this. The separation
between Dennie the public figure and the "Lay Preacher" of his columns
was vital to this pretense. Contemporary politicians and journalists
alike regularly reach for this kind of common touch, employing sports
metaphors or engaging in outdoor pursuits in a manner that can bur-
nish their manly mien, or leave them looking faintly ridiculous. What
Dennie, wholly disingenuously, offered his readers was a conservative
vision of the yeoman republic, a transplanted English idyll of country

squires and eccentrics ruled over by the greatest country gentleman of them all, the kindly and benign George Washington.

Dennie was able to do this because he was a part of a transitory generation of American journalists. He was by no means the first dedicated American editor—the salvos of the Philadelphia Newspaper War years earlier had seen to that—but he did enjoy a few unique advantages given his physical location and relative obscurity. He was afforded the opportunity to be a white-collar specialist in a field made up mostly of artisan jacks-of-all-trades and autodidacts. Outside of New York City, Boston, and Philadelphia, it is hard to find too many men of Dennie's background and education putting together quarto weeklies. When Carlisle hired Dennie, he did something unusual for the owner of a small-town provincial newspaper: he invested solely in intellectual capital. However dubious we might find the fruits of that intellectual labor to be, it did represent something of a departure for a town like Walpole, New Hampshire, to have a full-time wordsmith in its environs. Unfortunately, for the town and the paper, the national notice and success that Dennie achieved had no means of being translated into profitability. The *Farmer's Weekly Museum* had a greater national reach than any other New Hampshire paper, but it had a much shorter life span than publications like the *New Hampshire Gazette* of Portsmouth (1756–1847) or the *Courier* of Concord (1794–1805). Ultimately, local markets, subscription dues, and nonjournalistic printing (government contracts, book publication, and so on) sustained a small printer, not a renowned editor or beloved and respected columnist.

When considering the impact of individual journalists in the early national period, therefore, we have to think about a marketplace that transcends the singular influence of any one newspaper. Joseph Dennie was by no means a unique example of this phenomenon. Men like him had an influence that far exceeded their personal notoriety or the readership of their publication. In that sense, of audiences accessing a variety of branded content through the medium of a single publication, they resemble less the monolithic dailies of the twentieth century and more the blogosphere of the twenty-first. Dennie's pseudonymous celebrity may have allowed him, on a personal level, to reconcile personal vanity and conceit to a desire for influence and fame, but in fact it did for him what it did for other early essayists. In an age in which a physical copy of a newspaper could travel at the speed of a mounted horse or a favorable river current,[37] the widespread reprinting of the Lay Preacher and *Weekly Museum* serials ensured a much broader audience than Dennie could ever have hoped to reach through his own publication. As for many of his contemporaries, Dennie the dilettante law graduate was able to adopt and discard the guise of the evangelist and the hayseed as it suited his purpose and message, while protecting his private persona: the American natural aristocrat.

What the success of Dennie epitomized were the ways in which media and communications had fundamentally changed in the early American republic. Newspapers in rural areas did not exist merely to reprint news that had come from other, more important, places. While the news received from places like London and Philadelphia was an important component of their content, they also created a distinctive journalism of their own, which reflected the opinions and interests of both the authors and their readers. In addition to the editorial voice, these newspapers also provided a forum for the thought of Americans from different backgrounds, places, and classes. The general acceptance of pseudonymity and assumed identity protected these amateur journalists from social stigma and recrimination. If readership was an important ingredient of republican citizenship, then writing was another. When the editor of the *Rising Sun* of Dover established his "planetarium" feature, he invited contributions from his own readers. "As many, if not most of its patrons, have regular access to the very best sources of direct intelligence," Sidus wrote, "something in the line of literature might profitably fill up those columns which are left after a good summary of the *news* of the day is inserted."[38] This call for not just news but art was taken up with eagerness, if mixed degrees of technique, by his readers. Being asked to express one's finer feelings, even in a nakedly transparent attempt to pad out a newspaper, is a validating experience.

Other than encouraging the creative impulses of aspiring writers, this spread of writing from previously unheard quarters of society had another, further-reaching, consequence. These correspondents not only were new to the conversation but also had fundamentally different things to say. Often only tangentially concerned with the machinations of "high" politics, they had a variety of axes to grind and grudges to prosecute. The introduction of men writing "from their home, under the mountain," into the national conversation meant that the tenor of that conversation would be changed permanently. The opinions of John Fenno, Benjamin Franklin Bache, and even Joseph Dennie would have to jostle in an increasingly rambunctious marketplace of ideas with those of farmers, storekeepers, and clerks. The ensuing melee would, in no small part, shape the contours of the new nation.

CHAPTER SEVEN

"THESE FALSE AND SCURRILOUS LIBELS"

The Rancor of Early American Political Journalism

The villainy of the Jacobins is now so obvious, and their determination so great to overturn the Government of the United States, that they are not satisfied with spreading all the sedition in their power by their vile tongues, but are determined to establish a Jacobin Press in this town . . .

Arouse! Arouse every friend of his Country, and do all in your power to impede the progress of the above Villainy, and stop it while in embryo. But it is to be feared that nothing but the strong arm of Government can put a stop to these vile declaimers, and the base means, using in this town, to destroy one of the best of Governments on earth.

A FRIEND tO GOVERNMENT

—*Federal Observer*, May 16, 1799

The veneer of unanimity that characterized American politics at its inception was inevitably fleeting. The circumstances that created it, of a quasi-deified leader who modeled himself on the republican virtue of Cincinnatus, a tiny electorate of property-holding men, and a brief sense of collective purpose, were not the enduring conditions that sustain a nation. The 1790s were the decade in which Americans, trustees of a new republic, began to struggle over the nature of what they were to be. They weren't starting from first principles; in fact, they were all too aware of historical precedent, of how unlikely their precarious experiment was to succeed. In such febrile conditions, political identities formed around competing understandings of not just how best to conduct the experiment but what its ultimate ends might be. If the 1790s began with at least the outward appearance of a consensus, they did not end that way. "Far from being an age of classical virtue and republican self-restraint," Marcus Daniel has observed, "political life in the post-revolutionary United States was tempestuous, fiercely partisan, and highly personal."[1]

This dialectical process was carried out in various spheres of life. Of course, the best remembered are the disputations of men like Jefferson, Hamilton, Adams, and Madison. Variations on these conversations were, however, taking place in churches and taverns across the Union (although, in the latter case, with fewer Latin quotations and more expletives). For many Americans, the primary forum for these debates came in the weekly newspaper. There, they could follow the swirls and eddies of not just political events but the emerging demarcations between rival groups with fundamentally different perspectives on what America might be. They were shaped by, while helping to shape, these disputes.

"Political news" in the late eighteenth century was not the type of beat reportage it would later become. Most of the political content in newspapers came in one of two forms. The first was verbatim copies of legislation, election results, presidential addresses, and treaties. These, usually printed without comment, were the purview of the older-style "gazette," a publication whose primary purpose was the circulation of such official documents. The second were opinion columns, the work of either the editor or a reader-correspondent or else lifted from another newspaper. These articles could not exactly be described as "news"; they imparted little in the way of factual information and usually relied on a good degree of assumed knowledge on the part of the reader. In addition to these columns, rhetoric was also manifested in religious texts (whether written for the newspaper or transcribed from preaching), poetry, or records of public speaking, ranging from rostrum speeches to after-dinner toasts. Such slices of political culture appeared side by side with more traditional journalistic content.

As a result of this emphasis on opinion, early newspapers tended to be quite emotive. Neutrality and objectivity were not the aims of most of the people who wrote for them, even in the relative calm of the early 1790s. "Professions of impartiality I shall make none," wrote William Cobbett. "They are always useless, and are besides perfect nonsense, when used by a newsmonger; for, he that does not relate news as he finds it, is something worse than partial; and as the articles that help compose a paper, he that does not exercise his own judgement, either in admitting or rejecting what is sent him, is a poor passive tool, and not an editor." Cobbett, for his part, felt "the strongest partiality for the cause of order and good government" and claimed that "to profess impartiality here, would be as absurd as to profess it in a war between Virtue and Vice, Good and Evil, Happiness and Misery."[2] This avowed attachment to an ideal or principle was considered a healthy attitude for a news-paperman; indeed, why would someone go into the trade if they didn't have passionately held beliefs? The job of the "newsmonger" was not to drily parse facts and dates, but to impress on the reader the meaning of affairs and what ought to be done about them. The editor was not just a chronicler of political events but a participant in them, and journalism remained more art than science.

Even during the first Washington administration, the journalistic tenor of the first years of the republic was not altogether harmonious. Ongoing arguments over the adoption and interpretation of the U.S. Constitution, the Bill of Rights, the Hamiltonian economic program, and the Bank of the United States provided grist for many a mill. The polemical organs of the Federalist and Jeffersonian factions, the

Gazette of the United States and the *National Gazette*, respectively, steamed with political animosity and squabbles. Yet those papers, avowedly partisan and supported financially (albeit indirectly) by Hamilton and Jefferson, were atypical. Outside of these publications, the general tone of early 1790s newspapers, at least so far as the administration was concerned, was mild and deferential. Political allegiances were demonstrated primarily through effusive praise for heroes of the revolution and (in New England) the grandees of the Federalist Party. "We congratulate *America*, that her *favorite* Son, WASHINGTON, has in health, peace and love, returned from his Southern Tour to *Philadelphia*," gushed the *New Hampshire Gazetteer*. "Having now experienced, that however the different interests of *South* and *North*, may clash, yet Unity is the bond of affection toward him; that where he comes, Love fires the incense of adoration, and that esteem, veneration and respect, are shewn to him, unmixed, with envy, hatred or distrust."[3] This sort of language pervaded much of the political discourse found in small-town newspapers in the early years. Intentionally or not, editors and correspondents were participating in the first drafts of the sort of didactic mythmaking surrounding the founding fathers in general, and Washington in particular, that persists throughout popular accounts of American history.

There was bile in the New Hampshire newspapers of the early 1790s, although it tended to be directed toward foreigners (usually the French) or unnamed dissenting elements. This, however, would change with astonishing rapidity over the course of the decade. For example, three articles featuring the words *politics* and *hatred* appear in the New Hampshire press from 1790 to 1795. Four appear in 1798 alone and eight in 1799. By the end of the decade, the quantity and intensity of the invective became overwhelming. The language used to describe the first president stands in stark contrast to that used for the newly elected third in 1800. "Should the election of Mr. Jefferson to the first office of the United States take place," went a piece in the *Museum*,

> which is now ascertained to be a certainty, it will be attended with one blessing, which be a cessation of the clamor of Jacobins. From Georgia to New Hampshire, the whining of this disaffected, disorganizing crew

has resembled the croaking of a tuneful frog pond, and like this animal, as the fable narrated by Esop, they have wearied Heaven with their importunities to send them another man to rule over them. Should their prayers be heard, their fate might not be unlike that of the frogs of Esop. The expectations of these democrats with respect of a change in the administration are singularly extravagant and unreasonable. From the legislator, whose situation gives them opportunities to whisper his flatteries in the ear of his master, to the discontented democrat who belches out the praises of Jefferson in a bar room, are all anxious to see him fill the first office of government; and are on the tiptoe of expectation to have the gift of some lucrative or honorable post.[4]

Articles such as these abounded. Praise for Adams and other icons remained, but with greater and greater frequency, attacks on political foes were being substituted in place of positive reportage. If the general emotional complexion of 1790 was one of reverence, then 1800 was one of furious anger.

Political terminology morphed and evolved over time, with some words that had been applied to general principles becoming more narrowly partisan in their implications. In constitutional debates in the years leading up to and surrounding the American War of Independence, *federalism* referred not to the outlook of a clique of politicians but to a broader set of principles regarding governance and sovereignty. Or, put another way, it transmogrified from a common noun to a proper one. Yet this transformation did not erase the previous meanings of the word. When Thomas Jefferson famously declared in his inaugural address that "we are all republicans, we are all federalists," he did not merely mean that the two major political parties shared a common sense of purpose (not least because such a statement would have been patently absurd to anybody listening).[5]

During the 1790s, *Jacobin* became an epithet of abuse for Democrat-Republicans by Federalists and their fellow travelers, just as the Democrat-Republicans took up cudgels like *aristocrat* or *monocrat*. "The violence of the printed word," writes Daniel, "often flowed off the page and into the streets, provoking verbal and physical assaults, duels, public demonstrations, and riots."[6] It was more than a simply partisan designation. It signified, to the New England reactionary, an unholy nexus of amorality, dissolution, and nihilism. The French Revolution had an enormous effect not just on the first party system in the United States but on the entirety of antebellum political culture. It was a part of newspapers, religious discourse, fiction, art, and much else. Whether one admired it or abhorred it, it was a defining shibboleth to be clung to or stood against.[7] The evidence of this is available in abundance in New Hampshire. "Before you can make a Jacobin of an American," an anonymous author in the *Farmer's Weekly Museum* wrote, "you must strip him of his religion. When he no longer fears Gods, he will soon be induced to disrespect the laws of his country." One could lose more than religion: "MAD COW—Last week a Cow belonging to Mr Stevens, of this town, run mad, and died in extreme torture. . . . A Correspondent assures us, the above Cow was bitten by a JACOBIN, in the rage of political hydrophobia. . . . An infallible cure for the BITE on the human kind, is, a careful review of administration policy with regard to France, and a plaster of tar and feathers applied to the biter."[8] Also popular were attempts to explain the deranged Jacobin psyche. "*Recipe to make a Jacobin.* Take the herbs of hypocrisy and the roots of ambition, two ounces of pride and vain glory, bruise them in the mortar of contention and discord, boil them over the fire of sedition until you see the scum of falsehood that swims on the top," and so on for paragraphs. Attacks against fellow editors were also couched in these terms. "Duane, and after him Callender and Lyon," Dennie wrote, identifying three opposition editors, "with the rest of the Jacobin printers throughout the United States—laugh at virtue, religion and morality, and make as much noise as possible in the world at all events."[9] By 1800 the term could be used to describe practically anything of which a Federalist editor might disapprove.

Few journalists applied the term to their fellow Americans in the period 1790 to 1793, when it was exclusively confined to coverage of the French Revolution. From there on in, it slowly became adapted into the American political vernacular. Frequently, the term was used derisively to refer to other news sources, as with this from the *Courier*, "The Jacobins of New York, condemn the Treaty as wholly Grenville's: In Bache's Aurora, it is condemned as being written wholly by Mr. Jay, or Mr. Hamilton," or the *Mirrour*, "The Jacobin papers of Philadelphia as was expected, have began to abuse the French National Convention."[10] Others were general polemic, as with the historical glossary of terms of approbation, taken from the *Oracle of the Day*:

THE JACOBIN LADDER

ALTHOUGH there may be some well meaning people, who may condemn the Treaty, yet a great majority of loud brawlers against that instrument, ascended the ladder of demagogism by grades like the following:

They were
TIMID WHIGS, in 1775, when danger was near;
FURIOUS WHIGS, in 1783, when danger was past;
BANK INSURGENTS in heart, if not in deed, in 1786;
ANTI-federalists, in 1788;
APOLOGISTS for the whisky boys, *before they were humbled,*
    in 1794,
and to complete the climax, are
TREATY CONDEMNERS, in 1795.
VERITAS.[11]

This placed the term *Jacobin* in a longer tradition of troublemakers and double-dealers throughout American history. Words becoming signifiers for various types of undesirables was already, and remains, a tradition in American political culture, but *Jacobin* had a couple of special contexts. First, unlike terms like *Anti-Federalist*, it explicitly signaled a foreign allegiance. As Wendell Bird has explained, during the war hysteria of 1798, "many Federalists viewed sympathy with France as seditious, and saw the nascent Republican Party not as a legitimate opposition but as the Jacobin party, and the small number of Republican newspapers as not legitimate sentiments but as agents of France."[12] In much the same way that the eighteenth century used the term *papist* to refer not just to Catholics but to an undue adherence to Rome, *Jacobin* implied that one felt closer ties to France than to America. Second, *Jacobin* indicated a connection not just to the French Revolution per se, but to a specific intellectual and cultural strain of it—to the *sansculottes*, the mob, and the guillotine. The French Revolution as a project was something many Americans felt an instinctive kinship with, but they were repulsed by the terror, violence, and anti-Christian ethic that the Jacobins seemed to represent.

Jacobin-based attacks were frequently jarringly vituperative and often directed against competitors. "To compare either of them with the numerous *fog banks* which exhale from the *Jacobin canals* from *Portsmouth* to *Savannah*," the *Courier* thundered, "would be a prostitution of the powers of comparison." *Farmer's* had this to say in its "Index to Jacobinism": "One who can [be found] with in the Chronicle, or in the Aurora, is a determined jacobin."[13] Some pieces were written with a satirical (a less generous soul might say libelous) bent, with words falsely attributed to particularly hated enemy papers:

> *Creed of the Jacobins and Democrats being as follows:*
>
> I do not believe in anything that is permanent.
> I believe only in the virtues of change and experiment.
> I believe that is wiser to rush into any evils that may await
>   us, because life is not long enough to wait the flow
>   progress of simple reform.
> I believe that all good government are made the existing
>   members, and that they have nothing to do with
>   posterity.
> I believe that the succeeding generation has nothing to do
>   with us, and that we have nothing to do with the next
>   generation.
> I believe that every existing rich man, ought to be poor;
>   Democrats excepted.
> I believe that the only fit men to govern are Democrats, and
>   those, who wish to live independent of any established
>   government, as they only can know what freedom is.
> I believe in the virtues of corruption, without which there
>   can be no regeneration.
> And I believe, that all men who do no believe, as I believe,
>   ought to be hanged.
>
> AURORA[14]

Indeed, "Jacobin papers" became the common shorthand in the New Hampshire press for those publications that the editor found most objectionable, and the *Aurora* of Philadelphia, with its vehement attacks on John Adams during his administration, was the primary target of such assaults.

The following graph details the usage of the word *Jacobin* in New Hampshire news coverage in the 1790s. After entering regular American

circulation from 1792 onward, the term was initially used to refer specifically to French Jacobins or to Jacobin letters and publications original
to France or England. In 1795, 106 articles in New Hampshire referred
to Jacobins, but only 25 of those were written on American subjects. By
1796, the media panic about French Jacobins had apparently abated, but
it would soon be supplanted by a hysteria concerning radicals much
closer to home. By the final years of the decade, *Jacobin* had almost
entirely lost its technical meaning and was being used in political articles on a range of topics, including the XYZ Affair and Sedition Act.
By 1800, only 25 published articles that mentioned Jacobins referred to
France or European affairs, whereas 125 dealt with domestic politics.

The transformation of *Jacobin* from a term used to describe a French
political movement to a term of abuse was part of a broader linguistic
and tonal shift taking place in American journalism. "Any student pass-
ingly familiar with the early republic," Ronald Formisano asserts, "knows
that deference ended sometime during these years."[15] To test this notion,
all available articles explicitly concerning domestic government and

FIGURE 5. USES OF JACOBIN IN NEWS COVERAGE

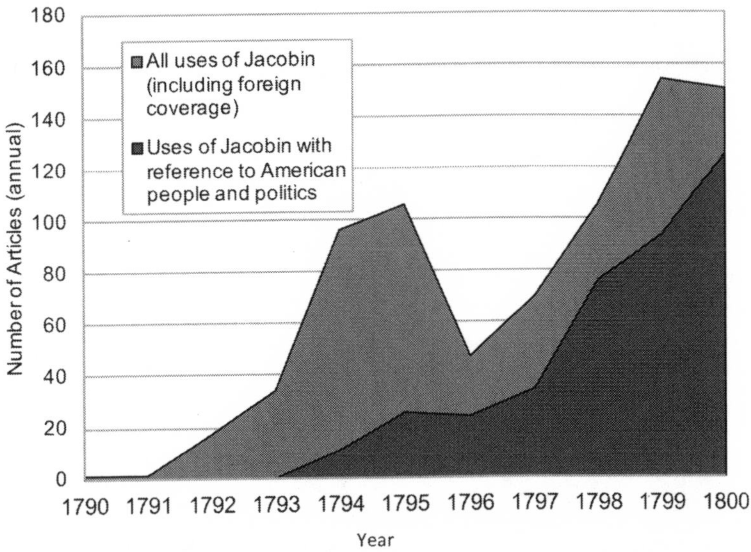

Data compiled from NewsBank.

politics printed in New Hampshire during the period 1790–1800 have been divided into three categories (which will be fully illustrated later), positive, neutral, and negative.[16]

The "positive" category includes general texts with a patriotic or nationalist sentiment, encouraging pride and exceptionalism. At its most elemental, the very fact of being American was celebrated, in a way that would become immediately familiar, indeed an intrinsic, part of American culture and identity. "It is a privilege in existing in the nature of our government—and secured to us by our constitutions and bills of rights," the *Mirrour* of Concord solemnly intoned. "It is a privilege necessary to the maintenance of our freedom." As the *Oracle of the Day* put it, "To have been born an American ... is a species of felicity which no other race of men have experienced. Those, born to behold and enjoy it, now see, that it has given dignity to human nature."[17] Both of these examples come from articles derived, at least in part, from New York and Boston papers, respectively. Sometimes, headlines alone give one all the necessary information: "An Oration: On the Rising Glory of America; Delivered on the Fourth of July, 1792, by a Student of Princeton College (N.J.)." Speeches were transcribed at length and distributed throughout America, amplifying the voice of the original speaker a thousandfold. One transcript, on the "ensuing session of Congress" in 1790, was reprinted throughout the country.[18]

Speeches were one form of public political act that were transcribed into the pages of American newspapers. Another was the popular[19] practice of toasting. Toasts were a less formal, but no less symbolic, means of celebrating a beloved figure. "A TOAST," the *Journal* reported, "give a few days since, at an entertainment, after a military parade at Ipswich. Deafness to the ear that would patiently hear, dumbness to the tongue that would utter a calumny against the immortal WASHINGTON." These toasts were taken from the feasts and patriotic binges of the public, recycled as column material, and then translated back into the vernacular by readers. "By the end of the 1790s," writes Simon Newman, "those who participated in these events knew that their actions were quite likely going to be read about and interpreted by citizens far beyond the confines of their own community. This sharing of information made possible the emergence of a common national language of ritual activity."[20] Through the medium of the newspaper, toasts could go from reaching their intended audiences of perhaps a few dozen to a readership of thousands dispersed across the United States.

Positive news coverage also included pieces more specifically supportive of the administration that made the case for stability, continuity, and the importance of public backing of the government. "The success which has attended the administration of the general government exceeds the most sanguine expectations of the warmest friends to the Union of these free states," one paper editorialized. "Every anticipation has been more than realized; and hitherto not one gloomy prediction has been verified."[21] Frequently, such articles were thinly veiled partisan electioneering in support of the local establishment, but they are notable by their mildness of tone and absence of aggression. "Good Government being among the most essential blessings the people of these highly favored states enjoy," one such article began, "and of which they have participated in a measurable degree upon the principles of the new constitution, and we may without deceiving ourselves anticipate various future advantages . . . of how much importance then is it that we view the approaching election of National Representatives as connected with a more full, equal and permanent enjoyment of those happy effects already attained under the present administration. A little variation in the next representation, will ensure to us the establishment of these, and will place us in a situation as enviable as any of our sister states." Statements such as these were often couched not in partisan terms but rather in the logic of continuity; why change the government, they asked, if it is working perfectly well already? "The debates in the first session of Congress, and a considerable part of the present," the article contended, "were conducted with a coolness, candor and unanimity, which commanded the admiration and applause of the world." Of course, it was easy to be so sanguine about avoiding the figurative changing of horses in midstream when one's own party was in power. For the most part, editors assumed readers knew who the proper candidates were and referred to them indirectly. "The public papers of New Hampshire propose several gentlemen for representatives, and by them it appears that the people contemplate a change; but it should be observed, that the gentlemen who not represent us, have near two years experience in the proceedings of Congress," the article explained, without ever pausing to mention who these gentlemen might be. "We make choice of those who inherit from nature, education and habit, a decided superiority in the essential points of genius, knowledge and eloquence, we shall gain nothing by it; and exclusive of the objections above mentioned, with will be most eligible to re-elect them."[22] By refusing to name its preferred candidates, the editor of the *Spy* could portray himself not as a campaigning hack but as merely offering sensible advice to his readers.

When it came to national political figures, however, journalists were far more direct in lavishing praise on specific public figures, as with this article addressed to George Washington: "We beg leave to join the general voice in most respectful congratulation on thy appointment to the highest office, and most extended trust which can be confided by a free people," and so on for many obsequious paragraphs.[23] Indeed, the almost religious language used in reference to the president in his first administration no doubt helped stoke the fears of those who suspected monarchists in their midst. A piece titled "An Essay towards the Character of the President of the United States" barely fell short of canonization. "By the mere natural strength and superiority of his genius, he broke out at once, a General, a Hero . . . Indefatigably laborious and active, coolly intrepid in action." These rapturous portraits did not merely focus on his personal qualities but also referred to his almost preordained mastery of command. "Modest and magnanimous . . . Arriving at a situation far more dignified than a King, you find him a citizen and a patriot," the author continued. "The arduous duties of his important station lose their weight in his hands, because of the comprehensiveness of his mind, and the clearness of his perceptions." It was not just the traits or the skills of the leader that were important to these writers, but a sort of intrinsic moral solidity that defined them. "Many a private man might make a great President," the essay concluded, "but, will there ever be a President who will make so great a private man as WASHINGTON?" In tracts such as these, the origin myths of nationhood were being hammered out in public forums in florid prose. Indeed, it is remarkable, given the supposed "island communities" of late-eighteenth-century America, just how national the preoccupations of the newspapers could be. Simon Newman has written persuasively on this subject, noting that "when the new Federal constitution went into effect a great deal of political power shifted from the peripheries to the center, and for the first time since Yorktown many Americans began to take note of their national government, a government that now enjoyed the power to make a difference in their lives. Newspapers reported congressional speeches, presidential messages, and the reports of cabinet members, and national politics captured the limelight."[24] Such a focus on figures of national importance not only served the purpose of reinforcing an American identity but also meant that articles could be reprinted more widely throughout the country.

Although the nationally known figures received more lavish and extensive coverage, local notables too could receive the hagiographic treatment. In these cases, such articles were much more likely to be written by those personally acquainted with the subject, and the readers were far more likely to know them, too. In one such treatment, written simply by "A Correspondent," the author professed "great opportunities of observing the activity, humanity, attention & zeal, which has marked the whole conduct of Col. George Gains, begs leave to express the high sense that he entertains of such praise worthy firmness, fortitude and perseverance." This sort of personal vouchsafe was common practice in early American politics, in which personal and public reputation often interwined. "He was literally been a father and a friend in the midst of a trying dispensation, which has unnerved the most robust and manly minds. There is no hour in the twenty-four, but what has borne affecting witness to his unremitted services." Also important was to convey the sense that here was a man who would not stoop (at least publicly) to ask for votes. The ideal republican gentleman would not sully himself with such a crass display, but a friend or admirer might, knowing of his unaffected modesty, do so on his behalf. "He has deserved honorably well of his fellow-citizens. The least they can bestow is the voice of universal approbation, pronouncing well done, good and faithful," the notice concluded.[25] Whoever wrote it, and it is not altogether impossible that the estimable Colonel Gains had a hand in it himself, such an article represented a common form of rural political writing in the early 1790s.

Early in the decade, official campaigning for national and state offices was beholden to a kind of informal gentlemen's agreement, in which to argue on behalf of one's candidate was perfectly permissible, but to directly criticize one's opponent was taboo. "The phrase 'being a candidate' has not the same meaning here as southward," wrote Jeremiah Smith, first a state and then a U.S. congressman in the 1790s, wrote to a friend in New Jersey. "It means with you a person who expresses a desire for office, solicits votes, perhaps treats the elections. *Here* it only means a person *talked of* for an office; not by himself or particular connections, for in that case he certainly would not be elected."[26] As such, when early partisans sought to run down their rivals, they usually resorted to nonspecific general aspersions. "Shall we not get out of the path of common prudence, and," one such article began, "give . . . NICHOLAS GILMAN and JEREMIAH SMITH, our united votes for a seat in the next Congress. Let us remember that their parents were both farmers, and they in their youth were used to drive the team and swing the ax—I formerly had the honor of a small acquaintance with MR. GILMAN, and well remember that I marked him to be a sensible, industrious man, and a good husband in his own affairs." Naming preferred candidates for office was perfectly acceptable. However, the eponymous "Farmer" who submitted his letter to the *Portsmouth Gazetteer* had more portentous forebodings about what might happen should Gilman and Smith *not* win. "But if you should so differ from me," he continued, "as to think you can willingly toil in sultry field from sun to sun, that the gentleman and merchant's bowl may flow cheaper, that your sons should sleep on straw to purchase down for theirs, then I say, give your votes for some strangers to the soil, whose hands never handled the plow, who never earnt their own bread, and who are totally unacquainted with fatigue of the laborer or cultivation of the field."[27] The Farmer, without directly smearing a candidate, employed negative imagery and left the reader to determine to whom the author might be referring.

Other positive political articles were employed to promote and support specific policies and often read like Federalist memos, some of which might easily have come from Hamilton or one of his colleagues. One piece written in support of a national bank claimed that its popularity was the "cement of the Union—the liberal principles on which it is bottomed—and the respectability of the gentlemen who are candidates for offices in it, must render the institution highly beneficial to the people, and government of the United States; and must command the confidence of Europeans—whose property cannot be as safe in the confusion which perpetually reigns there, as in this tranquil country."[28] This article, like most of its type, originated in the *Gazette of the United States* in Philadelphia, one of the chief sources of policy-specific propagandist writing of this sort. The extent to which this type of journalism tended to arrive in New Hampshire from big-city newspapers will be explored in the next chapter.

One of the primary fonts of support for the administration was the pulpit. While preachers often handled political matters indirectly, resorting to allegory and simile, correlating the heavenly order with the temporal was not uncommon. "What an eventful period is this?" a sermon delivered in Concord, and reprinted in the *Herald*, asked. "I am thankful that I lived to it; and I could almost say 'Lord now lettest thou thy servant depart in peace, for mine eyes have seen thy salvation' . . . And now methinks I see the ardor for liberty catching and spreading: a general amendment, beginning in human affairs; the dominion of kings, changed for the dominion of laws. . . . Be encouraged all ye friends of reason and conscience. . . . The times are auspicious." By invoking the hand of Providence in political affairs, preaching such as this reinforced a sense of divine mission in American politics and the righteousness of the administration. "Your labors have not been in vain. Behold kingdoms admonished by your starting from sleep, breaking their fetters, and claiming justice from their oppressors! Behold you light you have struck after *setting America free*." Indeed, the Almighty held no small responsibility for the justice and rectitude of American government. As the editor of the *New Hampshire Spy* opined, "Providence has been pleased to bless the people of this country with more perfect opportunities of choosing and more effectual means of establishing their own government, than any other nation has hitherto enjoyed; and for the use we may make of these opportunities and these means, as we shall be highly responsible to that Providence, as well as mankind in general." And, as the editor of the *Repository* pointed out, the relationship ran both ways: "The publisher of a Newspaper is highly responsible to God and his country for the sentiments which he propagates among the body of the people; as it is in his power, at choice to subserve the cause of virtue or of vice, of faction or of good government."[29] With such a sense of providential mission, it is not surprising that patriotic, public-minded reporting predominated in the first years of the republic.

In the early days of the Union, most political reportage was of the type sampled above: baroque, earnest, worthy, and tedious. One or two examples, however, of a different style of American political comment were emerging in the New Hampshire press, and they were as notable for their authorship as for their content. In a letter to Eliphalet Ladd, editor of the *Political and Sentimental Repository* of Dover, New Hampshire, "AN OLD SOLDIER" of Wolfsborough offered up a sample of this change in style: "I live in the country, Mr. Printer, and am guided chiefly by the great people in the lower towns; for they have greater opportunities to know who are men of ability—but they are so divided among themselves, that I am really afraid some undeserving, office-hunting rabscallions will git the office." Here there is a marked difference from the earlier quotations in language, spelling, and construction, as well as the unpretentious, conversational tone and frankness of expression. "I hope, however, that the good people of New Hampshire will consider, that a number of the gentlemen proposed are men of no principles, but the CHINK—confined merely to their own private views—one third of whom are men of no property or abilities—and the other two thirds have been, or ought to have in goal, for being rather TOO INTIMATE with that kind of beings some time since called TORIES!" The correspondent then went on to list those candidates who satisfied his criteria of public virtue and those who did not. Particularly exercised by "the exorbitant salaries now given to the officers under the federal government," he threw his support behind "the only one member from this state who used his influence to reduce" them.[30] While not engaging in the sort of direct attacks that would characterize a lot of political journalism in the late 1790s, the Old Soldier's rustic address and "plain speaking" (which, of course, was seldom plain at all) were a sign of things to come.

The Old Soldier was not the only voice of rural irascibility in New Hampshire in 1790. RUSTICUS, whose submission was "Done at my Cave, under the Mountain, March 1790," also affected an unpolished, sardonic style. He took aim against pseudonymous authors who descended into squabbling with one another rather than presenting realistic reforms. "Mr Hough, I OBSERVE a number of geniuses have *graced* (or rather some of them *disgraced*) your Herald, with their productions, Whether they consider themselves *politicians, place-seekers, squibblers, or wits*, I know not: but I can tell them, they are but little understood by the common people . . . ," he asserted, presumably speaking on behalf of those common people. "I have no doubt that each writer is known personally by his opponent, or the observations thrown out would not have been so accurately pointed. . . . [I]nstead of being ashamed of their performances, their virulence increases; the contest grows more warm; the breach more wide, and consequently a reconciliation the more impracticable." From there, Rusticus warned of the deleterious effect this might have not only on the press but on public trust in general. "It will soon be difficult for a man to call at your office for a newspaper, without being suspected of handing a piece for publication; and should *you* be seen more sociable with one person than another, you would immediately be set down a *partial printer*."[31] He then, at length, berated, by name, those authors who had most aggrieved him, thus (hopefully with some sense of irony) committing the very sin for which he chastised his targets. Rusticus, and correspondents like him, was proof of the intimacy of the community of journalism and correspondence in New Hampshire; technology extended the spittle-flecked, puce-cheeked political discourse of the drinking house and town square.

Indeed, some correspondents occasionally paused to celebrate this state of affairs, with a commentator in the *Journal* noting that "our government guarantees to every man a full right speak his mind freely on all subjects; and to be in heart a tory, an aristocrat, a Mahometan, a Jew, a Pagan, a Jacobin, or an *antifederal*,"[32] the correspondent defending both his subject's right to free expression and his right to loathe them in turn. Intellectual relationships (and indeed rivalries) were fostered in the exchanges, as the more prolific authors became, as happened to the Lay Preacher, minor celebrities. Rebuttals were, in addition to being acerbic, a good indicator of how intensely the debates framed in the pages of newspapers were experienced. "Pray Mr. Pierce, who is this *Old Whig*, that appears in your paper of the week current? So much dissatisfied with the federalists, as to charge them with various schemes and rank them with *Old Tories—Apostates, combined to ruin us, &c.—* High swollen words these?" ZELUCO, a correspondent to the *Oracle of the Day*, asked. "Let us examine a little who they come from, and see if there be not as great a difference between Old Whigs & real ones, as there is between Old Tories and real; perhaps upon investigation, he will appear to be one of those Old Whig's of 1791, who had the fingering of the public money, and by improving their talents, have been so *unfortunate*, as from private citizens of very little property, to become men of princely fortunes—and who now wish for another revolution, that they may be able to plunder this union again as much more. . . ." In a partial concession, Zeluco then took the unusual step of partly censoring the names of those he had taken issue with, in a way that suggests some adherence to the old formalities. "Was not R—d—h one of those old bastard Whigs?—was not W——m B————t an Old Whig of this sort? And was not Benedict Arnold one of these Old Whigs? And pray, which of those do you think the greatest *traitor?*"[33] Thus, the petty animus of village life, transferred to the printed page, was as much a part of the political culture of the early republic as any ornate passage from Freneau or Franklin Bache.

Sometimes, these correspondences fall into the "positive" category, espousing a homespun variant of republican simplicity. "MR. PIERCE, I'M for peace and good government. I don't like disputations, and there's no good comes from 'em—I'm for order and regularity, that's my way—My neighbor Short is grown quite beside himself—turn'd quite topsey turvey—He says we are all going to *rack and ruin*. . . ." The correspondent, who went under the name "Humphrey Steady," made a malapropism-riddled appeal to rural good sense: "You say every man should go to town meeting—I say not. . . . I'm for every man's being his own man—that's my way. . . . I'm no *town-meeting's* man nor *paper-signer's* man—I'm neither one side nor t'other—I'm for peace—I'm for every man's acting for himself—fair and square—that's my way." Humphrey Steady spoke for an apoliticized ideal of the yeoman farmer, who spent more time considering the soil than the Senate. "Now says I—go to work—and mind your trade—Let every man mind his own business. . . . I'm for order and regularity; that's my way, Mr. Printer."[34] In such letters, it can be difficult to sift sincerity from satire and to know which were penned by genuine backwoods philosophers and which were in fact rather mean-spirited mockeries of bumpkins. One letter that appeared in the *Concord Mirrour*, signed by a "Tom Clodhead," is representative of this school: "But at any rate, we up here dont thinks very good polaticks at this critikle juncter of fairs, to try to make the gals any more crochical than they natterly wood be, for you see wee hav turrible quarrels at Congress now a days about one thing another, and they are ruther too tite for us at the futhard—we want more representatives, and then weed make um have the Treaty."[35] In letters like these, the parochial style was employed not to convey wisdom but rather to invite the derision of the reader. For the most part, however, they were written in a good-natured, affectionate style.

As the 1790s progressed, and particularly once the presidency passed from George Washington to John Adams, this generally benign media landscape began to give way to a new, bleaker journalism. A gnawing sense of paranoia was in a gradual ascendancy as the decade wore on and became the characteristic trait of the negative news pieces. One article, by the self-dubbed WHISKY, who announced, "I AM a man of nature," declared "creditors worse than Indians" and asked, "Shall I be dragged into the militia?" By the middle of the decade, an undercurrent of disquiet and pessimism concerning the general direction of American national government was stirring amid the editorial circles. "We are surrounded with hordes of beings, most poisonous to a government . . . ," wrote VIGIL to the *Hanover Eagle* (the most remote New Hampshire town to have a newspaper in the 1790s). "These vermin are particularly anxious to disperse their pernicious principles more generally through these states; but in New Hampshire have hitherto failed in their attempts." While the New Hampshire press was not yet engaging in open partisan mudslinging, it was no longer the backwoods cranks alone who prophesied anarchy or despotism. "Venality and corruption are already so far advanced in this country, that, with certain characters, it is thought impossible for a man in any the least degree connected with government, to act, in other respects, from disinterested motives," wrote a correspondent to the *Concord Herald*. "Judging from themselves, and what would be their own conduct in a similar situation, they suppose every act, word, and thought, of such a man, must be rendered hypocritically conformable to the ideas of a supposed majority in the government, which, according to them, ought to maintain a complete sovereignty over the minds of those who may have been appointed to the performance of some of its duties."[36] Even as the mood was darkening, most correspondents still tried to restrict their criticisms to the realm of the abstract.

The impulse to remain above the hurly-burly of personalized politics, as well as the desire to avoid being served a libel suit, tied journalists in ever more convoluted knots to avoid specifying their targets, achieving a sort of glum resignation with an article from the *Connecticut Courant* (reprinted in the *New Hampshire Journal*), headed "To N*******L N***s, Esq; Vermont."[37] In time, however, specific issues began to recur in the pages of the New Hampshire papers with greater and greater frequency. Of the goings-on that agitated the newspaper readers and correspondents of New Hampshire in 1792 and 1793, the debates on public credit and revenue,[38] the controversies surrounding Citizen Genet and all that he would come to represent, and the emerging horrors of the French Revolution were the greatest irritants.[39] Genet seems to have provided one of the first hate figures for the New England journalists of the early republic. "It is said, that Mr Genet, has attached himself in a particular manner to the known enemies of the federal government," the *Gazette* clucked, "to the revilers of the President and of almost every public functionary of high rank in it."[40] Genet, the vainglorious ambassador of revolutionary France to the United States who became a hate figure for many Federalists while trying to recruit Americans to the cause against Britain, was an early emblem of Francophobia in the New England press.[41]

By 1794 a new specter had arisen to trouble the imagination of the New Hampshire newspaper reader. After an effusive paragraph on the general good sense and courageous disposition of the American public, the "Farmer" (possibly the same one as quoted earlier, although it is impossible to know; it was a popular pseudonym) wrote that "it must give pain to the true Patriot, disgust to those worthy of the privileges we enjoy, and grief to our valiant Sons, whose scars yet remind us of the price by which we purchased our Independence, to see the envious, designing and factious, making every possible exertion to raise prejudices against our government and stain the glory of our flourishing empire; to see the Demagogue at the head of a Democratic Society, circulating the effusions of hearts, influenced by influenced by the fell Demon, who presides in the grim Court of Pandemonium, and Satan-like, with infernal artillery, presuming the ruin and destruction of our happy country." The Farmer continued in a similar vein for four more paragraphs. Indeed, when considering that he, and a few other authors, took to substituting the neologism *Demoncratic* for *Democratic*, one only begins to grasp the acidity of the vitriol. The historian Rachel Cleves has convincingly written of the correlation between the increasing violence of language as it appeared in American newspapers and pamphlets to increasingly violent feelings in the hearts of people on both sides of the Atlantic.[42] The emergence of identifiable and named parties clearly had a pronounced effect on political journalism, as they provided commonly understood labels for otherwise nebulous groups and classes.

While the transition from one form of journalism to another took place incrementally, 1796 was the year in which the incipient disquiet transformed into outright anger. In the Federalist newspapers of New England, much of the year was preoccupied with drumbeating for John Adams and tributes to Washington, some of them plaintive entreaties against his resignation. Indeed, some of his particularly fervent admirers feared for the fate of the Union without him. "Faction! Curst offspring of hell, begot on mercenary interest! If faction come to dissolve, or disturb our harmonious system, all the splendid pictures that our patriotism and philanthropy have framed, shall be defaced and blotted out forever. Avaunt! Fell monster!" The staccato, exclamatory rhythms of articles like this represented not only a tonal move away from the more lyrical cadences of the positive news coverage but also a shift in imagery toward the hellish and the macabre. "Thou hast dared to shew thy horrid visage for a moment, crawling from infernal pit, and to spit thy venom and sulpher on the untarnished immortal glory of a WASHINGTON! His powerful genius shall crush thy head and plunge thee down again into the abyss from whence thou sprung; O WASHINGTON! Whose name, on every return of his anniversary, I shall pronounce with enthusiasm along the sacred name of country, as thou hast fought her battles, live to cement her union!" The author beseeched Washington to stay in office: "Let not heaven call thee too soon from the vows of mortals! Nor ever quit the helm of government, while one head remains of the hydra of disorganisation!"[43] Such desperate appeals indicate not only the fervor that the cult of Washington inspired but also the fear of what might follow his retirement.

While partisanship grew, even the most rigidly proadministration of the New Hampshire newspapers were not averse to publishing anti-Adams propaganda from elsewhere in the Union, as the following piece evinces:

Who drew the declaration of independence, that great charter of our enfranchisement?
Ans. Thomas Jefferson.
Who was the first prime minister under the federal government?
Ans. Thomas Jefferson.
Who appointed Thomas Jefferson to that office?
Ans. The patriot Washington
Who advised the proclamation of neutrality?
Ans. Thomas Jefferson.
Who defended our government against the interference of Genet, on his attempt to draw us into the European war?
Ans. Thomas Jefferson ...
Then must not the "Federalist" who charges Thomas Jefferson with being the leader of a faction against our government, adopt that signature from being a subject of one of the despots of the confederacy as Pilnitz?
Ans. Undoubtedly ...
Who planned the form of government submitted to the Convention by Alexander Hamilton, proposing a King, Lords and Commons?
Ans. John Adams.[44]

Whether the editor of the normally impeccably Federalist *Gazette* had been seized by a momentary lapse of faith, faced a deadline scramble for printable content, or, and this is not altogether impossible, had failed to read the copy can only be speculated upon. What is evident, however, is that the delineated adjectives that categorized newspapers, editors, and articles did not always hold true in the ad hoc, highly personalized world of late-eighteenth-century journalism.

The latter part of the decade provided a wealth of issues for newspapermen and correspondents to get excited, and antagonized, about. Direct attacks made against fellow editors became increasingly common. "A small paper, called the Bee, of New London, which began tolerably, but has since dwindled to most downright democracy and French principles, contains a proposal for printing a literary paper, to be baptised the Honeycomb," wrote Joseph Dennie, a particularly practiced exponent of the artful smear. "Mr C. Holt, printer and democrat, gives us a fine specimen of the learning of his publican tribe. . . . The illiterate state of a democrat's brain is well understood. We know that of genius they never exhibit a spark, but really supposed that they would not stumble over easy words of three syllables." Dennie could not even resist slipping in a little advertisement into his barrage. "As we are concerned for these people, we wish to take some little pains in their education, and cheerfully recommend certain elementary treatises, such as Mrs. Barbauld's Lessons for Children two years of age." While generally considered the low point of his presidency, Adams's Alien and Sedition Acts were warmly welcomed by many New Hampshire editors, providing ample opportunity for schadenfreude at the expense of political enemies. The *Courier*, perplexed as to what all the fuss was about, deemed it "the mildest law ever made to suppress seditious practises. . . . [W]e hope it will be promptly executed on every occasion." "The *Seditious* are highly alarmed at the *Sedition Bill*," the *Oracle* noted with glee. "Proof of its excellence! Government should be a terror to evil doers." Headlined "A Good Step," the following article did not suggest an abundance of solidarity across a burgeoning community of journalism: "The Editor of the Aurora (B. F. Bache) was yesterday arrested on a warrant from Judge Peters of the Federal Circuit Court, on the charge of libelling the

President and the Executive Government, in a manner tending to excite sedition, and opposition to the laws, by sundry publications and republications."[45] So much for fraternal feelings among tradesmen.

Aside from celebrating the downfall of their foes, editors noted with suspicion the activities of other Federalist scribes.[46] Editors competed with one another to demonstrate being particularly above reproach and in their posturing presented themselves as civic watchdogs, supervising the behavior of other newspapers. "The Editor of the Portsmouth ORACLE, who has hitherto been considered rather Jacobinical," wrote the editor of the *Concord Mirrour*, "proclaimed to the World in a late number, that his paper, for the future, should bear only the '*form* and *pressure* of *Federalism*.' He deserves credit for his conversion, though late. It is high time for all honest men to rally round the Government." Also in the *Mirrour*, Moses Davis wrote, "We are told by a gentleman from Portsmouth that in consequence of MR. PIERCE's declaring that 'he will print a Federal Paper,' seven Persons have withdrawn their names from his list—among them, the *liberal* MR. GARDNER, the *expiring* Senator LANGDON, and his *swearing* Brother."[47] Seditious editors were not the only subjects of condemnation; readers were also potential subjects of suspicion.

When they were not rejoicing in the misfortune of their colleagues, editors were heaping plaudits on Adams and his wisdom in shutting down their competitors and sycophantically demonstrated their own unswerving loyalty to the federal government. The editors of the *Federal Observer* wrote in November 1798 that they pledged "themselves, that nothing immoral, profane or seditious shall ever disgrace their paper, or dishonor its publishers." Lest their meaning be lost on anyone, they added, "Though highly appreciating the Freedom of the Press, and the liberty of discussing with candor and decency, every topic, yet more highly estimating the peace of society and welfare of their country, which under the mask of liberty have been so often violated, they are resolved with the utmost vigilance to discountenance, and to resist every attempt to depreciate morals, to slander religion, or vilify the government. No writings of this cast shall every find a place in the FEDERAL OBSERVER." This need to demonstrate their compliance with the administration and its sedition laws reached a sort of apex when the article concluded that "so far are they from supposing a Printer excusable in venting falsehood, calumny and sedition, merely because he did not invent them, they consider HIS CRIMES as greatly aggravated, and like the Trumpeter in the Fable, who made a similar plea, that he merits a tenfold punishment."[48] Eighteenth-century journalists were men of business first and crusaders for truth and liberty a very distant second.

It was not just the sedition legislation that won the approbation of many New Hampshire natives. Its restrictions involving migration were also warmly welcomed. "Wisdom comes often learnt too late," lamented the *New Hampshire Gazette* of Portsmouth. "It is supposed that there is no less than 100,000 active male *aliens*, in the U. States opposed to the government thereof—including emigrants from France, Ireland, and the West-Indies. . . . We have an *Alien Law*, but *"dead to infliction, to itself is dead."*[49] That immigrant journalists and printers were disproportionately Republican only reinforced the nativist undercurrent in the Federalist reactions to the Alien and Sedition Acts.[50] Another issue on which New Hampshire papers generally sided with the government, and against "a certain class of restless, seditious, disorganising Malcontents,"[51] was that of a proposed land tax, that which became the Federal Property Tax Act, an early example of the long and not always proud history of antitax campaigns in American life.

Old World conspiracies seem to have become a concern of newspaper correspondents only in the late 1790s. Freemasonry was a thorny issue; it was difficult for many to reconcile a natural suspicion regarding secret societies with the affiliation of George Washington and Benjamin Franklin.[52] "I am very sensible that that some of the Masons feel hurt at Barruel's [a critical historian of the Freemason movement] work . . . ," wrote one concerned citizen, "but Barruel does not criminate the common, simple Masonry. His reproaches are against the higher, more dark, or to use his own term, *occult* Lodges, whose practises not only he, but all honest men, *and Masons*, also will join in execrating."[53] The fraternal and civic values of the Masons seemed, to many of their members, to be not only self-evidently good but also essential. As one John Andrews explained, a member belonged "not to one particular place only, but to places without number, and in almost every corner of the globe; to whom, by a kind of universal language, he can make himself known—and from whom we can, if in distress, be sure to receive relief and protection."[54] To the skeptical, however, the avowed universality of the organization had chilling implications of shadowy machinations and secret governments.

For more cosmopolitan paranoids, developments in Europe provided yet greater provocation. "UNDER the name of ILLUMINEES, a separate band of conspirators arose, nearly at the same period, far more dangerous in their tenets, more artful in their plots and more extensive in their plans of devastation," explained an article in the *Museum*. "Of this sect, Adam Weishaupt, formerly Professor of Law at the University of Ingolstadt, was the founder. His character is a monstrous composition of everything odious, of everything depraved, of everything desperate. A remorseless atheist, and a profound hypocrite. . . . Every degree of vice, from the slightest error to the most consummate wickedness, appeared to him, like objects to the eye of the new born infant."[55] From Weishaupt, the author explains, begat Robespierre, and through him the Illuminated Seers of Bavaria became ancestors to the hard-liquor rabble of the American countryside.

Apparently, rural America was teaming with German occultists. "When we reflect on the political divisions, which have, for a long time, violently aggravated our empire; when we observe a numerous class of our citizens unremittingly abusing our wise and faithful rulers; when we see the virulent opposition, that is made to every measure of national defence and security; when we behold the same impious and disorganising principles disseminated here, which are avowed by the Illuminees in Europe," wrote Thomas Day, a college tutor, noted orator, and eminent member of the Williamstown community. "We have irreversible proof, from an authentic source, that the American Lodges are branches of the *Grand Orient of France*; who is so incredulous, who is so stupid, who is so obstinately blind, as not to perceive, that the conspirators of our country are preparing the same scene of devastation and horror for us, which has already bathed the European nations in blood?" The links between foreign cabals and plots at home were a recurrent theme. "Is it not highly probably, that the late insurrection in Pennsylvania, like the Revolution in France, was 'a sportive essay of their strength'? . . . How absolutely necessary, therefore, is it to your peace, to your safety, and, I may add, to your existence, that you be vigilant and active!"[56] Of the sixteen references to Weishaupt and the Illuminati made in the New Hampshire press from 1790 to 1800, all of them were made in 1799 and 1800, which becomes peculiar only when considering that his small organization had been stamped out in 1784. The concept of "Illuminism" was introduced into the American mind by a Scottish author, John Robinson, whose work was subsequently reprinted in New York. From there, the Massachusetts minister Jedidiah Morse took up the theme in his preaching, presenting the cabal as a threat to religious life.[57] Some perceived the malignant influence of shadowy forces in the pages of rival papers. In an *Oracle* article titled "ILLUMINATI and MASONRY," the Reverend Morse was quoted as saying, "The Aurora, the Argus and the Bee and every lying vehicle of slander, is industriously spread over the country, and put into the hands of credulous, ignorant men, to excite disaffection to our government." Paranoia, as is so often the case, took on a self-perpetuating quality. As Gordon Wood has acutely observed, "The conspiratorial interpretations of the age were a generalized application to the world of politics of the pervasive duplicity assumed to exist in all human affairs. Only by positing secret plots and hidden machinations by governments was it possible, it seemed, to close the bewildering gaps between what rulers professed and what t hey brought forth."[58] Many enlightened men of the eighteenth century were inclined to think systematically and mechanically. The primacy they gave to "reason" and "rationality" extended all the way to the divine; a century earlier, Isaac Newton had described God as a "watchmaker," an analogy that suggested a comprehensible and functional universe of measurable cause and effect, overseen by a celestial engineer. Chaos and disorder were perceived as not just undesirable but in some sense unnatural. When the French Revolution, with its classical motifs and quotations from Montesquieu, Voltaire, and Rousseau, descended into a maelstrom from persecution and retribution, it was not possible to accept that man was less a machine of reason than an animal of passion.[59]

"Far from being symptomatic of irrationality, this conspiratorial mode of explanation represented an enlightened stage in Western man's long struggle to comprehend his social reality," Wood argues. "It flowed from the scientific promise of the Enlightenment and represented an effort, perhaps in retrospect a last desperate effort, to hold men personally and morally responsible for their actions."[60] If the American experiment was providentially approved and grounded, then only unseen dark forces could account for any setbacks or reversals it might face.

However anxious the New Hampshire reading public was about Masons, the French, whiskey insurrectionists, seditious printers, atheists, Satanists, and the Illuminati, in 1800 a specter more dismaying than any of these arose: presidential candidate Thomas Jefferson. "Mr. Jefferson, and his party, have long endeavored to destroy our Federal Constitution," declared the *Courier*. "And here," it continued, "I shall remark once, for all, that I consider every effort which has been made, every plan which be been pursued, by the democratic party; as being directly; or indirectly, chargeable to Mr. Jefferson."[61] Indeed, more was at stake than the Constitution. "It is reported, and we wish to obtain correct information as to the fact, that Mr. Jefferson has introduced into his own family or among his dependants, the French Week or Decade. It is very interesting to know whether the United States are to have a man at the head of government, who countenances the abolition of the Christian sabbath."[62] BURLEIGH, a regular contributor to the *Connecticut Courant*, was widely reprinted throughout the state and became the leading polemical critic of Jefferson in New England. Others seemed to toy with the notion of abandoning the republican experiment altogether, should Jefferson emerge victorious. "There is, in the ardent spirit of democracy," wrote the editor of the *Gazette*, "more dangers to be apprehended, and more tyranny to endure, than under the rankest aristocracy that ever existed in the world. America, while increasing in strength and greatness, must increase also the energies of its government."[63] While "democracy" and the American government were by no means synonymous, casting such active doubt on the role of participating citizens betrayed the level of alarm felt by many Federalists.

The election of 1800, therefore, took on a very different timbre than those of 1792 and 1796. The election of 1792 had very little direct effect on the tone of newspaper content; Washington was so assured of reelection as to make even commenting on the fact banal. That of 1796, on the other hand, while more of a contest, saw a massive upturn, the largest in the decade, in positive news coverage (46 percent) and an attendant fall in negative content in both absolute (48 percent) and relative (18 percent) terms. Partisan authors focused on Adam's long career, his experience, and his virtues, as exemplified in the following piece (which was reprinted from the *Boston Columbian Centinel*, Boston's leading Federalist sheet). Writing of Adams, a reprint from the *Columbian Centinel* in the *Courier* insisted that he "was one of the principal leaders of his countrymen at the first dawn of revolution. His deep researchers into the principles of civil liberty, convinced him that the domination which Great Britain claimed over this country, was irrational, unfounded and subversive of the dearest interests of freemen." Articles such as these focused on his positive characteristics and accomplishments. "With undeviating firmness, he urged the claims of America to those prerogatives, without which liberty cannot exist; and seeing the ministry of the mother country, inexorable in their purposes, he endeavored to prepare the minds of the people for the contest which has terminated gloriously."[64] The election of 1796 was not without scuttlebutt and scandal, but the electioneering still consisted, in large part, of focusing on the merits of one's chosen candidate rather than the wickedness of one's enemy.

By 1800, however, things had changed beyond recognition. Most New Hampshire papers gleefully called the election for John Adams. "Nothing can exceed the 'tribulations and anguish' of the Pennsylvania Democrats," cackled the *Courier*. "Tench Coxe writes letters dolorously whimpering and disgustingly prolix, from Lancaster. Duane groans, Lloyd wishes himself again in Newgate; all the *young boys* of democracy, who panted for Jefferson's election, in the hope of obtaining office or preferment, change countenance and are preparing to accommodate themselves, as well as they can; to four more years of Federal *tyranny*." For a period of about two and a half weeks in New Hampshire, the victory of Adams was reported as a fait accompli. On December 6, the *Oracle* had Adams winning by seventy-three to sixty-five electoral college votes, the very figure by which he would lose. Much of the problem came from papers providing predicted outcomes and other papers reporting the estimated numbers as real results. With regard to the electoral mathematics, the misapprehension came from the newspapers' insistence that the Carolinas would be solidly Federalist, when in fact they would turn for Jefferson and Burr. As late as December 15, the *Farmer's Weekly Museum* of Walpole was confidently asserting, "From South-Carolina we continue to receive the most favorable accounts of a full vote there for Mr. Adams." On December 20, under the headline: "GREAT NATIONAL RETURNS: Correct List of Votes for PRESIDENT," the *Oracle* declared, "There cannot now be a doubt of the result of the great election. Mr. Adams and Gen. Pinckney will each have 73 votes. The House of Representatives will choose Mr. Adams President, and Gen. Pinckney will be Vice-President. Messrs Jefferson and Burr will each have 65 votes—unless South-Carolina should prove Jacobinical!" In fact, the exact reverse was true, and New York, which the *Farmer's Weekly* had also trumpeted as a Federalist bastion, would give its entire allotment to Jefferson. It was only by the end of the year that the chilling realization seeped through the state that Jefferson was the victor and president-elect. The *Courier* of Concord was the first paper to correctly declare Jefferson president and did so on December 26 in a late printed supplement sheet attached to the main body of the paper, the usual practice for "breaking news." The *Oracle* followed suit the next day. Readers of Keene's only paper, the *Sentinel*, would have to wait until January 3 for the correct result to be announced.[65] This was better than some got, however, as once Jefferson was understood to be the clear winner, some important papers, most notably the venerable *Gazette* of Portsmouth, failed to publish the election returns altogether. Most editors, having celebrated so exuberantly Jefferson's political demise, printed terse, short retractions (not one apologized) and moved on with their business, which remained the demolition of Thomas Jefferson's reputation and persona.

The election of 1800 was a milestone in American politics, and the ferocity at which it was fought was unprecedented. "The turbulent years between 1788 and 1801 were of tremendous significance in American political history," Newman has noted. "It was during this decade that the first truly national popular political culture began to develop and a national political party system began to take shape."[66] What emerges, however, is that the old style of political newspaper writing, with its toasts to Washington and independence, its reports of happy crowds greeting the chief magistrate, and its obsession with heroism of the Revolutionary War, did not in fact go away. Papers like Russell's *Boston Centinel*, Fenno's *Gazette of the United States* in Philadelphia, and Noah Webster's *New York Commercial Advertiser* (née *Minerva*) continued to produce widely distributed political content of this sort. Two things, however, are notable. First, on the whole, the local papers did not produce a great deal of the positive content themselves; when it appears, it was generally in the form of credited reprints. Second, although the quantity of positive content did not rapidly change (although it did enter into an apparently terminal decline from 1798 onward), it became swamped by a rising cacophony of personal attacks, scaremongering, and critical polemic. This content was generated by a much wider variety of sources. The editor, local reader-correspondents, transcripts of orators and preachers, serialized political treatise, and the big urban papers were all tributaries to the mainstream of partisan disputation.

CHAPTER EIGHT

AMERICAN INTELLIGENCE

The Hinterland Unleashed

Here tumult wild, and rude confusion reign,
And hoodwink'd PARTY heads the senseless train;
Here meets her motley tribe—here holds her COURT,
For pamper'd GLUTTONY, the grand retort.
From orgies to profane—stern FREEDOM flown,
CORRUPTION mounts her abdicated throne
Oh! Unhappy state—thy degenerate tribe,
Like Esau, barter birthright for a bribe.
—*Farmer's Weekly Museum*, May 19, 1800

The 1790s witnessed a dramatic shift in the content and style of political newspaper coverage. Old norms of deference and civility eroded and were replaced by a different set of journalistic values that emphasized partisanship, name-calling, and enmity. Relationships between editors, which had for the most part been professionally cordial and sometimes warmly fraternal, turned into bitter rivalries, not just in competition for readers but over the very idea of America. Some of these enmities were carried out over distances of hundreds of miles, frequently between men who had never met; sometimes, they might not even be aware of the other's real name. For readers, this meant that their newspapers not only were different in terms of content and style but effectively came to serve different purposes as well. At the start of the new republic, most printers fancied themselves public servants. The newspaper was an organ of social harmony, filled with salutary anecdotes from the lives of great men and exhortations to civic virtue. This idealized concept of the newspaper as the "cement" of the Union produced a lot of worthy, and dull, journalism. It was, unsurprisingly, the end of this era of smug complacency that coincided with the boom in print that saw the number of newspapers treble in a decade. If the newspaper of 1790 served, for the most part, as a sort of moral instructor, the same could not be said of its counterpart ten years later. Calumnies, libels, and invective poured forth and were eagerly taken up by a reading public who had been previously starved of such indulgences. "If the stiletto of newspaper slander may pierce, unredressed, the reputation of our first officers," the *Farmer's Weekly Museum* asked, "where shall we find men willing and able to fill the offices of our government?"[1] While the *Museum* might decry this collapse in the social contract, it had in its time delivered as many "stilettos" as any other paper. Few editors were truly able to hold out for long, if indeed they really wanted to; American journalism had simply, in the space of decade, become a crueler cultural space in which to work.

At the start of the decade, 5 percent of all political articles that appeared in the New Hampshire press were positive in tone, 35 percent were neutral, and only 10 percent were negative. The year 1795 was the first that the number of negative articles outweighed the number of positive ones, and from 1797 onward there were consistently more negative stories than positive. In 1800, 65 percent of all news stories in the New Hampshire press consisted of some sort of attack, compared to 27 percent that praised or otherwise made positive arguments for candidates or policies.[2] At the same time that negative newspaper content was replacing positive, the number of news articles that fell into neither category was also in decline. Not only were American receiving fewer favorable editorials and columns, but their newspapers contained fewer largely factual reports, too.

FIGURE 6. POLITCAL STYLE AND CONTENT, NEW HAMPSHIRE, 1790–1800

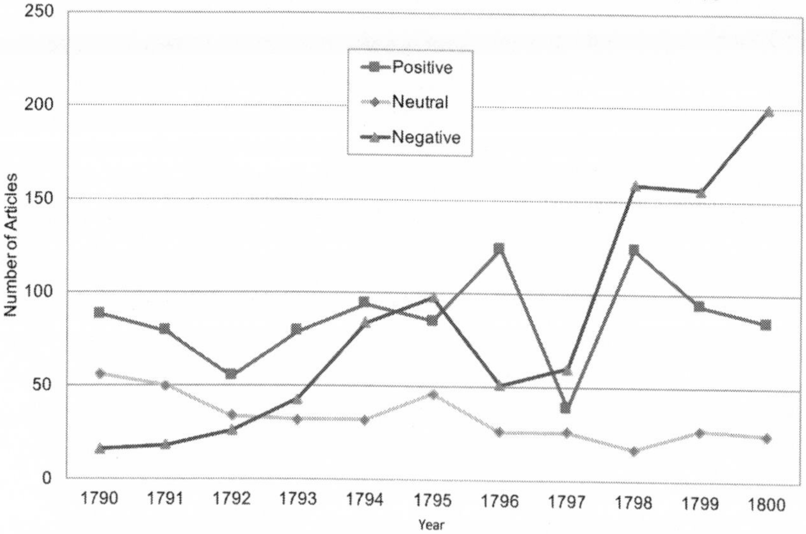

Data compiled from NewsBank.

These trends were borne out in the appearance of certain "keywords" that appeared in newspapers. Positive keywords, such as *celebrated*, *honorable/honourable* (both spellings appeared regularly), *noble*, and *patriotic* appeared with great regularity in political news and editorials at the beginning of the decade. These terms, which often appeared clustered together in articles, were part of a descriptive language of virtue that framed popular understandings of both private character and good governance. "This highest applause is due to him for the large and noble views that animated his conduct," read a eulogy in the *Spy*. "He was a sincere, an ardent and an enlightened friend to civil and religious liberty. The diffusion of civil and religious liberty, in the utmost extent, was the wish and joy of his heart."[3] The use of repetition and redundancy in adulation was a common trait of late-eighteenth-century writing, not just in journalism but also in prose and poetry. Contemporary readers were familiar with not just the words being used but the sonorous cadence that characterized this mode of writing as well.

In 1790, 69 percent of the keywords used in New Hampshire political articles were positive.[4] However, over the course of the decade, while they did not disappear, they ceased to constitute the prevailing idiom of political rhetoric. The affirmative terms that dominated the news in the early Federalist period had, by the end of the Adams presidency, been supplanted by other, more pernicious, adjectives, adverbs, and nouns: *corrupt, corruption, disgrace, disgraceful, evil, infamous, Jacobin, Jacobins, sedition, seditious, traitor,* and *traitorous*.[5] This language too conformed to a codified set of tropes and signifiers instantly recognizable to any frequent newspaper reader. Just as the earlier expressions attempted to evoke a classical sense of republican decorum, these others presented the darker side of the equation. "Will not federal men, as well as anti-federal," asked one attack on Thomas Jefferson, "believe that your ambition, pride and overbearing temper have destined you to be the evil genius of this country."[6] Vainglory and self-aggrandizement were the inverse of the humility and disinterestedness sought in ideal leaders and therefore required little explanation on how they might, or should, disqualify one from office. By 1800 the proportion of articles featuring positive terms had fallen to 37 percent, with the remaining 63 percent being made up of these negative words.[7]

This transition in style excited alarmed comment among those who worried that it boded ill for the future not only of decency and good manners but of the American project itself. In a lengthy treatise printed in the *Oracle of the Day* titled "Liberty of Speech and of the Press," Alexander Addison, a Pennsylvania jurist, questioned whether such a press ought to have a role in the life of a constitutional republic. "One would have thought," he wrote, "that the United States of America, blessed with the best practicable model of republican liberty, which human wisdom hath yet been able to suggest, would have escaped this greatest of all plagues, the corruption of public opinion; and that all men would have united in approbation of a system of government, which must be acknowledged excellent, and an administration, which must be acknowledged to have been wise, enlightened and honest." Addison, who noted that such "plagues" were endemic throughout Europe and afflicted France in particular, despaired of the seeming inevitability of the press as a disruptive force. "Unfortunately, this plague hath reached us also; and our government has been assailed with the grossest slanders, by many who perhaps believed, and by many who surely could not believe, the slanders which they uttered." The infection, he thought, was not just carried by newspapers. "The tongue, the pen, and the press; conversation, letters, essays & pamphlets have represented our truly republican and balanced Constitution as a system of tyranny, and our upright and wise administration, as mischievous and corrupt." This decay of public trust, Addison believed, not only was deleterious to the stability of the nation, but also rendered it vulnerable to foreign attacks and interference. "Without suppressing slander and sedition against the government, the support of public opinion cannot be preserved to it; and without the support of public opinion, all other defence against France is in vain." Measures like the Alien and Sedition Acts were a necessary step to protect Americans both from unsavory foreigners and from those who would ferment insurrection at home. "This law," he wrote of the legislation, "takes from no man liberty but the liberty of doing mischief."[8] Addison's argument was representative of a growing unease, particularly among an older generation of Americans with memories of colonial rule and the dawn of the revolution, that an unruly and unchecked press was not merely distasteful but dangerous. The circulation of Paine's *Common Sense* had helped spur the battle for independence, and *The Federalist Papers* had galvanized support for the Constitution. What else could print, turned loose, accomplish?

For some correspondents, this change in the character of the American newspaper was not merely a temporal political problem. Newspapers were not, these authors tended to argue, simply responsible for informing the public of current affairs. "I am no party-man, but a faithful subject and friend to our Government," wrote someone under the initials "YZ" to the Portsmouth *Oracle*. "I am much secluded from company and conversation, but I cast my eyes sometimes over Newspapers, if perchance I may see what remarkable events are taking place." The shocking rhetoric that YZ encountered was not only a debasement of the nation's civil discourse but an existential threat to its spiritual well-being. "The newspapers teem with this—They are an index of the general taste, and of what is pleasing to the world—They please and they corrupt it—They have lately announced many examples of the dreadful abuse of the word of God, in lay-preachers, toasts and songs." The newspapers were culpable in spreading such blasphemies, even if they did not create them. For correspondents such as these, the newspaper ought not to be simply a window onto a base and profane world but should act as a gatekeeper, letting through what was elevating and shutting out the detritus. Violent rhetoric poisoned the political atmosphere as well as the very fabric of a God-fearing American society. "However true these remarks may hereafter appear, there is little ear for them now," YZ concluded, "I can only convey them to the opening of a canal—There I conclude they will rest with the rubbish, as being too unpopular for publication."[9] Yet the remarks were published and then reprinted in the Concord *Courier*; at least two editors agreed enough to save the article from the rubbish pile.

Printers and editors themselves generally concurred with the alarmists, with one small but vital caveat. While they agreed wholeheartedly that the venomous tirades pouring forth from the presses of the *opposition* were a mortal danger to the Union, and in the interests of public safety and national security would be better off abolished, the violence of their *own* rhetoric was entirely justified and provoked. "Why do we find them using the most irritating and abusive language at this important juncture?" asked the *Portsmouth Price Current*. "If these persons were disposed for peace, it is probable they study such numberless epithets to provoke the resentment and excite the jealousy?" A noble sentiment, perhaps, but somewhat undermined by a later reference to the other side as a "blasphemous banditti" characterized by "outrageous depredations."[10] Such Janus-faced reasoning was not uncommon among editors who would cheerfully call for the ruin, or even imprisonment, of a fellow editor on political grounds but cried foul when aspersions were made against themselves or their allies. Given the contentious atmosphere of the late 1790s, with Democrat-Republicans fearing the Alien and Sedition Acts on one side, and Federalists fearing revolutionary bloodshed on the other, it is little wonder they could be so thin-skinned.

While the national and international dimensions of these print wars were important, no less significant were more localized conflicts between editors. The controversial sedition trial, and imprisonment, of

Matthew Lyon,[11] which received considerable coverage in Vergennes, Vermont, was gleefully taken up by editors across New Hampshire. One piece, which described his arrest in exultant detail, mentioned with perhaps just a tinge of disappointment that "one of his company, as soon as they passed the street of houses, in attempting to huzza for Lyon, the vessel losing its ballast, fell over-board, but though seas-over was not drowned!"[12] This reveling in Lyon's plight was becoming perfectly ordinary by 1799, but the difference between the coverage of this story in the New Hampshire press was based, in large part, on firsthand experience. The vilification of, for example, Benjamin Franklin Bache was based almost entirely on essays and newspapers that were produced in Pennsylvania; the invective against Lyon was homegrown. Even the local clergy were not spared such attacks. "The despicable Jacobin party stop at nothing however false and base to carry their point, and clog the wheels of government," began a letter to the editor of the *Oracle* from a correspondent in York County.[13] "It is not almost incredible that Parson Webster should suffer himself to become a tool to such a scandalous junto—that a leader in religion should thus stoop to lend his aid in support of that horrid combination against religion and government."[14] These were not articles written about remote figures, but were produced by correspondents and editors with personal knowledge of their subjects.

This phenomenon, of an increasing quantity of negative news and opinion coming from New Hampshire newspapers, was not limited to the cases of Matthew Lyon or the Reverend Webster. In an article under the headline "The Reign of Terror!" the *Oracle* of Portsmouth reprinted a story from the Concord *Courier* that inveighed against events closer to home. "The success of the anti-federal candidate for Congress in Boston," the article began, using the outdated and insulting term for an opponent of the Constitution to describe a Democrat-Republican, "had encouraged the sanguinary Jacobins to propose hanging in Effigy those who voted for the Federal candidate, Mr Quincy, a man of unblemished political character." This piece, written and published across New Hampshire about events over the border in Massachusetts, reflected a growing pool of local journalism. "This is their pure republicanism," the article concluded, "this is the Liberty which the leaders of our pretended Republicans wish form, and this is the sort of government which we shall soon have, if the people elect French politicians to take charge of our public concerns!!!!!"[15] Pieces such as these tended to deal with political events either within New Hampshire or nearby. Another took aim at those who sought to discredit the governor of the state, John Taylor Gilman, and was submitted to the editor of the paper by a local reader who signed themselves "DETECTOR." The author took particular issue with the appropriation of simple and trustworthy pseudonyms by such individuals when he wrote, "The hackneyed nicknames of Anti-federalist, Democrat, Disorganiser, Jacobin, etc., do not answer their purpose—Among the motley variety of scribblers none seem more agitated than An Old Farm—as he falsely styles himself in the Oracle of Saturday last."[16] It was not only the editors of newspapers that were going to war with one another but readers, too.

Two trends in American journalism were, therefore, running parallel to one another. First, during the 1790s, newspapers were drawing on an ever-greater diversity of sources of news, particularly from rural and small-town newspapers and local reader-correspondents. Second, there was a simultaneous shift in both language and subject matter toward a harsher, more vindictive style of political newspaper content. These two phenomena were not unrelated to one another.

In 1790, 148 political news and opinion articles featuring the "positive" keywords discussed earlier in this chapter appeared in the New Hampshire press, as compared to just 68 articles with "negative" keywords. The sources for these keywords, however, were not evenly distributed. Of the 148 positive articles, 58 came from newspapers in the cities of Philadelphia, Boston, and New York, 39 percent of the total. Of the negative articles, however, only 17 came from these three large cities, a quarter of the overall number. Throughout the decade, with the exception of the year 1797 (the year, not coincidentally, of John Adams's inauguration), the big-city newspapers continued to contribute a higher proportion of positive news than negative to the New Hampshire press. In 1800 positive and negative articles came to 205 and 345, respectively, totaling 550. Of the positive articles 75, or 37 percent, came from America's three largest cities, while only 83 negative articles, or 24 percent, came from those places. The newspapers of Philadelphia, Boston, and New York City, many of which were daily publications with many thousands of subscribers, produced a disproportionate amount of praise and positive keywords.

One explanation for this is that the big-city papers had the closest ties to national politicians. While they, like all newspapers, increasingly resorted to ad hominem diatribes, the ones most closely connected to significant figures in the administration, particularly during the Washington years, tended to not only produce more content favorable to their patron but also exercise slightly more restraint in the sorts of criticisms they dished out. Given how widely known the connections between politicians and the newspapers they affiliated themselves with could be, editors had to tread more carefully, lest they tarnish the reputation of their powerful supporters. The personal relationships that existed between big-city editors and prominent individuals were also a natural brake on the very worst of the bile, and the gentlemen's accord lasted the longest among the large daily newspapers. Newspapers in Philadelphia, Boston, and New York published plenty of unpleasant material, but they were also under greater pressure to create types of content that exalted as well as execrated.

In the latter part of the decade, the matter of who could and couldn't criticize the administration was complicated by the introduction of the Sedition Act of 1798. American libel and sedition laws were formed, as were many judicial matters, in the context of the broader Anglo-American legal sphere. In both America and England in the eighteenth century, attitudes toward writing and speech made in opposition to the government were beginning to change. As Emerson writes, "The First Amendment was drawn up and ratified during this period of transition. Whether the framers intended to abolish outright the English law of seditious libel is a matter of historical dispute. Certainly the First Amendment was adopted by men who had just achieved a successful revolution against autocratic power, who were attempting to establish a popular form of government, and who were aware of the uses to which the law of seditious libel could be put. . . . Whatever ambiguity there may have been about the meaning of the First Amendment at the time of adoption, the passage of the Alien and Sedition Acts of 1798 brought the matter to a head."[17] The most pertinent section of the law for printers and editors was the second:

> That if any person shall write, print, utter or publish, or shall cause or procure to be written, printed, uttered or published, or shall knowingly and willingly assist or aid in writing, printing, uttering or publishing any false, scandalous and malicious writing or writings against the government of the United States, or either house of the Congress of the United States, or the President of the United States, with intent to defame the said government, or either house of the said Congress, or the said President, or to bring them, or either of them, into contempt or disrepute; or to excite against them, or either or any of them, the hatred of the good people of the United States, or to stir up sedition within the United States.[18]

The act produced more than twenty-five arrests, and fifteen indictments, including four prominent Democrat-Republican editors. While a challenge to the law never made it all the way to the Supreme Court, it was met with general affirmation in the lower courts; the opposition to it was more political than judicial, as it was a target of Jefferson and Madison's Kentucky and Virginia Resolutions. Ultimately, the fate of the law was tied to that of the Adams administration, and the newly elected Thomas Jefferson allowed it to lapse in 1801.[19]

The debates surrounding the passage of the legislation, and furor around its implementation, provided Americans with the first substantial opportunity to publicly debate the role of the free press in America. "The story of the storm over the First Amendment brought by the Sedition Act," writes Wendell Bird, "is a story of a struggle about a narrow or a broad First Amendment."[20] The Sedition Act was something of a Rorschach test for contemporaries and remains so for contemporary scholars. For its critics, it represented the grossest betrayal of the principles of free expression, as they had been enshrined in the First Amendment to the U.S. Constitution. However, for others, the act was not quite such a radical break. They reject the notion that "the First Amendment was designed to abolish the English common law of seditious libel" and that in fact the authors of the Constitution expected courts to continue to enforce common law where it wasn't explicitly superseded by the Constitution. Rather than a repudiation of the Bill of Rights, the act's defenders considered it "merely declaratory" of existing law and custom. Its only innovation was, they contended, a progressive one: it transferred the final deliberation in sedition cases from the judge to the jury. No less a libertarian hero than Thomas Jefferson would later urge "a few prosecutions" of libelous printers.[21]

The reason for the Sedition Act's infamy is perhaps not, Elkins and McKitrick argue, due to the law itself, but owing to the ineptitude with which it was enforced. It is possible that if the law had not seemed quite so blatant and blunt a political cudgel of the Federalist Party, then it might not have attracted quite the same level of vitriol. In the bungling of the prosecutions of individuals such as Matthew Lyon, the populist printer and politician from Vermont, they turned a divisive and relatively obscure figure into a national symbol of free speech suppressed. According to Paul Starr, the Sedition Act ultimately failed because "the traditional basis of a free press lay not in courts, but in politics and in the fragmented and decentralised structure of American institutions. Americans had accepted a journalism that was often scurrilous in its criticism of government and politicians. Controlling the press from the federal level was difficult, while it was relatively easy to start new publications."[22]

If the big-city newspapers were producing more than their share of positive political journalism, then other parts of the country had to be producing the negative coverage at greater rates. The New Hampshire newspapers themselves, even from the golden age of journalistic civility that was the first Washington administration, were more likely to produce negative coverage than their big-city counterparts. In 1790, 43 percent of the political articles featuring positive keywords were produced by editors or correspondents within the state, while 50 percent of the negative stories were homegrown. In 1800, 30 percent of the positive stories had a New Hampshire provenance, as compared to 37 percent of the negative ones. Even within the state, the number of sources was multiplying. In addition to newspaper towns like Portsmouth, Concord, and Dover, letters and reports from smaller communities like Boscawen, Gilmanton, Salisbury, and Sandbornton started to appear with growing regularity toward the end of the decade. Places such as these, which has been practically invisible in the media, became minor sources of news in the late 1790s. "We are greatly obliged to Mr Oliver Davis, merchant of Boscawen," one story began in the *Concord Mirrour*; David had passed on various tidbits to the editor, including the movements of General Pinckney and the outbreak of a fever in Boston.[23] A "Farmer" Gilmanton started writing under the heading of his own "Rural Museum," decrying "speculators" and "money-changers."[24] Benjamin Whittemore, a correspondent from Salisbury, New Hampshire, wrote a detailed account of a scandal involving a local parson's political interference; New Hampshire parsons, it would seem, could scarcely refrain from meddling in local elections.[25] It was not just that New Hampshire editors were creating and distributing more negative political content than their counterparts in Boston or Philadelphia, but that they were receiving it from increasingly wide networks of contributors.

However, New Hampshire editors did not only have big-city newspapers and their own readers on which to draw. They had access to publications from across the United States, and the availability of these other newspapers increased as time went on. In 1794 political news stories that originated in twenty-seven different towns and cities in the United States appeared in the pages of New Hampshire newspapers.[26] By 1799 political news from sixty-four different communities, dispersed across the country, made its way into the New Hampshire press.[27] By the end of the Adams administration, political dispatches from New Orleans (still, at that time, part of the Louisiana Territory) had appeared in New Hampshire newspapers, as had stories from Wheeling, West Virginia, and Cincinnati in what was soon to become the state of Ohio. These articles generally dealt with frontier politics. Articles from the "legislature of the Territory of the North West of the Ohio" started to appear with some regularity in various New Hampshire newspapers from the late 1790s onward.[28] "How crowded are the newspapers of the present day," began a piece in the *Political and Sentimental Repository*, reprinted from the *Newark Gazette*, 'With accounts from the westward."[29] In the 1790s, newspapers outside of New Hampshire and the "big three" newspaper cities were the source of 18 percent of the state's positively worded news but 26 percent of its negative stories, a trend that continued throughout the decade. Put simply, editorials or commentaries that came from the newspapers of Boston, Philadelphia, and New York City were more likely to be celebratory or hagiographic than those that came from within New Hampshire itself or from other small or midsize towns around the country.[30]

In addition to relatively remote places like New Orleans and Ohio, new communities from existing states were also producing news that was finding its way into the New Hampshire press. The aptly named Newtown (now Elmira) of New York State, incorporated in only 1792, first had an attributed political article published in New Hampshire seven years later, in 1799. The most notable developments in news sources took place closer to home, in New England and the mid-Atlantic states. Hartford's *Connecticut Courant*, with its popular columns "The Moralist," "Memoirs of Jacobinism," and, especially, "To

FIGURE 7. SOURCES OF POSITIVE DOMESTIC NEWS TERMS, AS PERCENTAGES

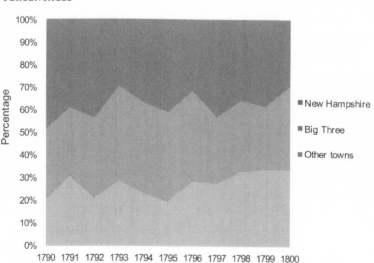

Data compiled from NewsBank.

FIGURE 8. SOURCES OF NEGATIVE DOMESTIC NEWS TERMS, AS
PERCENTAGES

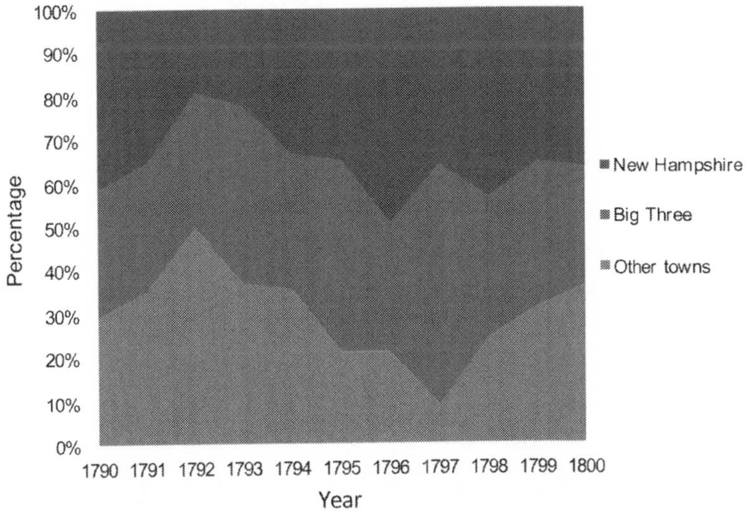

Data compiled from NewsBank.

the People of the United States," was serialized over most of the New
Hampshire press. As with the sources of foreign news, beneath Hartford there was a network of midsize to large towns that each supplied
significant amounts of news. Providence, Rhode Island; Newburyport,
Massachusetts; and Portland, Maine, were all examples of this type.
Where domestic news distribution differed from foreign in this sphere,
however, was in the growing variety of minor contributors, small towns
from across the region that each provided one or two stories per year.
Windsor, Vermont; Danbury, Connecticut; Byfield, Massachusetts;
and Vassalboro, Maine, all began cropping up on an occasional basis.
As these places became a part of the news cycle, the networks of news
were growing not just in thousands of square miles, to places like New
Orleans and Nova Scotia, but in depth of penetration, too. Not only
were such farm communities recipients of political journalism, but they
were beginning to have their stories and controversies heard in the wider
world as well. And those voices were, for better or worse, of a coarser
timbre than those of urban editors and correspondents. Even within the

small and medium-size towns that produced news in the 1790s, there was a clear stratification that reflected the differences between the types of content places produced. The contribution of the "other towns" to the "positive" category was quite heavily concentrated in a number of key secondary towns: Hartford, Connecticut; Salem, Massachusetts; and the like. The negative category, however, while still containing significant contributions from these larger towns, consisted of a wide assortment of smaller communities.

What becomes clear from looking at both the above data and the text of the newspapers is that the authorial voice of editors developed throughout the 1790s. While they continued in their existing role as curators of second- and third-party content, the persona and opinions of the editor became increasingly important components of the newspaper, and the content they created, particularly when it was political, became more distinctive and more important. The small-town newspaper remained a patchwork quilt, pieced together from found parts of variable quality and sometimes clashing hue, but in some newspapers change was afoot. Some journalists, correspondents, and editors achieved notice in the wider community, and not just those based in the big city. Joseph Dennie failed when he founded his literary magazine the *Tablet* in Boston.[31] It was only when he took over the *Farmer's Weekly Museum* that he became a nationally known figure. The increasingly familiar terms that editors would adopt as time passed can be seen in this piece of Dennie's, published in 1799, offering a rare insight behind the scenes of newspaper production and composition: "Amid the numberless curiosities, and interesting groups of Europe, it might be readily supposed, even by the vainest writer, that a weekly sheet from an American *village* would hardly fix a momentary attention. To be assured, and in a manner most flattering, that the 'Museum' was examined with interest in the *elder* world, is a strong incentive to exertion."[32] This promise of "new articles" was not frequently made, but in fact readers of small-town newspapers like the *Museum* were receiving much more original content than they had just ten years earlier. Whether this came in the form of editorials or reader correspondence, the result was that while international news became more universally available, knowledge of local events and controversies became more pervasive than ever before.

Likewise, the politics and literary styles of the various New Hampshire editors were of equal or greater importance to their local readers than the grandees of American daily journalism. It is difficult to know whether the news consumers of New Hampshire abhorred the parochial fare generated in their home state, or put greater stock by, and whether they formed their opinions on the *Boston Gazette*, the *New York Daily-Advertiser*, and the *Pennsylvania Packet*. Or, just as possibly, they detested the pretensions and superiority of big-city editors, with their famous friends and unknown interests, and instead relied for knowledge on members of their own communities, with whom they often had social and commercial relations. Sometimes newspaper correspondents demonstrated a remarkable degree of familiarity with their printer. "To infants at the breast the inoculation has proved peculiarly successful, for I have now had a very considerable of private patients of this description," wrote a Dr. William Woodville to the *New Hampshire Gazette*. "In none of whom was the inoculation attended with and pustules, and even very rarely with any perceptible disorder of the constitution," he added, "an instance of this kind, Mr Editor, you had in your own family."[33] Such intimacy doubtless played a role in developing not just trust in journalism, but bonds of friendship, too.

Print did not hold a monopoly on news communication. A host of other means informed and shaped political views: conversation, both at home and in public places, such as taverns and general stores; personal correspondence; town criers; ministers; popular entertainers; and other public speakers. Speech and print, however, were not separate. The argot of late-eighteenth-century print media was, in rhythm and composition, a text that was meant to be spoken. Susan J. Douglas points out that the ways in which news media were experienced and passed on from person to person played a pivotal role in this process. "Different media," she writes, "favor different senses and cognitive, emotional engagements." The intersection between the published word and the oratory, debate, and dispute of the village forum is plain to anybody who opens a Federalist-era newspaper. "Newspapers," Simon Newman has observed, "played a vital role in the transformation of the rites and symbols of festive culture into part of the currency of political exchange." The rhetoric of newspaper journalism was drawn directly and indirectly from what was being said in the town square and drinking house, and those conversations were, in turn, shaped by the reading material at hand. As Newman states, "Political festivals and celebrations from all over the nation were continually created and re-created in the newspapers of cities, towns and rural hamlets alike. Therefore, a succession of essentially non-literary political activities assumed a textual existence in the early national press, creating a nexus of old and new, urban and rural, and northern and southern forms of politics. A national popular political culture was created simultaneously on the streets in the actions of ordinary Americans, and on the pages of the newspapers that reported them."[34] The boundaries between an oral and written culture were permeable.

Not only did newspapers draw on toasts and public addresses for content, but the newspaper often provided information and inspiration for such performances. "At Schraalenburg, the students of Divinity and of Physic, toasted, among other things, Thomas Jefferson and the Aurora . . . ," noted the *Oracle*, referring to the Democratic-Republican newspaper of Philadelphia, "a newspaper devoted to the cause of the infidel in France, and issuing from the same press with Paine's Age of Reason, and many of the anti-Christian writings of the present day." The permeable line between what people read and what people said meant that the political tone and content of newspapers both drew on wider ranges of sources than those who directly contributed to them and reached a greater and more diverse audience than subscription numbers might suggest. "Without newspapers," the *New Hampshire Gazetteer* opined, "our coffee-houses, and barber's shops, would undergo a change next to a depopulation; and our country villagers, the curate, the excise-man, and the blacksmith, would lose the self-satisfaction of being as wise as WP."[35] The newspapers gave the blacksmith and the barber, and indeed anyone with little connection to power, the raw materials necessary to participate in political discourse.

American politics changed dramatically over the course of the 1790s, and part of the explanation has to be found in the history of its jour-nalism. Of course, the relationship between politics and journalistic discourse can be, as it was then, a vicious cycle: politicians used inflam-matory rhetoric, which became a part of the journalistic vernacular, which incited divisions, which then fed back into the nation's politics. Editors, politicians, and the public were all participants in that process. When explaining why journalism changed, the whole milieu needs to be accounted for. No moving part in the sprawling and complex appa-ratus of American news was independent of any other. Influence was not the sole province of the daily newspapers in America's biggest urban centers. They played a large part, but outside their immediate sphere of influence their voices and narratives were among many, competing for column inches and readers' attention. People on the fringes of society and public debate, geographically, culturally, and socially, spoke loudly, and often angrily, in the national debate. To an increasingly great extent in Federalist-era America, the local was the national. The affairs and distinctive political problems of the Eastern Seaboard, and to a growing extent the frontier, were finding their way into the pages of New Hamp-shire newspapers with ever-greater regularity. It is one thing to talk of a national community and to mean the debates between Jeffersonians and Hamiltonians, the XYZ Affair, or the death of Washington. It is quite another to mean college students in Hanover, dry-goods merchants in Portsmouth, and farms in Walpole reading about corruption in the New Jersey state senate; a flood in Winchester, Virginia;[36] or the district court in Woodfield County, Kentucky.[37] This did not, as subsequent events would surely prove, make America a unified or even coherent national entity, but it did its part in making it what it is.

"FROM THE EDITOR"

The Evolution of the Early American Newspaper

A newspaper, whose magnitude is so much superior, and where the chief of its contents are not sanctioned by royal or official authority, is obliged to become the receptacle of invention. It is made a museum of *we hear—they write—it is said—a correspondent remarks*—with a long list of *ifs* and *supposes*—that at once serve to please, amuse, divert and inform; and yet the evils of PAN-DORA'S BOX do no operate more extensively—than these paragraphs do over the face of the earth. *We hear*, can alter a man's face as the weather would a barometer & *It is said* can distort the features like an electrical shock. *If* can make a man cry; and *suppose*, on the contrary, provoke a fit of laughter. Thus do they operate, like physicians, according to the constitutions, tempers, and principles of the patients.

—*New Hampshire Gazetteer*, October 28, 1791

To the naked eye, the American newspaper was a similar artifact in 1800 to what it had been for most of the proceeding century. There were a lot more of them, to be sure; in terms of their physical dimensions, print quality, and aesthetic design, though, no great leap forward had occurred. Nor did a revolution take place in the technology that governed their manufacture or distribution. The same cumbersome equipment, wrought of iron and wood, was employed. Inks, mainly imported from England, were still often made of traditional ingredients such as lampblack and linseed oil and varied wildly in quality.[1] Paper manufacturing, which in New Hampshire began in Exeter in 1778, still relied on the use of rags and methods that dated back to the Middle Ages.[2] The methods by which newspapers reached readers had not changed overly much, either. While the number of American newspapers traveling on stagecoaches along roads did increase, the majority were still delivered by men on horseback, much as they had done in colonial America and in England beforehand. Roads benefited from incremental improvements, but most Americans, particularly in rural areas, still made do with rough-hewn tracks and improvised pathways.

No great mechanical or material innovation took place to compare to the transformative impact on communications that the railroad and telegram had on nineteenth-century America or that the introduction of ever more sophisticated systems of rotary printing had on the publishing industry. The eighteenth century was an age of scientific experiment and discovery, but in the things that mattered to the dissemination of information, transportation, and printing, the practicalities of 1800 resembled far more closely those of 1700 than they would 1900. The peak velocity of news remained the gallop of the horse or the speed of a wind-powered sailing vessel. The fundamental limitations of human beings in the physical world, some of which had remained basically unchanged since antiquity, held fast. Even the most fervent believer in enlightenment and human progress could not anticipate the ways in which those barriers would collapse, repeatedly, over the next two centuries. The exponential character of modern alacrity had not yet taken hold.

Yet a transformation was under way, one that could be entirely explained neither by invention nor by demographics. The American population grew from 3,918,000 in 1790 to 5,236,000 in 1800, a substantial growth but one insufficient to explain the trebling in newspaper publishing that took place in the same period. New Hampshire was a microcosm of this trend. The state's population grew from 141,885 to 183,858 from 1790 to 1800, in which time it went from six newspapers publishing 10,552 articles to ten newspapers containing 23,942 pieces.[3] This proliferation did not escape the notice of printers and editors. "It appears by the debates in Congress," ran one short note in the *New Hampshire Gazetteer*, "that the amount of all the Newspapers, circulated from the different Presses of the United States has been nearly Four Millions a year for the two last years. The number of these periodical publications is about eighty five, some of which are printed daily, some thrice, some twice, and some once in a week." Newspapermen, aware of their role in this cultural transformation, were not oblivious to its possibilities. "About the year 1718," wrote one, "when the brother of Dr Franklin was about to establish a newspaper in Boston, his friends endeavored to dissuade him from the undertaking, alleging, that there was one newspaper already in that town, and that one was sufficient for America." After describing the ongoing explosion in the numbers of newspapers being established, as well as the numbers of copies being printed, the editor noted that "we cannot but form high expectations of the improvement in virtue and science which will be discussed amongst the people through these channels of intelligence." This article was written in 1790, before the true boom in newsprint had really begun. By the end of the decade, although the quantity of publications had multiplied, not everyone was so buoyant about the ramifications. "That newspapers enlighten and instruct society," wrote the "Hermit" to the *Farmer's Weekly Museum* in 1800, "is a fact indubitable, and their circulation, when they have a tendency to promote the public good, merits encouragement; but when they become the vehicles of falsehood, slander and false rumours, the strong arm of government should crush their existence."[4] Despite the Hermit's misgivings, the culture of American print had changed.

Nor could the acceleration in the speed of news be explained by any single development. News from Boston took twelve days to appear in the Concord newspapers in 1790 and six days in 1800. Printers and editors did not often notice or comment on this change, as people tend not to with large but diffused developments going on around them. The quiet revolution in communications was brought about by a confluence of different events. The establishment of the Post Office Department helped speed up the long-distance transmission of letters and news-papers, and increasingly intricate and penetrative networks for private post riders and stagecoaches got the mails into the hands of editors and readers. Broader developments also sped up the transmission of news. The long unfolding of the eighteenth-century "market revolution," which turned America into what T. H. Breen has called a "consumer society," quickened the movement not only of goods but of informa-tion as well.[5] The influx of manufactured goods into American homes required not only the aforementioned improvements to transportation infrastructure, but also a print culture in which these goods could be marketed and sold. The proliferation of booksellers (many of whom were also involved in the newspaper trade) grew in symbiosis with the press.[6] By 1800 paid advertisements in New Hampshire's newspapers portrayed a vibrant commercial society. Transportation links, set up by private enterprise, sprang up across the state, not only linking towns and cities but also splintering off into rural communities and backwoods. Business owners in neighboring states hawked their wares aggressively to New Hampshire consumers, and the vistas of possibility for rural shoppers opened ever wider. It would be an exaggeration to suggest that New Englanders were, by 1800, traveling extensively, but the markets that the newspapers served grew apace, in both population and square miles, during the Federalist period. And, of course, the very newspapers that carried these blandishments were consumer products themselves and provided their own form of circulating currency. Many Americans, including many white men, were still without the franchise; they could, however, express a political preference through their consumption, not least in their choice of newspaper.

While life in 1800 might not seem quite so frenetic from a twenty-first-century remove, the new pace of things raised some interesting questions. What difference did it make to a cooper in Merrimack County whether he knew the outcome of a battle in Hungary seven weeks after the fact or nine? Did a doctor in Exeter suffer for waiting three weeks to read of a fire in Charleston? "If we read of one man robbed, or murdered, or killed by accident, or one house burned, or one vessel wrecked, or one steamboat blown up, or one cow run over on the Western Railroad, or one mad dog killed, or one lot of grasshoppers in the winter," Henry David Thoreau would insist a half century later, "we never need read of another. One is enough. If you are acquainted with the principle, what do you care for a myriad instances and applications?"[7] Thoreau's exasperation was not, of course, representative. Human beings have been, throughout recorded history, insatiable devourers of what he derisively termed "gossip" and take no less of an interest in murder or catastrophe now than they ever have. This function is what some scholars of journalism have dubbed the "monitorial" role, by which the press fulfills the elementary societal need for information.[8] Yet the question of *time* remains. Did the acceleration of media diffusion described in this book have meaningful consequences in the lives of most Americans?

News can have almost a narcotic quality, and people in late-eighteenth-century America were not immune to its allure. In conversation, in correspondence, in their reading matter, they demonstrated a hunger for the latest intelligence. Living on what they thought to be the edge of the world instilled only a greater need for up-to-date information. Not only did they want to know what was happening both at home and abroad, but they especially prized the most up-to-date reports and rumors. In an environment of uncertainty, with different accounts traveling at different speeds, people sought out the most recent story. "Several articles in the London papers of the latest dates," one article began, "mention the rupture in the American negotiation at Paris, and of the preparations making by the Envoys to return; but we have before us a letter from a very respectable gentleman, which fully contradict the London statements."[9] Immediacy was of the essence. In the abstract the time lag between an event and its reaching newspaper readers made little practical difference; for the news-consuming public, however, learning of an occurrence sooner heightened both their sense of connection and their emotional reaction to it. News, to achieve maximal impact, must be, at least comparatively, new.

Speed was not merely a matter of how quickly people received the news; it also determined the extent that they could participate in it. The newspapers were not simply inert vectors of information. Their distribution, and dependence on participatory readership, created vital cultural networks. Around the town of Concord, thanks to developments in short- and medium-range transportation, and to informational infrastructure in the form of post riders and stagecoaches, the "public sphere" of that town extended out into the surrounding countryside. Residents of communities like Charlestown, Dunstable, Marlborough, and Hampton Falls were taking out advertisements and entering political correspondence in the Concord papers. One can draw a semicircle, with Concord at its fulcrum, about ninety-five miles in diameter that sweeps from the Atlantic Ocean, down into Massachusetts, and across to the Connecticut River and the Vermont border. This area does not simply describe where the subscribers to the Concord papers lived; it contained the people who participated in their creation. News from Philadelphia, London, and Paris was eagerly appropriated, but so were the opinions of a man living on the southern shore of Lake Winnipesaukee, not to mention the citizens of communities that no longer even exist, in what is now the White Mountain National Forest.

Just as the post rider delivered the weekly paper to readers, they handed him in return a half-remembered joke, or a toast given at a recent celebration, or a treatise on constitutional government. These scraps and fragments, political and otherwise, found their way over the subsequent weeks to the offices of the newspapers. Many journeys terminated there, but some did not. A printer-editor, looking to fill a remaining half page, would insert what took his interest or what best fitted the space. Of course, even when an editor was simply reprinting stories, they had a degree of discrimination in what they chose to publish. In some cases, this winnowing process might have been explicitly political, and stories may have been discarded for partisan or ideological reasons. More prosaically, stories might have been passed over for stylistic reasons, or for being reminiscent of something else in that week's issue, or for the most elementary reason of simply not being of sufficient interest to the reading public. The choices of the "gatekeeper" were, Michael Schudson has written, a function of individual subjectivity and also reflected a broader "bureaucratic phenomenon," by which a variety of imperatives determined what did and did not see print.[10]

If newspapers served a "monitorial" function, acting as a record of events, then they also fulfilled what academics of the media call the "facilitative role."[11] A few hundred copies of that paper would then be run off, and a few weeks after the words left the pen of their author, they would be sent out to subscribers. Here again, many more stories reached their terminus. A handful of these papers, however, would end up in the hands of printers in other towns, perhaps even in other states. When composing newspapers, some whim or expediency might cause them to include a portion of that paper in their own, and sometimes it would be that penned by the original correspondent. His words, perhaps dashed off in a flushed moment of passion after hearing a rousing sermon, or downing a glass of whiskey before turning in for the night, would eventually be seen by readers across the Union. He would most likely never know he had touched so many lives, and he would likely receive no financial reward for his effort. But his thread was woven into the sprawling and ragged fabric of American political culture. His individual contribution was, indubitably, not as significant as that of Benjamin Franklin Bache or William Cobbett. The truly salient fact, however, is that this simple narrative took place many times, in many places, with many different individuals. Historians have a detailed and nuanced understanding of the savvy operators of the major urban presses, with their transatlantic contacts and intricate political connections. The people whom the expanding communications network encompassed were less sophisticated in their manipulation of the media, but this in itself seems to recommend them as sources of an early national ideology. The growth of a culture is a process that is sedimentary rather than volcanic. It accumulates imperceptibly, in uncountable tiny accretions.

What the case of New Hampshire demonstrates is the manifold intersections of local life with regional, national, and transnational affairs. The state was at once a part of the Atlantic world, but also a place of dispersed settlements scattered amid imposing wilderness. It was neither an "island community" nor a model of early modern cosmopolitanism. The culture and politics of the state were shaped by Boston and broader New England, but the hinterlands were not in passive thrall to the metropole, in terms of either information or opinion. New Hampshire was possessed of a peculiar and sometimes rabid strain of politics, but Boston and places like it were influenced in turn by the writings and thoughts of their cousins to the west.

These contrasts took place in microcosm within the state. Towns like Portsmouth and Exeter looked to the east; as coastal and inlet towns that relied on trade, wharves, and merchants from Europe and the Caribbean, they also shared a common currency of language and culture with these far-flung partners. The New Hampshire media of the Federalist era reveals two overlapping cultures. The first, facing the Atlantic, was preoccupied with global commerce and the Old World of William Pitt, Edmund Burke, and Maximilien Robespierre. The second New Hampshire was an agricultural society, not unconcerned with the wider world and national politics but viewing those broader events through the lens of the local. The newspapers of those communities portray an existence that was conducted through small-scale trade, churches, and the institutions of village life, be they the new schoolhouse or the old tavern. These two worlds were not segregated. They intersected, not only geographically but also socially, and influenced each other in myriad ways. This interaction can be observed in the state's newspapers. The press of Portsmouth provided the rest of the state with thousands of news items, advertisements, and other content over the course of the period, but it also drew on the towns and villages of the interior. In turn, the fragments of oral culture from the countryside that surface are laced with references to France, Haiti, and the Barbary Coast. What the case of New Hampshire demonstrates is that an exclusive focus on either macroscale transatlantic communication networks or parish notices and county fairs is an inadequate way of approaching both newspaper studies and political culture. A synthesis of the two is necessary because American culture was itself being synthesized from an array of sources from the parochial to the global and back again.

The consequences of this leveling reverberated through American society. The circulation of these cultural artifacts contributed to some sense among Americans of a common set of rites and political vocabulary. As Waldstreicher puts it, "American nationalism emerged from the conjunction of local celebrations and their reproduction in the press." His conception of a "reciprocal dynamic of celebrations and print" in fact applies to a variety of newspaper content: ranging from the commercial to the religious. In the New Hampshire press, the substance of this nascent nationalism was passed from hand to hand in a growing network of communities and eventually throughout the whole republic. Common stores of information and political intelligence were gathered by printers from a huge array of sources, dispersed in strata of both location and status. What Michael Durey has written in reference to the Democrat-Republicans applies to both sides in this case. "Their propagandising," he asserts, "was effective in vulgarizing Republican discourse, making it more suitable for a society that was becoming increasingly politicized and in which popular participation in politics was coming to be taken for granted. They therefore continued [Thomas] Paine's role of demystifying political principles and offering them to the masses."[12] This tendency extended across American journalism and political culture in the Federalist period. The New Hampshire papers, in the late 1790s, staged a conflict (as did the papers of many states) between the competing philosophies that were shaping the young nation.

As the politics of the early United States were coalescing around new competing factions and ideologies, newspapers became active conduits of the struggle. The Federalist press in New Hampshire began the decade producing patriotic poems, eulogies to the great and the good of the founding generation, and genteelly encouraging those fortunate enough to have the vote to back their honest incumbent senator or representative. By the decade's end, this cool urbanity had been largely, though not wholly, replaced by panicked exposés of immorality and corruption across society, blatant character assassinations (sometimes of the very men celebrated a half-dozen years earlier), and even attacks on fellow editors and printers. Some of this change, of course, came from the top. The uneasy truces that held together the ruling elite during the first Washington administration were, from their very inception, living on borrowed time. By the Adams administration, and particularly after the divisions caused by both the XYZ Affair and the Alien and Sedition Acts, the fragile consensus had fractured altogether. The combined forces of personal enmities between national figures, and irreconcilable ideological differences, laid waste to utopian dreams of a republic led by a class of amicable gentleman. The wars in Europe, the meaning of the French Revolution, differing visions about the financial and economic role of the state, and a suspicion of centralized banking and speculation all contributed to the schism. And, of course, looming above all else, delayed but inevitable, was the apparently insoluble question of slavery. The newspapers reflected these problems.

They did more than simply reflect, however. In providing a platform for a dizzying array of opinions and perspectives, the fault lines that lay just below the surface of American politics became impossible to ignore. Some men, like the acerbic Joseph Dennie, built careers on the acidity of their pens and in courting provocation. A newly emerging generation of editors and journalists, distinct from the artisanal printers who preceded them, put their time and educations into sculpting authorial identities that championed, with increasing degrees of vehemence, partisan positions. Such journalists could become lauded and despised in equal measure and achieved levels of fame attained by only a handful of preindependence journalists.

Less celebrated, but no less significant, were the multitudinous voices of the public. "Farmers," "Old Soldiers," "Hermits," and "Patriots" all made themselves heard through the medium of their local newspaper. While in some respects they conformed, one way or another, to the broad outlines of the first American party system, most of them disavowed any explicit allegiances. "Ranking myself with no party," read one letter signed "Lycurgus" in the *Republican Ledger*, "I am neither a dupe of their professions, nor a victim of their intrigues. . . . I AM NEUTRAL. Who enjoys this office, or that office, can never shake my repose."[13] Neutral they may have been (although in many cases with these protestations, a healthy dose of skepticism is in order), but they were far from uninterested. They spoke for a set of values that is difficult to put shortly and that managed to be the sole domain of neither the

Federalist nor the Democrat-Republican Party. They almost all stood for "good government," as most people presumably do. They tended also to be for "religion," by which presumably Christianity was meant, but tended to avoid denominational affiliation. And, with each passing year, they succumbed ever more to a hysterical paranoia. Correspondents disagreed on who the shadowy cabal undermining the strength and prosperity of the nation might be: the diabolical "Demoncrats," the Federalist financiers, French Jacobin radicals, or perhaps the Masonic Order and the Bavarian Illuminati. What they could generally agree on, however, is that a cancerous force was sapping America of virtue and vitality and needed to be rooted out.

These early instances of the paranoid style in American political writing did not solely come from the geographic fringes of the country; there were plenty of urban authors who were overtaken by a darkening view of the American prospect in the late 1790s. However, as demonstrated in chapter 7, correspondents and editors in places like rural New Hampshire, as well as along the country's western frontier, were disproportionately responsible for producing content that encouraged readers to view themselves as the victims of a shadowy and all-encompassing conspiracy. For Richard Hofstadter, the modes of political thought that emerged in New England in the 1790s, with its reactions against the "swarming" Illuminati, became the progenitor for a lineage of reactionary thought that begat anti-Masonry in the 1820s and '30s, anti-Catholicism in the 1890s, and the John Birch Society in the 1950s. The common denominator, he argued, was that such a worldview projected a "'vast' or 'gigantic' conspiracy as the *motive force* in historical events. History *is* a conspiracy, set in motion by demonic forces of almost transcendent power, and what is felt to be needed is not the usual methods of political give-and-take, but an all-out crusade."[14] Since Hofstadter proposed his theory, events in the past half century have served only to strengthen his case. Perhaps the only real change is that conspiracy theories once confined to the fringes of popular discourse are now propagated before audiences of millions rather than thousands, on platforms offering instantaneous access and a degree of interaction beyond the wildest dreams of John Osborne, Isaiah Thomas, or Joseph Dennie.

Terms such as *citizen-journalist* and *open access* had not been coined in 1800, but that is not to say that the circumstances they describe did not exist, or that people did not have misgivings about them. "The world grows more enlightened. Knowledge is more equally diffused. Newspapers, magazines and circulating libraries have made mankind wiser. Titles and distinctions, ranks and order, parade and ceremony, are all going out of fashion," wrote John Adams in his *Discourses on Davila*. But while Adams would allow himself a cautious optimism, he remained apprehensive. "This is roundly and frequently asserted in the streets, and sometimes on theatres of higher *rank*. Some truth there is in it; and if the opportunity were temperately improved, to the reformation of abuses, the rectification of errors, and the dissipation of pernicious prejudices, a great advantage it might be. But, on the other hand, false inferences may be drawn from it, which may make mankind wish for the age of dragons, giants and fairies."[15] Whatever the cumulative effect of what Adams called the "more equally diffused" media of the early United States, whether in the balance its effects were for good or ill, the changes it wrought on the political culture of the young country were profound and echo through the sweep of American history.

The temptation to draw lessons from history is an impulse usually best resisted. From the vantage point of the later years of the 2010s, the negative turn of early American journalism feels at once intimately familiar and singularly ominous. We are living in an age of disintegrating trust, not just in the possibility of an equanimous journalism but in the ability of our fellow citizens to responsibly participate in a civil mass conversation. Indeed, we are haunted by a sense that things have in fact gotten *worse*, that as toxic as the letter pages of the *Oracle of the Day* or the *Political Repository* might have been, they were at least policed spaces, in which some standard of editorial moderation was being imposed. Newspapers readers of the 1790s knew that all was not well in the commanding heights of American politics, but they were not exposed to a daily flood of petty sniping and recriminations from the chief actors themselves. Nor could they, with no requirement of reflection, immediately give voice to their own most instinctual reflex. They could not ignore the need for quill and ink, the need to wait for the post rider's weekly appearance at the gate, the possibility of a moment's introspection or empathy. The inescapable lesson, it seems, is that the democratization of journalism, the admittance of the cacophonous multitude into the delicate business of making the news, dooms the possibility of a rational and harmonious public debate and, by extension, a rational and harmonious society.

Should we choose to draw such a conclusion, however, we are faced with a number of troubling questions. If the entry of hinterland Americans into the mainstream of American opinion making through the newspapers was deleterious to the tone of political discourse, as it surely was, what was the alternative? A media that would seek to deny its public a voice might do so with the lofty goal of leading rather than following popular fashions, although it would surely do so at the expense of its own bottom line. Journalists and editors of the eighteenth century, just like their twenty-first-century counterparts, well understood the fiduciary value of giving their readers a forum, not least because if human beings crave one thing more than the news, it is the opportunity to air their grievances about it. A customer that felt heard, and felt like a part of the process, was and is more likely to be a returning customer. It also alleviates the need for paid journalists to produce enough content to satisfy a content-hungry marketplace; why go to the expense of hiring journalists, with their troublesome insistence on abstract principles and ethics, when people are lining up to pay *you* for the privilege of appearing in your publication?

Commercial considerations aside, the closing off of the media presents a rather greater philosophical problem. We might, with good cause, be leery of the dangers inherent in giving everybody a voice. Such an environment has the tendency to amplify and magnify the extreme wings of movements and to lend legitimacy and even glamour to reprehensible views. It allows people to retreat into comfortable bubbles in which their prejudices and intuitions are endlessly reinforced and affirmed. Rather than encouraging healthy debate, it instead creates warring camps who don't so much speak to one another as bellow. Such was true of the Federalist and Democratic-Republican newspapers of the early national period, and such is axiomatically true today. Yet what if such voices could be silenced? What if a test for reasonableness and moderation could be imposed?

First, it is not altogether clear that such an elysian calm would necessarily redound to the benefit of humanity. The abolitionist press, which would emerge in the generation after the one described by this book, was hardly a model of serenity. Fiery, rough-hewn language is sometimes a necessary agent of change; the correspondence that took place in the pages of newspapers run in the nineteenth century by William Lloyd Garrison, Frederick Douglass, and Ida B. Wells ran hot with passion and more than a little righteous anger. Second, such an approach might serve to obfuscate problems, but it can never solve them. The dark imaginings of New England Federalists might have taken on vernacular form at the end of the eighteenth century and perhaps broken free to touch a host of Americans whom they otherwise might never have troubled. The consequences of an anger unspoken, however, are normally not apparent until too late.

The only lesson that leaves us, if we care to draw one, is that the problems that, to we bewildered inhabitants of the digital age, feel insurmountable are seldom as peculiar as we might suppose. The dilemma that confronted Adams, the unwelcome choice between truths manufactured by the mob or in hermetically sealed bastions of elite professionalism, between deference and democracy, confronts us still. We believe, to the point of dogma, in letting all voices be heard, in all perspectives being shared—until, that is, we stop to listen.

NOTES

INTRODUCTION

1. Women are largely absent from this book, as they are from most concerning early American journalism. Women appeared in newspaper stories on a fairly regular basis, but the people writing and manufacturing the papers were almost all male. Many of the printers who appear in this book were bachelors, and those who were married seldom had much to say regarding their spouses. The lot of a printer's wife entailed all of the economic uncertainty of their husband's profession but none of the cachet or fame.

2. Jeffrey Pasley, *The Tyranny of Printers: Newspaper Politics in the Early American Republic* (Charlottesville: University Press of Virginia, 2002), 24.

3. Other than via immigration, apprenticeships were the main source of skilled printers.

4. James Tagg, *Benjamin Franklin Bache and the "Philadelphia Aurora"* (Philadelphia: University of Pennsylvania Press, 1991), 93.

5. Simon P. Newman, *Parades and the Politics of the Street: Festive Culture in the Early American Republic* (Philadelphia: University of Pennsylvania Press, 1997), 8.

6. Thomas C. Leonard, *News for All: America's Coming-of-Age with the Press* (Oxford: Oxford University Press, 1995), 31; Richard D. Brown, *Knowledge Is Power: The Diffusion of Knowledge in Early America, 1700–1865* (Oxford: Oxford University Press, 1989), 7.

7. Charles E. Clark, *The Public Prints: The Newspaper in Anglo-American Culture, 1665–1740* (Oxford: Oxford University Press, 1994), 211–12; Howard Tumber, introduction to *Journalism: Critical Concepts in Media and Cultural Studies*, ed. Howard Tumber (London: Routledge, 2008), 5.

8. The Post Office Department charged one cent for the postage of newspapers up to a distance of a hundred miles. Longer distances cost a cent and a half. An equivalent-size private letter could cost up to twenty-five cents. Richard B. Kielbowicz, *News in the Mail: The Press, Post Office, and Public Information, 1700–1860s* (New York: Greenwood Press, 1989), 34.

9. Will Slauter, "The Paragraph as Information Technology: How News Travelled in the Eighteenth-Century Atlantic World," *Annales HSS* 67, no. 2 (2012): 271; Jean K. Chalaby, "Journalism as an Anglo-American Invention," *European Journal of Communication* 11, no. 3 (1996): 303; Michael Durey, *Transatlantic Radicals and the Early American Republic* (Lawrence: University Press of Kansas, 1997), 245–46; Forrest McDonald, *Alexander Hamilton: A Biography* (New York: W. W. Norton, 1979), 227–30, 334–36.

10. A prudent printer of course checked his work before going to print, but errors do abound in late-eighteenth-century newspapers. Books tended to be held to somewhat better standards.

11. A printer's assistant, if he was lucky enough to have one, would often be responsible for this. He was the "printer's devil."

12. Jerry W. Knudson, *Jefferson and the Press: Crucible of Liberty* (Columbia: University of South Carolina Press, 2006), 8.

13. Durey, *Transatlantic Radicals*, 201.

14. Dan Berkowitz, "Why a 'Social Meanings of News' Perspective?," in *Social Meanings of News: Text Reader*, ed. Dan Berkowitz (Thousand Oaks, CA: Sage, 1997), xii.

15. Note that this does not apply to other elements of the printer's trade. Books, one-off pamphlets, religious texts, sheet music, and the like were commonly purchased directly from the print shop.

16. Tagg, *Bache and the "Philadelphia Aurora,"* 94.

17. Ibid., 105.

18. Pasley, *Tyranny of Printers*, 47.

19. Allan R. Pred, *Urban Growth and the Circulation of Information* (Cambridge, MA: Harvard University Press, 1973), 24.

20. Ibid., 37.

21. Ibid., 36.

22. Some of the work that had been done recently in the field of the digital humanities has incorporated historiographical research with digital methods. For example, *Oceanic Exchanges: Tracing Global Information Networks in Historical Newspaper Repositories, 1840–1914* is a project that demonstrates the ways in which different national newspaper databases can be used in concert to explore the idea of global networks of communication. Work like this, in which the NULab for Texts, Maps, and Networks at Northeastern University plays a leading role, is expanding our knowledge of mass culture.

23. Rachel Hope Cleves, *The Reign of Terror in America: Visions of Violence from Anti-Jacobinism to Antislavery* (Cambridge: Cambridge University Press, 2009), 283.

24. Pred, *Urban Growth*, 34.

25. Lynn Warren Turner, *The Ninth State: New Hampshire's Formative Years* (Chapel Hill: University of North Carolina Press, 1983), 98; Paul Starr, *The Creation of the Modern Media: Political Origins of Modern Communication* (New York: Basic Books, 2004), 52; Trish Loughlan, *The Republic in Print: Print Culture in the Age of U.S. Nation Building, 1770–1870* (New York: Columbia University Press, 2007), 22–23; Kielbowicz, *News in the Mail*, 45.

26. James Curran, "Communication and History," in *Explorations in Communication and History*, ed. Barbie Zelizer (London: Routledge, 2008), 50.

27. William J. Gilmore, *Reading Becomes a Necessity of Life: Material and Cultural Life in Rural New England, 1780–1835* (Knoxville: University of Tennessee Press, 1989), 114; Charles G. Steffen, "Newspapers for Free: The Economies of Newspaper Circulation in the Early Republic," *Journal of the Early American Republic* (University of Pennsylvania Press) 23, no. 3 (2003): 419.

28. Note that this data was gathered using the NewsBank/Readex *Early American Newspapers (1690–1870)* series.

29. Josh Durham Peters, "History as a Communication Problem," in *Explorations in Communication and History*, ed. Zelizer, 24.

30. Newman, *Parades and the Politics of the Street*, 3.

31. Starr, *Creation of the Modern Media*, 86.

32. Richard R. John, "Expanding the Realm of Communication," in *A History of the Book in America*, vol. 2, *An Extensive Republic: Print, Culture and Society in a New Nation, 1790–1840*, ed. Robert A. Gross and Mary Kelley (Chapel Hill: University of North Carolina Press, 2010), 211–12.

CHAPTER ONE: "DOMESTICK SUMMARY"

1. *New Hampshire State Papers*, 10:639–89, 13:767–72, http://sos.nh.gov/Papers.aspx.

2. *First Census of the United States, 1790* (Washington, DC: Bureau of the Census, 1907), 8. Population density was calculated from the state's total area, 9,304 square miles (of which 4.1 percent is water)

3. https://www.census.gov/population/documentation/twps0027/tab02.txt. No other New Hampshire town appeared in the top twenty-four.

4. Some end numbers are missing from the 1790 Census, which makes precise calculations impossible here, but this figure should be accurate to the nearest thousand.

5. *First Census of the United States, 1790: New Hampshire*, 9–10.

6. William J. Gilmore, *Reading Becomes a Necessity of Life: Material and Cultural Life in Rural New England, 1780–1835* (Knoxville: University of Tennessee Press, 1989), 31.

7. http://www2.census.gov/prod2/decennial/documents/1800-re-turn-whole-number-of-persons.pdf.

8. New Hampshire, Population and Housing Unit Counts (U.S. Census Bureau, August 2012) 23, table 1.

9. Lynn Warren Turner, *The Ninth State: New Hampshire's Formative Years* (Chapel Hill: University of North Carolina Press, 1983), 190.

10. George Barstow, *The History of New Hampshire: From Its Discovery, in 1614, to the Passage of the Toleration Act, in 1819* (Boston: Little, Brown, 1853), 285.

11. Julian Ursyn Niemcewicz, *Under Their Vine and Fig Tree: Travels through America in 1797–1799, 1805, with Some Further Account of Life in New Jersey,* trans. Metchie J. E. Budka (Elizabeth, NJ: Grassman, 1965), 162.

12. Timothy Dwight, *Travels in New England and New York,* ed. Barbara Miller Solomon and Patricia M. King (Cambridge, MA: Belknap Press of Harvard University Press, 1969), 1:312.

13. Robert W. Lovett, "A Tidewater Merchant in New Hampshire," *Business History Review* 33, no. 1 (1959): 60–61.

14. Jere R. Daniell, *New Hampshire Politics and the American Revolution, 1741–1794* (Cambridge, MA: Harvard University Press, 1970), 219.

15. Richard M. Candee, "Social Conflict and Urban Rebuilding: The Portsmouth, New Hampshire, Brick Act of 1814," *Winterthur Portfolio* 32, nos. 2–3 (1997): 119.

16. Dwight, *Travels in New England and New York,* 1:312. Interestingly, Dwight challenges the findings of the 1800 Census, believing the population to be in excess of six thousand.

17. *New Hampshire Gazette,* December 30, 1802, 3.

18. Michael A. Baenen, "Books, Newspapers, and Sociability in the Making of the Portsmouth Athenæum," *New England Quarterly* 76, no. 3 (2003): 381–83.

19. University of New Hampshire, Milne Special Collection Exhibit, *The Popular Press in New Hampshire, 1756–1800,* https://web.archive.org/web/ 20080609071839 /http://www.library.unh.edu/special/index.php/exhibits/popular-press-in-new -hampshire/daniel-fowle.

20. Baenen, "Books, Newspapers, and Sociability," 381–83.

21. Saul Cornell, *Anti-Federalism & the Dissenting Tradition in America, 1780–1828: The Other Founders* (Chapel Hill: University of North Carolina Press, 1999), 26.

22. Gilmore, *Reading Becomes a Necessity of Life,* 21.

23. Barstow, *History of New Hampshire,* 288; Turner, *Ninth State,* 97.

24. Turner, *Ninth State,* 98.

25. Alexis de Tocqueville, *Democracy in America* (New York: Colonial Press, 1835), 1:281; Russell M. Lawson, *Ebenezer Hazard, Jeremy Belknap and the American Revolution* (London: Pickering & Chatto, 2011), 4.

26. J. M. Opal, "The Politics of 'Industry': Federalism in Concord and Exeter, New Hampshire, 1790–1805," *Journal of the Early Republic* 20, no. 4 (2000): 640–41.

27. Jeremiah Mason, *Memoirs of Jeremiah Mason*, ed. George S. Hillard (Boston: Boston Law Book, 1917), 28.

28. *First Census of the United States, 1790: New Hampshire*, 9.

29. Elting E. Morison, *From Know-How to Nowhere: The Development of American Technology* (Oxford: Basil Blackwell, 1974), 16–17, 18–19.

30. Cornell, *Anti-Federalism and the Dissenting Tradition in America*, 23.

31. Philip S. Foner, *The Democratic Republican Societies, 1790–1800: A Documentary Sourcebook of Constitutions, Decelerations, Addresses, Resolutions and Toasts* (Westport, CT: Greenwood Press, 1976); Jere Daniell, *Experiment in Republicanism: New Hampshire Politics and the American Revolution, 1741–1794* (Cambridge, MA: Harvard University Press, 1970), 276.

32. Stanley Elkins and Eric McKitrick, *The Age of Federalism: The Early American Republic, 1788–1800* (Oxford: Oxford University Press, 1993), 22–23.

33. Daniell, *Experiment in Republicanism*, 237.

34. *New Hampshire Recorder*, October 21, 1790, 3; *New Hampshire Spy*, June 4, 1791, 3.

35. Turner, *Ninth State*, 99, 107.

36. Sullivan was a well-regarded Revolutionary War hero, having served as a major general in the Continental army. He had served a New Hampshire delegate in both the first and the second Continental Congresses, was a prominent member of Exeter society, and had served as governor of New Hampshire. See Paul W. Wilderson, *Governor John Wentworth & the American Revolution: The English Connection* (Hanover, NH: University Press of New England, 1994), 243–53; and Richard Francis Upton, *Revolutionary New Hampshire: An Account of the Social and Political Forces Underlying the Transition from Royal Province to American Commonwealth* (Port Washington, NY: Kennikat Press, 1970), 40.

37. Plumer, a New Hampshire lawyer, was elected at the precocious age of thirty-one to be Speaker of the state house of representatives. He later served as U.S. senator and governor of New Hampshire. Like so many of his generation, his career was characterized by a transition in partisan affiliation from Federalist to Democrat-Republican.

38. Daniell, *New Hampshire Politics*, 234.

39. Even once the Federalist Party was all but dead, Exeter remained one of its last redoubts.

40. Turner, *Ninth State*, 144.

41. *Journal of the New Hampshire House of Representatives*, November 1798 sess. (Portsmouth, NH, 1799), 13.

42. Gordon Wood, *Empire of Liberty: A History of the Early Republic, 1789–1815* (Oxford: Oxford University Press, 2009), 175–77.

43. Wilderson, *Governor John Wentworth*, 250.

44. Newman, *Parades and the Politics of the Street*, 93.

45. Upton, *Revolutionary New Hampshire*, 139.

46. Max Ferrand, ed., *The Records of the Federal Convention of 1787* (New Haven, CT: Yale University Press, 1966), 3:323. Robert Morris, the first senator for Pennsylvania (along with William Maclay), was a renowned financier and speculator, who owed much of his political success to his vast riches. He would die in poverty and ignominy.

47. Turner, *Ninth State*, 142.

48. Modern-day Berlin, New Hampshire, on the northern cusp of the White Mountains, experiences regular snowfall from November to April. The higher elevations are regularly impassable in the winter months. See *Climatography of the United States, No. 20, 1971–2000* (Berlin, NH: National Oceanic and Atmospheric Administration, 2000).

49. Turner, *Ninth State*, 174.

50. Ibid., 89.

51. New Hampshire State Constitution and Bill of Rights.

52. Turner, *Ninth State*, 89.

53. *Rising Sun*, July 5, 1796, 4; *New Hampshire Spy*, July 20, 1791, 4.

54. Turner, *Ninth State*, 163, 155.

55. *Dartmouth Gazette*, March 10, 1800, 1.

56. Donald S. Cole, *Jacksonian Democracy in New Hampshire, 1800–1851* (Cambridge, MA: Harvard University Press, 1970), 16.

57. Ferrand, *Records of the Federal Convention of 1787*, 3:87, 3:232.

58. Joseph C. Morton, *Shapers of the Great Debate at the Constitutional Convention of 1787* (Westport, CT: Greenwood Press, 2006), 116.

59. Sean Wilentz, *The Rise of American Democracy: From Jefferson to Lincoln* (New York: W. W. Norton, 2005), 91; *Courier of New Hampshire*, January 11, 1800, 3; *Republican Ledger and Portsmouth Price Current*, December 30, 1800, 2.

CHAPTER TWO: "DEVILS AND DIATRIBES"

1. Eighteenth-Century American Newspapers in the Library of Congress, http://www.loc.gov/rr/news/18th/newhampshire.html.

2. Ralph Adams Brown, introduction to *The Country Printer: New York State, 1785–1830*, by Milton W. Hamilton (Port Washington, NY: Ira J. Friedman, 1964), xi; Jeffrey Pasley, *The Tyranny of Printers: Newspaper Politics in the Early American Republic* (Charlottesville: University Press of Virginia, 2001), 24; Gordon Wood, *Empire of Liberty: A History of the Early Republic, 1789–1815* (Oxford: Oxford University Press, 2009), 151.

3. Matthew Rainbow Hale, "On Their Tiptoes: Political Time and Newspapers during the Advent of the Radicalized French Revolution, circa 1792–1793," *Journal of the Early Republic* 29, no. 2 (2009): 213.

4. Pasley, *Tyranny of Printers*, 249.

5. E. Wilder Spaulding, "The *Connecticut Courant*, a Representative Newspaper," *New England Quarterly* 3, no. 3 (1930): 461.

6. Alfred McClung Lee, *The Daily Newspaper in America* (New York: Macmillan, 1937), 728–30.

7. Ebenezer Andrews to Isaiah Thomas, Isaiah Thomas Papers, box 2, November 3, 1792, American Antiquarian Society, Worcester, MA.

8. Ibid., February 8, 1792.

9. Carville Earle and Ronald Hoffman, "The Foundation of the Modern Economy: Agriculture and the Costs of Labor in the United States and England, 1800–60," *American Historical Review* 85, no. 5 (1980): 1086.

10. Thomas Papers, box 1, August 16, 1786.

11. James Green, *The Rise and Fall of Isaiah Thomas' Bookselling Network* (Worcester, MA: American Antiquarian Society, 1996), 3.

12. Andrews to Thomas, Thomas Papers, box 1, August 7, 1791.

13. Ibid., July 10, 1791.

14. Leonard Worcester to Thomas, ibid., box 4, January 1796.

15. Ibid., February 1796.

16. Elisha Waldo to Thomas, ibid., box 3, January 16, 1795.

17. Ibid., February 12, 1795.

18. Ibid., February 17, 1795.

19. Ibid., February 12, 1795.

20. Ibid., April 4, 1795.

21. Ralph Adams Brown, "The New Hampshire Press, 1775–1789" (unpublished manuscript), 30, quoted in Donald H. Stewart, *The Opposition Press in the Federalist Period* (Albany: SUNY Press, 1969).

22. Stewart, *Opposition Press in the Federalist Period*, 16.

23. Isaiah Thomas, *The History of Printing in America: With a Biography of Printers, and an Account of Newspapers* (Worcester, MA: Isaiah Thomas, 1874), 2:62; Hamilton, *Country Printer*, 248.

24. Peter Whitney to Isaiah Thomas, Thomas Papers, box 1, August 3, 1789.

25. Du Rouveller to Thomas, ibid., box 2, November 18, 1792.

26. Waldo to Thomas, ibid., box 3, August 9, 1795; Isaiah Beese to Thomas, ibid., box 1, March 10, August 3, 1789; Isaac Story to David Carlisle, ibid., box 3, April 30, 1800.

27. *Courier of New Hampshire*, February 6, 1798, 3.

28. *New Hampshire Sentinel*, March 30, 1799, 3.

29. Jack Larkin, "'Printing Is Something Every Village Has in It': Rural Printing and Publishing," in *A History of the Book in America*, vol. 2, *An Extensive Republic:*

Print, Culture and Society in a New Nation, 1790–1840, ed. Robert A. Gross and Mary Kelley (Chapel Hill: University of North Carolina Press, 2010), 148.

30. Michael Durey, *Transatlantic Radicals and the Early American Republic* (Lawrence: University Press of Kansas, 1997), 181.

31. Andrews to Thomas, Thomas Papers, box 2, July 16, 1793.

32. Michael J. Everton, *A Grand Chorus of Complaint: Authors and the Business Ethics of American Publishing* (Oxford: Oxford University Press, 2011), 15.

33. Lewis Hyde, *Common as Air: Revolution, Art and Ownership* (New York: Farrar, Straus and Giroux, 2010), 56, 106.

34. Section 5 of the act extends its protections only to American citizens.

35. Copyright Act of 1790, Section 1.

36. Thomas Papers, box 1, March 13, 1788.

37. Green, *Rise and Fall of Thomas' Bookselling Network*, 218; Timothy Pickering to Thomas, Thomas Papers, box 1, November 28, 1791.

38. Marcus Daniel, *Scandal and Civility: Journalism and the Birth of American Democracy* (Oxford: Oxford University Press, 2009), 39.

39. Pasley, *Tyranny of Printers*, 14.

40. Samuel Goodrich, *Recollections of a Lifetime* (New York, 1857), 86, quoted in David H. Hall, "The Uses of Literacy in New England, 1600–1850," in *Printing and Society in Early America*, ed. William C. Joyce, David Brown, and John B. Hench (Worcester, MA: American Antiquarian Society, 1983), 21.

41. Hamilton, *Country Printer*, 211; Pasley, *Tyranny of Printers*, 85.

42. James Tagg, *Benjamin Franklin Bache and the "Philadelphia Aurora"* (Philadelphia: University of Pennsylvania Press, 1991), 108.

43. Thomas C. Leonard, *News for All: America's Coming-of-Age with the Press* (Oxford: Oxford University Press, 1995), 31.

44. James Giles to Carlisle, Thomas Papers, box 3, July 30, 1798.

45. *New Hampshire Sun*, January 3, 1798, 1.

46. *New Hampshire Phoenix*, February 7, 1795, 4.

47. *New Hampshire Journal*, December 6, 1796, 1.

48. Pasley, *Tyranny of Printers*, 24; Brown, introduction to *Country Printer*, by Hamilton, xi; *Political and Sentimental Repository*, October 7, 1790, 3.

49. George Barstow, *The History of New Hampshire: From Its Discovery, in 1614, to the Passage of the Toleration Act, in 1819* (Boston: Little, Brown, 1853), 284–85.

50. Richard D. Brown, *Knowledge Is Power: The Diffusion of Knowledge in Early America, 1700–1865* (Oxford: Oxford University Press, 1989), 203.

51. Pamela Shoemaker, "A New Gatekeeping Model?," in *Social Meanings of News: Text Reader*, ed. Dan Berkowitz (Thousand Oaks, CA: Sage, 1997), 57.

52. Harold Milton Ellis, "Joseph Dennie and His Circle: A Study in American Literature from 1792 to 1812," *Bulletin of the University of Texas*, no. 40 (1915): 9, 14, 18.

53. Isaiah Thomas, *Three Autobiographical Fragments* (Worcester, MA: American

Antiquarian Society, 1962), 15. Thomas had signed on as an indentured apprentice in 1756 to Boston printer Zechariah Fowle, at the age of seven.

54. Andrew P. Peabody, "The Farmer's Weekly Museum," *Proceedings of the American Antiquarian Society*, vol. 6, *April 1889–1890* (Worcester, MA: American Antiquarian Society, 1890), 109.

55. Clifford K. Shipton, *Isaiah Thomas: Printer, Patriot and Philanthropist, 1749–1831* (Rochester, NY: Printing House of Leo Hart, 1948), 61.

56. Joseph Buckingham, *Personal Memoirs and Recollections* (Boston: Ticknor, Reed, and Fields, 1852), 2:25–26.

57. Peter H. Lindert and Jeffrey G. Williamson, *American Incomes, 1774–1860*, Working Paper no. 18396 (Cambridge, MA: National Bureau of Economic Research, 2012), 38.

58. Pasley, *Tyranny of Printers*, 249.

CHAPTER THREE: "DEAR MR. EDITOR . . ."

1. Published in Exeter, NH, in 1799.

2. Published in Haverhill, MA, from 1795 to 1797.

3. *New Hampshire Spy*, April 4, 1792, 3.

4. *New Hampshire Spy*, April 23, 1791, 4. This article appeared in the *Spy* again, unaltered, on March 24, 1792, suggesting the editor was either unscrupulous when it came to filling column inches or merely forgetful.

5. *Hanover Eagle*, June 6, 1796, 2.

6. *Concord Herald*, September 14, 1790, 4.

7. *New Hampshire Spy*, February 1, 1792.

8. *Mirrour*, September 6, 1796, 1.

9. *New Hampshire Spy*, June 6, 1792, 3.

10. *Courier of New Hampshire*, June 7, 1800, 3.

11. *Concord Herald*, September 29, 1792, 4.

12. *Rising Sun*, March 17, 1798, 4.

13. *United States Oracle*, March 1, 1800, 3.

14. *Oracle of the Day*, January 24, 1795, 3; *Courier of New Hampshire*, June 8, 1799, 3.

15. *Mirrour*, April 27, 1795, 1.

16. *Mirrour*, May 3, 1795, 1.

17. *Concord Herald*, September 26, 1793, 2; Andrew R. Murphy, *Conscience and Community: Revisiting Toleration and Religious Dissent in Early Modern England and America* (University Park: Pennsylvania State University Press, 2001), 13; *Federal Observer*, April 4, 1799, 4; *Oracle of the Day*, May 26, 1796, 1.

18. *New Hampshire Gazette*, February 15, 1792, 3.

19. *Gazette*, November 7, 1792, 2.

20. Jeffrey A. Smith, *Printers and Press Freedom: The Ideology of Early American*

Journalism (Oxford: Oxford University Press, 1988), 50; *New Hampshire Gazette,* October 7, 1756; *Oracle of the Day,* July 26, 1794.

21. Newspapers in the 1790s frequently published articles accusing political opponents of corruption and calumny. However, the lack of reporters and any system of fact checking means that it is very different from the kind of investigative journalism for which the nineteenth century is famous.

22. *Eagle,* February 10, 1794, 4.

23. *Federal Observer,* May 29, 1800, 4.

24. *Farmer's Weekly Museum,* January 20, 1800, 3.

25. *Oracle of the Day,* July 7, 1795, 3; *New Hampshire Gazette,* April 28, 1790, 3; *New Hampshire Sentinel,* November 9, 1799, 3.

26. *New Hampshire Gazette,* February 6, 1799, 3.

27. *New Hampshire Gazetteer,* October 28, 1791, 4.

28. *Oracle of the Day,* March 24, 1798, 3.

29. *New Hampshire Sentinel,* June 28, 1800, 3.

30. *New Hampshire Gazetteer,* January 8, 1791, 2.

31. *Eagle,* May 19, 1794, 3.

32. *Oracle of the Day,* March 22, 1794, 3.

33. *Mirrour,* November 26, 1798, 3.

34. *Rising Sun,* December 30, 1797, 3.

35. *Concord Mirrour,* October 21, 1793, 3.

36. *Dartmouth Gazette,* October 20, 1800, 3.

37. *New Hampshire Gazetteer,* October 5, 1792, 4.

38. Michael Durey, *With the Hammer of Truth: James Thompson Callender and America's Early National Heroes* (Charlottesville: University Press of Virginia, 1990), 55.

39. *New Hampshire Gazette,* February 3, 1790, 2.

40. *New Hampshire Gazette,* March 26, 1791, 1.

41. Peter Stallybrass, "Printing and the Manuscript Revolution," in *Explorations in Communication and History,* ed. Barbie Zelizer (London: Routledge, 2008), III.

42. *New Hampshire Sun,* September 12, 1798, 3.

43. *Eagle,* February 10, 1794, 4; Marcus Daniel, *Scandal and Civility: Journalism and the Birth of American Democracy* (Oxford: Oxford University Press, 2009), 9.

CHAPTER FOUR: "WE HAVE IT BY A RELIABLE GENTLEMAN IN THAT PLACE"

1. Richard L. Merritt, *Symbols of American Community, 1735–1775* (New Haven, CT: Yale University Press, 1996), 62.

2. This figure was calculated by tabulating the total issues for each newspaper according to the NewsBank American Historical Newspapers list.

3. Michael Durey, *Transatlantic Radicals and the Early American Republic* (Lawrence: University Press of Kansas, 1997), 164; *Courier of New Hampshire*, July 11, 1797, 3.

4. This was a known factor in the late eighteenth century. Benjamin Franklin's map of the Atlantic Gulf Stream in the Library of Congress demonstrates a remarkably sophisticated appreciation of maritime currents and climatology.

5. James Tagg, *Benjamin Franklin Bache and the "Philadelphia Aurora"* (Philadelphia: University of Pennsylvania Press, 1991), 315–24.

6. *London Gazette*, July 21, 1789.

7. *London Gazette*, July 14, 1798.

8. *Farmer's Weekly Museum*, February 21, 1797, 3.

9. *New Hampshire Gazette*, February 26, 1800, 3.

10. *Amherst Village Messenger*, October 12, 1799.

11. *New Hampshire Gazette*, September 16, 1794.

12. Kenneth Morgan, "Bristol and the Atlantic Trade in the Eighteenth Century," *English Historical Review* 17, no. 424 (1992): 629.

13. Jamaica appears in 1,523 articles, St. Kitts in 296, and Trinidad in 165.

14. Individual newspapers and their stories traveled at wildly different rates to one another. Some papers in 1790 got to American from England faster than some in 1800. However, the aggregate trend was one of acceleration.

15. R. G. Marsden, "The *Mayflower*," *English Historical Review* 19, no. 76 (1904): 672.

16. Durey, *Transatlantic Radicals*, 168.

17. *Farmer's Weekly Museum*, March 1, 1796, 1.

18. *Oracle of the Day*, October 26, 1793, 3; *Mirrour*, November 3, 1793, 3.

19. *Oracle of the Day*, June 4, 1793, 1.

20. *New Hampshire Gazette*, May 16, 1797, 3.

21. *New Hampshire Recorder*, December 9, 1790, 4.

22. *Concord Herald*, May 23, 1793, 3; *Federal Observer*, January 24, 1799, 3.

23. *Concord Mirrour*, August 19, 1794, 3; *New Hampshire Gazette*, August 5, 1790, 3; *New Hampshire Spy*, October 20, 1790, 1.

24. This study is made up of articles with a clear location and date of initial publication.

25. Editors tended to use their own preferred nomenclature for papers they made use of regularly. The *Columbian Centinel* also went by the *Boston Centinel*, the *Massachusetts Centinel*, and simply the *Centinel*, depending on the newspaper.

26. *Rising Sun*, December 1, 1795, 3; *Courier of New Hampshire*, November 22, 1800, 2.

27. *Mirrour*, May 13, 1793, 4; *New Hampshire Sentinel*, September 6, 1800, 2.

28. *Concord Herald*, September 14, 1790, 3.

29. *New Hampshire Gazette*, March 21, 1791, 1.

30. *New Hampshire Gazette*, November 1, 1792, 3.

31. *Farmer's Weekly Museum*, December 13, 1793, 3.

32. *Courier of New Hampshire*, February 16, 1799, 4.

33. Trish Loughlan, *The Republic in Print: Print Culture in the Age of U.S. Nation Building, 1770–1870* (New York: Columbia University Press, 2007), 21; *New Hampshire Gazetteer*, June 17, 1791, 2.

34. *Republican Ledger*, October 28, 1800, 4.

35. *Oracle of the Day*, May 26, 1798, 3.

36. *Farmer's Weekly Museum*, March 31, 1800, 3.

37. *Concord Herald*, November 4, 1792, 3.

CHAPTER FIVE: CLIMATE, COMMERCE, AND COACHES

1. *New Hampshire Gazette*, January 25, 1792, 3.

2. William J. Gilmore, *Reading Become a Necessity of Life: Material and Cultural Life in Rural New England, 1780–1835* (Knoxville: University of Tennessee Press, 1989), 180–81, 193, 194.

3. Grafton, Canaan, Lebanon, Orford, Piermont, Haverhill, Warren, Wentworth, Rumney, Plymouth, Boscawen, Salisbury, North Crantham, Hanover, Lyme, New Chester, Gilmantown, Meredith, Northfield, Sandborton, Canterbury, Loudon, Chichester, Epsdom, Deerfield, Hopkinton, Warner, Sutton, New London, Fisherfield, Bradford, Henniker, and Weare. These locations of subscribers were compiled from subscriber notices, usually requesting payment from delinquents, but sometimes thanking subscribers or addressing individual readers and their place of residence This list, compiled from fragmentary evidence, is almost certainly incomplete.

4. *Farmer's Weekly Museum*, December 10, 1798, 3.

5. *Political and Sentimental Repository*, July 29, 1790, 3; George Barstow, *The History of New Hampshire: From Its Discovery, in 1614, to the Passage of the Toleration Act, in 1819* (Boston: Little, Brown, 1853), 288; *Concord Herald*, January 27, 1790, 3.

6. *New Hampshire Spy*, October 23, 1790, 1.

7. Jurgen Habermas, *The Structural Transformation of the Public Sphere: An Inquiry into a Category of Bourgeois Society* (Cambridge, MA: MIT Press, 1991), 15–21.

8. *New Hampshire Journal*, March 7, 1797, 4.

9. The average transmission time from London to New Hampshire, by month, 1790–1800: January, 80.81 days; February, 88.83 days; March, 88.47 days; April, 82.59 days; May, 72.55; June, 64.58 days; July, 66.81 days; August, 70.6 days; September, 68.84 days; October, 65.78 days; November, 64.13 days; and December, 72.59 days.

10. http://lwf.ncdc.noaa.gov/oa/climate/online/ccd/snowfall.html.

11. The term originates with the geographer François E. Matthes, who described a period of relative chilliness after the "medieval warm period." The author

is indebted to the geologist Martin Sykes for invaluable advice on historical meteorology.

12. *Oracle of the Day*, June 1, 1799, 1.

13. *Political and Sentimental Repository*, December 2, 1790, 3.

14. *Concord Mirrour*, January 25, 1792, 3; *New Hampshire and Vermont Magazine and General Repository*, October 1797; *Concord Mirrour*, March 6, 1798, 4.

15. *New Hampshire Gazette*, March 18, 1797.

16. Paul Johnson, *The Birth of the Modern* (New York: HarperPerennial, 1992), 171.

17. For reference, see William Kaszynski, *The American Highway* (Jefferson, NC: McFarland, 2000).

18. *New Hampshire Eagle*, July 18, 1796, 1; Ronald Jager and Grace Jager, *The Granite State: New Hampshire* (Sun Valley, CA: American Historical Press, 2000), 84–85.

19. *New Hampshire Journal*, March 22, 1796, 1.

20. *Courier of New Hampshire*, August 3, 1799, 2.

21. Milton W. Hamilton, *The Country Printer: New York State, 1785–1830* (Port Washington, NY: Ira J. Friedman, 1964), 60–61.

22. An average of 486 advertisements across the state in November, as compared to 341 in February, in the years 1790 to 1800.

23. *New Hampshire Gazette*, March 14, 1798.

24. Ian K. Steele, *The English Atlantic, 1675–1740: An Exploration of Communication and Community* (Oxford: Oxford University Press, 1986), 213.

25. As compared to 96,868 news articles, 11,738 legislative records, 5,022 pieces of poetry, 2,343 obituaries, 1,785 dispatches of shipping news, and 213 election returns. These classifications come from the NewsBank Early American Newspapers series. It is worth pointing out that the numbers refer to the number of individual content pieces rather than column inches.

26. *New Hampshire Spy*, January 16, 1790, 1; Peter Mathias, "Risk, Credit and Kinship in Early Modern Enterprise," in *The Early Modern Atlantic Economy*, ed. John McCusker and Kenneth Morgan (Cambridge: Cambridge University Press, 2001), 24, 30; *New Hampshire Spy*, January 1, 1790, 3; *New Hampshire Spy*, December 4, 1790, 3.

27. *New Hampshire Gazette*, March 21, 1798, 1.

28. A couple of advertisements a year being taken out in one town from another might seem insignificant, but as a host of other towns, including Dover, Hanover, Exeter, and Keene, contributed larger numbers, the latticework of connections between communities, businesses, and newspapers emerges.

29. Paul Starr, *The Creation of the Media: Political Origins of Modern Communication* (New York: Basic Books, 2004), 87–89; David M. Henkin, *The Postal Age: The Emergence of Modern Communication in Nineteenth-Century America* (Chicago: University of Chicago Press, 2006), 42.

30. *New Hampshire Gazette*, April 29, 1797, 1; *Dartmouth Gazette*, March 24, 1800.

31. Douglas C. North, *The Economic Growth of the United States, 1790–1860* (New York: W. W. Norton, 1966), 249.

32. Allan R. Pred, *Urban Growth and the Circulation of Information* (Cambridge, MA: Harvard University Press, 1973), 19.

33. *New Hampshire Sentinel*, June 21, 1800, 4.

34. *Courier of New Hampshire*, July 4, 1795, 4.

35. *Courier of New Hampshire*, July 10, 1798, 4.

36. Pred, *Urban Growth and the Circulation of Information*, 80.

37. Richard B. Kielbowicz, "The Press, Post Office, and Flow of News in the Early Republic," *Journal of the Early American Republic* (Autumn 1983): 256; *New Hampshire Eagle*, August 18, 1794, 4.

38. There were thirty-three advertised postal coach services in 1795, as compared to two in 1793. From 1790 to 1792, there were none advertised at all.

39. Barstow, *History of New Hampshire*, 288–300.

40. Not an amount that would support man and horse for a year, but a crucial and reliable supplement to the rider's income.

41. Portsmouth, Exeter, Concord, Amherst, Dover, Keene, Charlestown, Hanover, and Haverhill.

42. *New Hampshire Courier*, May 1, 1794, 4. By the mid-1790s, a half dozen or so of these advertisements were appearing in the New Hampshire press every year, compared to scarcely any at the beginning of the decade.

43. *New Hampshire Gazette*, June 6, 1797, 4; *United States Oracle*, July 12, 1800, 3.

44. *Courier of New Hampshire*, May 22, 1794, 2.

45. *Rising Sun*, March 8, 1796, 4; *Rising Sun*, October 25, 1796, 4; *New Hampshire Journal*, August 4, 1795, 3.

46. *New Hampshire Gazette*, July 1, 1800, 4; *Farmer's Weekly Museum*, August 29, 1800, 3.

47. Richard R. John, "Expanding the Realm of Communication," in *A History of the Book in America*, vol. 2, *An Extensive Republic: Print, Culture and Society in a New Nation, 1790–1840*, ed. Robert A. Gross and Mary Kelley (Chapel Hill: University of North Carolina Press, 2010), 218; Jurgen Habermas, "The Public Sphere," in *Journalism: Critical Concepts in Media and Cultural Studies*, ed. Howard Tumber (London: Routledge, 2008), 25; Simon Newman, *Parades and Politics of the Street: Festive Culture in the Early American Republic* (Philadelphia: University of Pennsylvania Press, 2000), 187.

48. *Amherst Village Messenger*, January 3, 1797, 3.

49. *Amherst Village Messenger*, January 16, 1796, 3.

CHAPTER SIX: "THE LAY PREACHER"

1. *New Hampshire Gazetteer*, January 9, 1790, 2; *Oracle of the Day*, December 28, 1798, 1.

2. These figures were calculated by using the control group of stories first printed in New Hampshire concerning London. The rationale for using this sample was that such articles would attract relatively even rates of interest across regional lines (a piece about the House of Lords might attract as much attention in Charleston as in Newburyport, but an article about shipping in Portsmouth would be of more interest to the latter than the former) and that they were one of the most common available article types.

3. Rachel Hope Cleves, *The Reign of Terror in America: Visions of Violence from Anti-Jacobinism to Antislavery* (Cambridge: Cambridge University Press, 2012), 3.

4. Douglas C. North, *The Economic Growth of the United States, 1790–1860* (Englewood Cliffs, NJ: Prentice Hall, 1961), 250.

5. M. N. S. Sellers, *American Republicanism: Roman Ideology in the United States Constitution* (New York: New York University Press, 1994), 9.

6. Carl J. Richard, *The Founders and the Classics: Greece, Rome and the American Enlightenment* (Cambridge, MA: Harvard University Press, 1994), 41.

7. Eran Shalev, "Ancient Masks, American Fathers: Classical Pseudonyms during the American Revolution and Early Republic," *Journal of the Early Republic* 23, no. 2 (2003): 157, 164.

8. Barbie Zelizer, "Has Communication Explained Journalism?," in *Social Meanings of News: Text Reader*, ed. Dan Berkowitz (Thousand Oaks, CA: Sage, 1997), 25.

9. Even then, with the increasingly partisan nature of the press in the 1790s, some readers could quite easily discern the publication of origin based on locale and political bias.

10. *Farmer's Weekly Museum*, June 26, 1798, 4.

11. *Farmer's Weekly Museum*, April 1, 1799, 4.

12. *Farmer's Weekly Museum*, April 15, 1799, 4.

13. *Eastern Herald* (Portland, ME), June 7, 1797, 4.

14. *Farmer's Weekly Museum*, June 17, 1798, 4.

15. *Farmer's Weekly Museum*, August 26, 1799, 3.

16. *Columbian Museum* (Augusta, GA), August 24, 1798, 4.

17. *Norwich Courier* (Norwich, CT), August 30, 1798, 2.

18. *Farmer's Weekly Museum*, March 7, 1797, 1.

19. *Farmer's Weekly Museum*, December 10, 1798, 3.

20. *Philadelphia Gazette*, August 24, 1798, 3; *Commercial Advertiser* (New York), August 28, 1798, 3.

21. *Daily Advertiser* (New York), October 11, 1800, 3; *Mercantile Advertiser* (New York), October 11, 1800, 3.

22. William Clapp, *Joseph Dennie: Editor of the "Port Folio" and Author of the "Lay Preacher,"* 31–32.

23. *Porcupine's Gazette* (Philadelphia), July 24, 1798, 3; *Salem Gazette*, July 28, 1797,

3; *Rising Sun*, December 7, 1796, 1; Andrew P. Peabody, "The *Farmer's Weekly Museum*," in *Proceedings of the American Antiquarian Society*, vol. 6, *April 1889–1890* (Worcester, MA: American Antiquarian Society, 1890), 109; Clifford K. Shipton, *Isaiah Thomas: Printer, Patriot and Philanthropist, 1749–1831* (Rochester, NY: Printing House of Leo Hart, 1948), 61; Frank Luther Mott, *American Journalism: A History of Newspapers in the United States through 250 Years, 1690–1940* (London: Macmillan, 1941), 101.

24. Laura Green Peddler, ed., *The Letters of Joseph Dennie, 1768–1812* (Orono: University of Maine Press, 1936), 159.

25. *Farmer's Weekly Museum*, August 19, 1799, 4.

26. Peddler, *Letters of Joseph Dennie*, 161–62. Belknap was a leading New Hampshire intellectual and perhaps the state's first great historian.

27. *Farmer's Weekly Museum*, April 8, 1799, 4.

28. *Farmer's Weekly Museum*, July 24, 1798, 4.

29. Note that this counts only accredited versions of the articles. If we were to factor in the quantity of reprints without reference to the *Museum*, this number would be much higher. However, as we're mainly interested in the *Museum*'s "brand visibility" here, it is helpful just to count those articles that were directly attributed to it.

30. An Act to Establish the Post-Office and Post Roads within the United States, *Second Congress*, sess. 1, chap. 7, February 20, 1792.

31. Donald H. Stewart, *The Opposition Press of the Federalist Period* (Albany: SUNY Press, 1969), 16.

32. *Farmer's Weekly Museum*, December 10, 1798, 3.

33. *Farmer's Weekly Museum*, July 24, 1797, 1.

34. To put this in context, in addition to the *Gazette of the United States* and *Porcupine's Gazette*, Dennie was published in Philadelphia by the *Independent Gazetter*, *Philadelphia Gazette*, *Claypoole's American Daily Advertiser*, *Philadelphia Minerva*, and *Carey's United States Recorder*, all on multiple occasions.

35. *Philadelphia Aurora & General Advertiser*, June 11, 1799, 2.

36. His name appears more than three thousand times in his own paper during the 1790s alone.

37. This would have been an optimal state of affairs; newspapers on a cart or postal stage would be slower still. In 1793, the first year with a sufficient sample size to begin to calculate meaningful statistics, it took two weeks for a news story from Walpole to reach Boston, just ninety-three miles away, and an additional week to arrive in Philadelphia. By 1799 these travel times had fallen to ten days and two weeks, respectively.

38. *Rising Sun*, December 7, 1796, 1.

CHAPTER SEVEN: "THESE FALSE AND SCURRILOUS LIBELS"

1. Marcus Daniel, *Scandal and Civility: Journalism and the Birth of American Democracy* (Oxford: Oxford University Press, 2009), 5.

2. *Porcupine's Gazette*, March 5, 1797.

3. *New Hampshire Gazetteer*, July 22, 1791, 3.

4. *Farmer's Weekly Museum*, December 29, 1800, 3.

5. Alison LaCroix, *The Ideological Origins of American Federalism* (Cambridge, MA: Harvard University Press, 2010), 214–15.

6. Daniel, *Scandal and Civility*, 5.

7. Rachel Hope Cleves, *The Reign of Terror in America: Visions of Violence from Anti-Jacobinism to Antislavery* (Cambridge: Cambridge University Press, 2009), 2.

8. *Farmer's Weekly Museum*, October 9, 1797, 3; *New Hampshire Gazette*, August 28, 1798, 3.

9. *Courier of New Hampshire*, December 7, 1799, 2; *Farmer's Weekly Museum*, July 28, 1800, 3.

10. *Courier*, August 8, 1795, 3; *New Hampshire Mirrour*, May 22, 1795, 2.

11. *Oracle of the Day*, October 28, 1795, 3.

12. Wendell Bird, *Press and Speech under Assault: The Early Supreme Court Justices, the Sedition Act of 1798, and the Campaign against Dissent* (Oxford: Oxford University Press, 2016), 252.

13. *Courier*, September 19, 1795, 2; *Farmer's Weekly Museum*, December 18, 1797, 3.

14. *Courier*, March 21, 1795, 3.

15. Ronald Formisano, "Deferential-Participant Politics: The Early Republic's Political Culture, 1789–1840," *American Political Science Review* 68, no. 2 (1974): 483.

16. The creation of these categories was based on what Riffe, Lacy, and Fico call the "conceptual" rather than "operational" definition, which is to say that the statistics generated by this methodology show what I conceived of as being positive, neutral, and negative, rather than being scientifically replicable. However, since no scientific standard exists as to what a "positive" or "negative" piece of news coverage looks like, my own subjective appraisal is all that remains. See Daniel Riffe, Stephen Lacy, and Frederick Fico, *Analyzing Media Messages: Using Quantitative Content Analysis in Research* (New York: Routledge, 2014), 94–98.

17. *New Hampshire Mirrour*, December 2, 1793, 1; *Oracle of the Day*, December 14, 1793, 1.

18. *Gazetteer*, January 23, 1793, 1; *New Hampshire Recorder*, December 16, 1790, 2.

19. Not least because it combined two early American passions: speechifying and boozing. For more on this, the best source is Peter Thompson's *Rum Punch*

and the Revolution: Taverngoing and Public Life in Eighteenth-Century Philadelphia (Philadelphia: University of Pennsylvania Press, 1999).

20. *New Hampshire Journal*, 3; Simon P. Newman, *Parades and the Politics of the Street: Festive Culture in the Early American Republic* (Philadelphia: University of Pennsylvania Press, 1997), 3.

21. *Political and Sentimental Repository*, August 17, 1791, 3.

22. *New Hampshire Spy*, August 4, 1790, 4.

23. *Concord Herald*, May 25, 1790, 2.

24. *New Hampshire Gazette*, June 30, 1791, 1; Newman, *Parades and the Politics of the Street*, 39.

25. *Oracle of the Day*, September 15, 1798, 3.

26. John H. Morrison, *The Life of Jeremiah Smith* (Boston: Little, Brown, 1845), 124–25.

27. *Portsmouth Gazette*, August 24, 1792, 2.

28. *Gazette*, October 20, 1791, 3.

29. *Herald*, June 1, 1790, 2; *New Hampshire Spy*, June 2, 1790, 1; *Repository*, December 16, 1790, 4.

30. *Repository*, August 26, 1790, 3.

31. *Herald*, March 23, 1790, 3.

32. *New Hampshire Journal*, May 23, 1794, 4.

33. *Oracle of the Day*, August 26, 1797, 1.

34. *Mirrour*, October 16, 1795, 4.

35. *Mirrour*, September 13, 1796, 1.

36. *New Hampshire Spy*, March 28, 1792, 2; *Hanover Eagle*, November 24, 1794, 1; *Concord Herald*, September 15, 1792, 3.

37. *New Hampshire Journal*, November 21, 1793, 1.

38. Hamilton's magisterial series of reports on credit, banking, currency, and manufacturing polarized readers. His prescient depiction of American capitalism appealed to entrepreneurs and speculators but alienated many physiocrats.

39. Francophobic sentiment wasn't the universal rule across the state. Citizens of Portsmouth turned out to sing the Marseillaise in salute to French ships in harbor during the French Revolution. See Newman, *Parades and the Politics of the Street*, 142.

40. *Gazette*, August 27, 1793, 2.

41. For further details, see Stanley Elkins and Eric McKitrick, *The Age of Federalism: The Early American Republic, 1788–1800* (Oxford: Oxford University Press, 1993), 349–52.

42. *Concord Mirrour*, June 23, 1793, 1; Cleves, *Reign of Terror in America*, 73–103.

43. *Oracle of the Day*, July 28, 1796, 1.

44. *New Hampshire Gazette*, December 8, 1796, 2.

45. *Farmer's Weekly Museum*, December 10, 1798, 3; *Courier*, August 21, 1798, 2; *Oracle*, July 28, 1798, 3; *Courier*, July 10, 1798, 3.

46. It is worth observing that Republicans were not always the avid proponents of the free press that we might initially suppose. Jefferson once wrote to Washington, "No government ought to be without censors; and where the press is free, no one ever will be." James R. Wiggins, "Jefferson and the Press," in *Thomas Jefferson: The Man, His World, His Influence*, ed. Lally Weymouth (London: Weidenfeld and Nicolson, 1973), 142.

47. *Mirrour*, August 28, 1798, 2.

48. *Federal Observer*, November 22, 1798, 3.

49. *Gazette*, May 14, 1799, 2.

50. Michael Durey, *Transatlantic Radicals and the Early American Republic* (Lawrence: University Press of Kansas, 1997), 228.

51. *Mirrour*, December 27, 1798, 2.

52. Washington was a prominent member of the Virginian Grand Lodge (http://www.aw22.org/history.html). Franklin was a grand master of the Pennsylvania Lodge. See Stacy Schiff, *Benjamin Franklin and the Birth of America* (London: Bloomsbury, 2005), 214.

53. *Courier*, August 31, 1799, 2.

54. Gordon Wood, *Empire of Liberty: A History of the Early Republic, 1789–1815* (Oxford: Oxford University Press, 2009), 172.

55. *Farmer's Weekly Museum*, July 22, 1799, 4.

56. Ibid.

57. Richard Hofstader, *The Paranoid Style in American Politics* (Cambridge, MA: Harvard University Press, 1964), 11–13.

58. *Oracle*, June 29, 1799, 1; Gordon S. Wood, "Conspiracy and the Paranoid Style," *William and Mary Quarterly* (1982): 427.

59. Not everybody felt this way. The Marquis de Sade, upon hearing some canard about the dignity of "natural man," replied: "Nature averse to crime? I tell you that nature lives and breathes by it, hungers at all her pores for bloodshed, yearns with all her heart for the furtherance of cruelty." De Sade was a man apart from the intellectual currents of his day, but regrettably he seems to have provided a better explanation for the mayhem than his contemporaries were able to muster.

60. Wood, "Conspiracy and the Paranoid Style," 411.

61. *Courier*, August 9, 1800, 2.

62. *Farmer's Weekly Museum*, July 7, 1800, 3.

63. *Gazette*, August 12, 1800, 3.

64. *Courier*, November 8, 1796, 3.

65. *Courier*, December 6, 1800, 2; *United States Oracle*, December 6, 1800, 2; *Farmer's Weekly Museum*, December 15, 1800, 3; *United States Oracle*, December 20, 1800, 2; *Courier*, December 26, 1800, 3; *United States Oracle*, December 27, 1800, 2; *New Hampshire Sentinel*, January 3, 1801, 3.

66. Newman, *Parades and the Politics of the Street*, 9.

CHAPTER EIGHT: AMERICAN INTELLIGENCE

1. *Farmer's Weekly Museum*, December 15, 1800, 3.

2. The determination of "positive," "neutral," and "negative" articles of course entailed a degree of subjective judgment on the part of the author. The "neutral" category mainly consisted of legislative and judicial insertions, as well as shorter anecdotal notices. The positive and negative pieces fell into the two broad categories described in the previous chapter. While the rest of the data in this chapter was analyzed using content-analysis methodology, the broader "positive" and "negative" categories were done on the basis of knowing it when one sees it. As Daniel has pointed out, "Party identity in the 1790s was extraordinarily fluid and unstable, and its nomenclature and definition were never fixed. Not only were meanings of terms like 'Republican' and 'Federalist' hotly contested, but other labels of party allegiance and affiliation competed with them for primacy: 'American,' 'Alien,' 'Aristocrat,' 'Democrat,' 'Jacobin,' 'Monocrat.'" Marcus Daniel, *Scandal and Civility: Journalism and the Birth of American Democracy* (Oxford: Oxford University Press, 2009, 17). The sample size was 2,228.

3. *New Hampshire Spy*, June 2, 1792, 1.

4. The total number of incidences for the positive words was 5,044 (*celebrated*, 1,351; *honorable*, 775; *honourable*, 583; *noble*, 1,516; *patriotic*, 819). However, once the non-U.S. political articles were extirpated, the working sample was 2,228.

5. The only articles that have been included are American political articles and editorials, biographical pieces (of American politicians), and letters from correspondents on the same subject. As with the previous political data, a degree of human selection is at work on the part of the author; if a word appeared in a context that clearly precluded it from consideration as being a part of these broad categories (the term was being used with obvious irony or in a way that did not relate at all to the political argument of the piece), it was discarded. Sometimes context makes this obvious enough, as with the following piece from the *Concord Mirrour* (May 19, 1794): "PATRIOTIC TOAST. The American Printers. May their fingers be attacked with the shaking-palsy, their type boxes hurled in confusion, whenever they attempt to compose matter which can in the least degree tend to depreciate the merit of those sentiments, which guided the hearts, and strengthened the hands of the sons of freedom, at the ever memorable and critical period of 1775." While this text clearly has patriotism at its heart, in its regard for the revolutionary generation (and one would have to search long and hard for an article published in criticism of *that*), it would stretch credulity that it could be included in the positive category as presented in the previous chapter. On the other hand, and staying with the theme of patriotism, some articles might not necessarily address specific political figures or events, but are clear enough in their general sentiment, as with this article

from the short-lived *Amherst Journal* (May 1, 1795, 4), which also gives a clear sense of the way that hardheaded country pragmatism and bucolic sentimentality often kept close company in the pages of New Hampshire's newspapers: "AGRICULTURE, whether considered in a moral or political point of view, is an object of the greatest importance to society. It forms the only firm base and support of government. Its professors are more generally virtuous, and patriotic, than any other class of citizens. The practise of husbandry tends to strengthen the body, and invigorate the mind. It induces a manly firmness and independency of spirit, equally removed from savage moroseness, and fawning servility. No situation in life is so propitious to the cultivation of the more important moral and social virtues, to patriotism, benevolence and real greatness of mind. To the man of leisure, it affords a rational and agreeable amusement, to the philosopher, a boundless source of contemplation. To the industrious professor it ensures, as to wealth, that happy state of mediocrity, which most conduces to procure, and preserve, a calm and unruffled security of mind; the cause of true happiness." In these cases, the article has been included and in the final tabulation put into the positive column. Examples of both types (misleading use of keywords in ambiguous contexts and articles that indirectly tackle political issues) can also be found among the negative words studied, and the author has sought to be as consistent as possible in both cases. Such examples are an extreme minority within the total sample size, however, and the "judgment calls" amount to less than 1 percent variance.

6. *Portsmouth Price Current*, November 18, 1800, 2.

7. The total number of incidences for the negative words was 5,012 (*corrupt*, 318; *corruption*, 260; *disgrace*, 321; *disgraceful*, 105; *evil*, 1,352; *infamous*, 404; *Jacobin*, 823; *Jacobins*, 817; *sedition*, 226; *seditious*, 127; *traitor*, 225; *traitorous*, 34). However, once the non-U.S. political articles were extirpated, the working sample was 2,228.

8. *Oracle of the Day*, June 15, 1799, 1.

9. *Courier of New Hampshire*, July 26, 1800, 4.

10. *Republican Ledger and Portsmouth Price Current*, April 9, 1800, 3.

11. Matthew Lyon was the editor of the *Farmer's Library* who was controversially prosecuted under the Sedition Law, due to his Democratic-Republican affiliation. See Gordon Wood, *Empire of Liberty: A History of the Early Republic, 1789–1815* (Oxford: Oxford University Press, 2009), 262.

12. *Concord Mirrour*, March 18, 1799, 1.

13. York County is now in the state of Maine.

14. *Oracle of the Day*, November 3, 1978, 3.

15. *United States Oracle*, November 22, 1800, 2.

16. *Portsmouth Price Current*, March 19, 1800, 3.

17. Thomas Irwin Emerson, *The System of Freedom of Expression* (New York: Random House, 1970), 99.

18. *Alien and Sedition Acts*, 1 U.S.C. § 74 (1798).

19. Emerson, *System of Freedom of Expression*, 100.

20. Wendell Bird, *Press and Speech under Assault: The Early Supreme Court Justices, the Sedition Act of 1798, and the Campaign against Dissent* (Oxford: Oxford University Press, 2016), 251.

21. Stanley Elkins and Eric McKitrick, *The Age of Federalism: The Early American Republic, 1788–1800* (Oxford: Oxford University Press, 1993), 700.

22. Paul Starr, *The Creation of the Modern Media: Political Origins of Modern Communication* (New York: Basic Books, 2004), 81.

23. *Concord Mirrour*, August 7, 1798, 3.

24. *Sun*, March 19, 1800, 3.

25. *Courier of New Hampshire*, August 9, 1800, 1.

26. The towns were Albany (NY), Baltimore (MD), Boston (MA), Concord (NH), Dover (NH), Dumfries (VA), Elizabethtown (NJ), Hanover (NH), Hartford (CT), Haverhill (MA), Lexington (KY), New Bedford (MA), Newburyport (MA), New Haven (CT), Newport (RI), New York (NY), Northfield (MA), Philadelphia (PA), Pittsburgh (PA), Portsmouth (NH), Richmond (VA), Salem (MA), Stockbridge (MA), Trenton (NJ), Walpole (NH), Windsor (VT), and Worcester (MA).

27. The towns were Albany (NY), Alexandria (VA), Andover (MA), Annapolis (MD), Augusta (GA), Bennington (VT), Boston (MA), Brattleboro (VT), Brookfield (MA), Burlington (VT), Byfield (MA), Charleston (SC), Chesterfield (NH), Concord (NH), Cooperstown (NY), Danbury (CT), Dedham (MA), Derby (CT), Dover (NH), Elizabeth (NJ), Elizabethtown (NJ), Exeter (NH), Fairhaven (VT), Georgetown (DC), Greenfield (MA), Halifax (NC), Hanover (NH), Hartford (CT), Haverhill (MA), Hull (MA), Keene (NH), Kennebunkport (ME), Montpellier (VT), Nashville (TN), Newburyport (MA), New Haven (CT), New London (CT), Newport (RI), New Providence (NJ), Newtown (NY), New York (NY), Norfolk (VA), Northampton (MA), Philadelphia (PA), Plymouth (MA), Portland (ME), Portsmouth (NH), Princeton (NJ), Providence (RI), Raleigh (NC), Richmond (VA), Salem (MA), Savannah (GA), Springfield (MA), Stamford (CT), Trenton (NJ), Vassalboro (ME), Vergennes (VT), Walpole (NH), Warren (RI), Washington (DC), Westminster (VT), Windsor (VT), and Worcester (MA).

28. *Oracle of the Day*, March 22, 1800, 2.

29. *Political and Sentimental Repository; or, Strafford Recorder*, September 21, 1791, 1.

30. Only towns with stated locations of origin were used in this sample. As with the graphs in chapters 4 and 5 of this book, the pie charts have been arranged to show the three general categories together; clockwise, they show the New Hampshire towns, the other towns, and the big cities.

    Positive sources, 1790: Boston, 20; New York City, 18; Philadelphia, 20; other towns, 27; New Hampshire, 63

Negative sources, 1790: Boston, 7; New York City, 4; Philadelphia, 6; other towns, 18; New Hampshire, 34

Positive sources, 1791: Boston, 14; New York City, 5; Philadelphia, 29; other towns, 45; New Hampshire, 54

Negative sources, 1791: Boston, 3; New York City, 1; Philadelphia, 7; other towns, 25; New Hampshire, 22

Positive sources, 1792: Boston, 10; New York City, 16; Philadelphia, 24; other towns, 56; New Hampshire, 48

Negative sources, 1792: Boston, 2; New York City, 7; Philadelphia, 9; other towns, 13; New Hampshire, 22

Positive sources, 1793: Boston, 21; New York City, 17; Philadelphia, 18; other towns, 31; New Hampshire, 40

Negative sources, 1793: Boston, 14; New York City, 9; Philadelphia, 12; other towns, 16; New Hampshire, 24

Positive sources, 1794: Boston, 24; New York City, 17; Philadelphia, 18; other towns, 26; New Hampshire, 40

Negative sources, 1794: Boston, 12; New York City, 9; Philadelphia, 12; other towns, 22; New Hampshire, 41

Positive sources, 1795: Boston, 30; New York City, 10; Philadelphia, 25; other towns, 33; New Hampshire, 67

Negative sources, 1795: Boston, 19; New York City, 7; Philadelphia, 30; other towns, 34; New Hampshire, 76

Positive sources, 1796: Boston, 36; New York City, 16; Philadelphia, 20; other towns, 34; New Hampshire, 37

Negative sources, 1796: Boston, 14; New York City, 23; Philadelphia, 17; other towns, 37; New Hampshire, 98

Positive sources, 1797: Boston, 19; New York City, 8; Philadelphia, 19; other towns, 25; New Hampshire, 60

Negative sources, 1797: Boston, 27; New York City, 9; Philadelphia, 18; other towns, 15; New Hampshire, 77

Positive sources, 1798: Boston, 34; New York City, 12; Philadelphia, 19; other towns, 70; New Hampshire, 89

Negative sources, 1798: Boston, 27; New York City, 19; Philadelphia, 50; other towns, 116; New Hampshire, 161

Positive sources, 1799: Boston, 37; New York City, 13; Philadelphia, 19; other towns, 71; New Hampshire, 101

Negative sources, 1799: Boston, 46; New York City, 36; Philadelphia, 47; other towns, 107; New Hampshire, 160

Positive sources, 1800: Boston, 39; New York City, 10; Philadelphia, 26; other towns, 69; New Hampshire, 61

Negative sources, 1800: Boston, 29; New York City, 21; Philadelphia, 33; other towns, 129; New Hampshire, 127

31. Milton Ellis, "Joseph Dennie and His Circle: A Study in American Literature from 1792–1812," *Bulletin of the University of Texas* (1915): 42.

32. *Farmer's Weekly Museum*, March 4, 1799, 3.

33. *New Hampshire Gazette*, August 19, 1800, 1.

34. Susan J. Douglas, "Does Textual Analysis Tell Us Anything about Past Readers?," in *Explorations in Communication and History*, ed. Barbie Zelizer (London: Routledge, 2008), 73; Simon P. Newman, *Parades and the Politics of the Street: Festive Culture in the Early American Republic* (Philadelphia: University of Pennsylvania Press, 1997), 187.

35. *Oracle of the Day*, August 16, 1800, 3; *New Hampshire Gazetteer*, October 28, 1791, 4. "WP" is not identified, but the author's best guess is that it refers to William Penn.

36. *New Hampshire Journal*, October 27, 1795, 3.

37. *Federal Observer*, October 31, 1799, 3.

CONCLUSION: "FROM THE EDITOR"

1. Lawrence C. Wroth, *The Colonial Printer* (New York: Dover, 1994), 115–19; William J. Barrow, "Black Writing Ink of the Colonial Period," *American Archivist* 11, no. 4 (1948): 291–307.

2. John Bidwell, *American Paper Mills, 1690–1832: A Directory of the Paper Trade with Notes on Products, Watermarks, Distribution Methods, and Manufacturing Techniques* (Dartmouth, NH: Dartmouth College Press, 2012), 239–47.

3. Newspaper data compiled from NewsBank.

4. *New Hampshire Gazetteer*, January 28, 1792, 3; *New Hampshire Gazette and General Advertiser*, June 24, 1790; *Farmer's Weekly Museum*, August 18, 1800, 4.

5. T. H. Breen, "'Bauble of Britain': The American and Consumer Revolutions of the Eighteenth Century," *Past & Present*, no. 119 (May 1988): 77.

6. William J. Gilmore, *Reading Becomes a Necessity of Life: Material and Cultural Life in Rural New England, 1780–1835* (Knoxville: University of Tennessee Press, 1989), 165.

7. Henry David Thoreau, *Walden* (New York: Thomas Cromwell, 1910), 122.

8. Clifford G. Christians et al., *Normative Theories of the Media: Journalism in Democratic Societies* (Urbana: University of Illinois Press, 2009), 139.

9. *Jenk's Portland Gazette*, October 27, 1800, 2.

10. Michael Schudson, "The Sociology of News Production," in *Social Meanings of News: A Text-Reader*, ed. Dan Berkowitz (Thousand Oaks, CA: Sage, 1997), 9.

11. Christians et al., *Normative Theories of the Media*, 158.

12. David Waldstreicher, "Rites of Rebellion, Rites of Assent: Celebrations, Print Culture, and the Origins of American Nationalism," *Journal of American History* 82, no. 1 (1995): 38; Michael Durey, "Thomas Paine's Apostles: Radical

Emigrés and the Triumph of Jeffersonian Republicanism," *William and Mary Quarterly* 44, no. 4 (1987): 686.

13. *Republican Ledger and Portsmouth Price Current*, November 25, 1800, 2.

14. Richard Hofstader, *The Paranoid Style in American Politics* (Cambridge, MA: Harvard University Press, 1964), 11–28.

15. John Adams, *Discourses on Davila: A Series of Papers on Political History* (Boston: Russell and Cutler, 1805), 84–85.